Classic Cars

Classic Cars

LEGENDARY AUTOMOBILES: DESIGN AND DEVELOPMENT

CRAIG CHEETHAM

METRO BOOKS
NEW YORK

Metro Books
122 Fifth Avenue
New York, NY 10011

Editorial and design by
Amber Books Ltd

Project Editor: James Bennett
Copy Editors: Chris McNab, Siobhan O'Connor
Picture Research: Kate Green
Design: Brian Rust

ISBN-13: 978-0-7607-9448-7
ISBN-10: 0-7607-9448-0

Printed and bound in China

1 3 5 7 9 10 8 6 4 2

Contents

Introduction

Defining what makes a classic car isn't easy. With over a century of designs to choose from, it's tempting to apply the term 'classic' indiscriminately, in reference to any vehicle that is no longer in production. But for a car to be considered a true classic, its design must stand the test of time. It must have a style or engineering facet that moves the motor industry forward, and be remembered for introducing something to the world of motoring that wasn't there before it existed.

Some of the cars in this book are here for the brilliance of their engineering. The Audi Quattro, for example, made four-wheel-drive a common feature on mainstream cars, while the Land Rover practically invented it. The Chevrolet Corvette is remembered for many things, not least its position as an icon of America's social history. Yet aside from its desirability, the Corvette is best known for being the first series production car to be made from glass-reinforced plastic – a

technical innovation that set the precedent for generations of sports cars that followed.

Other cars in this cross-section of classic motoring mobilized generations of people. Cars such as the Citroen 2CV, the Mini, the Fiat 500,

▼ **Aston Martin DB MkIII**
The Aston Martin DB series of cars was one of the most elegant ever made – the trademark 'coat hanger' grille survives even on the company's latest models.

▲ **Chevrolet Corvette Sting Ray**
Chevrolet's Corvette was one of the true innovators, bringing new manufacturing methods and a whole new image to the Chevrolet brand. Every successive generation was different, but the 1963 Sting Ray was the most distinctive.

the Ford Mustang and the VW Beetle are models that became part of the very fabric of society in their domestic markets, and in the case of the VW, all over the world. Their classic credentials are there simply because their design was so right; so perfect for the market into which the cars were launched.

Other cars are classics simply because of their beauty. Cars such as the Aston Martin DB series, Jaguar E-Type and Mercedes SL require no justification. On looks alone, they are true greats.

There are other cars here, though, that may seem a little unusual. Choices that may at first seem odd, but were specifically picked because the very fact that their basic design sired an important series of subsequent models. Cars such as the Volvo 140/240 Series – a design so fit for purpose it required almost no updates over a 25-year life – finally get the recognition they so richly deserve.

In each case, the cars in this book are related by series. They are cars that started off as one and became many, their constant evolution spawning new and more varied spin-offs that ensured a production run, in all cases, of over a decade. Given how fast-moving the car industry has become, a decade is a very long time indeed – but as the detailed technical specifications and production records demonstrate, these cars were never off the pace, despite their longevity.

The only frustration is that to document every car that could legitimately claim to be a classic would require a book of encyclopedic proportions, meaning we've had to be extremely strict on what could and couldn't be let in. Choosing the cars to star in these pages was a difficult task, but we believe the finished book documents a broad and fascinating cross-section of the most influential classic cars from all over the world, and is not just a collection of glitzy sports models or mega-expensive fashion icons.

AC Cobra
1962–73

What connects a British maker of handbuilt luxury cars, Ford's motorsport campaign and a chicken farmer from Texas? Why, the AC Cobra, of course.

Ace

Until the Ace appeared in 1953, AC had a reputation for building luxury touring cars. But the Ace was different – it was a true sports model, built on a chassis developed by American engineer John Tojeiro. It was also the first British car to have fully independent suspension all round. The Ace had great handling, but was let down by its powerplant – a 1991cc (121ci) six-cylinder unit carried over from the AC 2-Litre saloon (sedan), producing only 74bhp (55kW).

The car was gradually improved, though. A coupe version, called the Aceca, appeared in 1954, while in 1956 it acquired overdrive and a new 2.0-litre (121ci) engine courtesy of Bristol, which gave a 60 per cent power increase. Front disc brakes came in 1957, while in 1961 a 2.6-litre (159ci) Ford engine, taken from the Zephyr and tuned by Ruddspeed, finally gave the Ace the performance it so richly deserved. The Ace was a great sports car, and it became the basis for a true legend.

◀ ▼ **AC Cobra 289**
The Cobra 289 was closest in styling terms to the original Ace – its grille was identical and the wheelarches were much slimmer than those of the 427.

Specifications	
Engine type: V8	Length: 3.8m (151.5in)
Displacement: 4736cc (289ci)	Width: 1.6m (63.0in)
Maximum power: 202kW (271bhp) at 5750rpm	Height: 1.2m (48.0in)
Top speed: 225km/h (140mph)	Wheelbase: 2.3m (90.0in)
0–96km/h (0–60mph): 5.5sec	Weight: 916kg (2020lbs)

AC was adamant it would maintain its identity, even if the engines were a core part of Ford's motorsport programme. As such, the only Ford badges to appear on the Cobra were on the front wings (fenders) above the air ducts, on plaques that also revealed whether or not the car had a 289 or a 427 block.

Cobra 260/289

Nine years after its launch, the AC Ace was a well-respected car, but one which wasn't doing the business for its manufacturer. Not for the first, or indeed the last time in its life, AC was on the verge of bankruptcy, with a British government contract to build invalid carriages keeping it afloat, but doing little to save its reputation.

Meanwhile, across the Atlantic, a chicken farmer from Texas was busy trying to build up his career as a racing driver. Carroll Shelby had approached Ford, which had volunteered to support him with racing engines, but had no vehicle in which he could compete. By pure chance, Shelby realized that the Ace was the smallest and lightest sports car into which Ford's

compact V8 could be installed, and the very first Cobra was produced. It was an instant success, its blistering acceleration enough to raise the eyebrows of many a circuit racer. By the end of 1963, just one year after coming up with the idea, Shelby had built 25 AC Cobras, and a legend was born. The following year, the original 4.2-litre (260ci) engine was upped to 4.7 litres (289ci) and resulted in the first truly successful Cobra. Incredibly quick, a real handful to drive and a multiple race winner, the Cobra 289 rescued AC from obscurity, turned Carroll Shelby into a household name and rightly earned itself recognition as one of the most important classic cars of all time.

Cobra 427

Despite the phenomenal success of the Cobra 289, Carroll Shelby was not a man to rest on his laurels. The 289 might still have been winning the world's endurance races, but Shelby wanted more – and more he got, courtesy of Ford's

▼ **AC Cobra 427**

When it debuted in 1966, the Cobra 427 was the fastest car in the world, with a top speed of around 290km/h (180mph) – a figure that still sounds impressive today.

▲ **AC 428**

With styling by Frua and long, elegant bodywork, the AC 428 looked like a civilized Grand Tourer, but under the skin it had the bite of a Cobra.

6984cc (427ci), 425bhp (317kW) big block V8 – a power output that wouldn't look out of place in even a modern supercar. To shoehorn the enormous engine under the bonnet (hood), Shelby and Ford helped AC redesign the original Ace bodywork to feature outwardly flared wheelarches, power bulges in the bonnet and heavily revised suspension, this time with coil springs all round.

The 427 was awesomely fast. The 0–60mph (0–96km/h) could be despatched in less than four seconds, and while no top speed was ever officially recognized, a standard 427 was once tested up to 291km/h (180mph), making it the fastest car in the world – a record it held right up until the Porsche 959 debuted in 1986. Allegedly, AC did much of its speed testing on the M1 motorway in the UK, and it was an incident with racing driver Jack Sears travelling in excess of 243km/h (150mph) on the road that led to Britain introducing a 110km/h (70mph) maximum speed limit in 1965.

AC 428

With more money in the bank and a far rosier future outlook, AC decided to use the Cobra's success to capitalize on its more traditional market by launching the 428 in 1965. Based on a Cobra chassis, but with elegant bodywork styled by Frua of Turin, the 428 was a Grand Tourer in AC's traditional mould, with leather trim, a wooden dashboard and room for four passengers. A beautiful handmade car, it was nonetheless expensive, and only a handful were built. As well as the coupe, AC built a convertible version of the 428, which was even prettier but – thanks to the use of poor-quality Italian steel – was badly rust-prone, leading to the premature death of many an example.

▼ ▶ **AC Superblower**

From the front, it is hard to tell a late-model Superblower from an original Cobra – the air scoop to accommodate the Mustang-sourced V8 is the only major difference.

The 428's engine was slightly larger than that of the Cobra at 6997cc (428ci), but despite the extra capacity it was nowhere near as powerful, and most owners chose to have their car fitted with an automatic gearbox.

Superblower

Many a kit car manufacturer tried to replicate the legendary Cobra over the years, but none could claim to be the real deal. The closest was perhaps the Dax Tojeiro, which had a John Tojeiro–designed chassis, but even this example had Jaguar running gear and was built from a box of parts.

AC itself had gone bust in 1984, its ill-fated 3000 ME sports car wiping out all of its previous profits in one of the most badly planned launches of all times. But elements of the company were kept alive, and under new ownership the AC Car Group (as it became) unveiled the Superblower in 1996. Built to the original 427 moulds, the car didn't have the backing of Shelby so couldn't carry the Cobra name, although it was obvious that this was the real car reincarnated. A 427 engine was not possible, either, but true to tradition AC equipped the car with the most powerful Ford V8 of the time – a 5.0-litre (302ci) Mustang unit

Model	Years Built	0–96km/h (60mph)	Top Speed km/h (mph)
Ace	1953–64	11.4sec	168 (103)
Cobra 289	1962–68	5.5sec	223 (138)
Cobra 427	1966–69	3.8sec	291 (180)
428	1965–73	5.9sec	225 (139)
Superblower	1996–2002	4.1sec	259 (160)

developing 320bhp (239kW). That obviously didn't make the Superblower as fast or as powerful as the 427, but it was still plenty fast enough to cause a stir, and was as true to the brand's heritage as enthusiasts could dream of.

The Superblower was a genuine AC car, not to be mistaken with the many Cobra replicas that popped up over the years. Most of these were powered by either Rover V8 or Jaguar V12 engines, although one example – the Dax Tojeiro – was a semi-official variant, built to the original Cobra measurements.

Cabins of modern Superblowers are more luxuriously appointed than those in the original, more hardcore Cobras. The central half-crescent instrument pod remains, but is trimmed with light alloy and leather to give the car a more bespoke, handbuilt feel.

Specifications

Engine type: V8	Length: 4.2m (165.4in)
Displacement: 5000cc (305.1ci)	Width: 1.7m (68.7in)
Maximum power: 265kW (55bhp) at 5700rpm	Height: 1.2m (47.2in)
Top speed: 250km/h (155mph)	Wheelbase: 2.3m (90.0in)
0–96km/h (0–60mph): 4.2sec	Weight: 31.2kg (68.7lbs)

Aston Martin DB Series
1948–

The Aston Martin DB series is renowned throughout the world for its combination of great performance, alluring looks and supreme quality.

DB1

More commonly known as the 2-Litre, the Aston Martin DB1 was the first of a series of cars to take its name from the initials of the company's chief, David Brown. It was also the first post-war model to emerge from the factory in Newport Pagnell, England, and was designed primarily for competition use.

Despite this, it wasn't especially quick – its engine produced only 90bhp (67kW). Thanks to its robust build and superb handling, however, the car was still very competent in the right environment, and enjoyed particular success in rallying, where its endurance helped it to outlast some faster rivals.

▲ **Aston Martin DB1 (2-Litre)**

With such bulky bodywork and rather asymmetrical styling, it's hard to believe that the original Aston Martin 2-Litre gave rise to one of the most elegant and successful lines of cars ever known.

The most prized models among collectors are 1949-onward Sports versions, identifiable by their fold-flat windscreens.

DB2

Much more of a luxury tourer than the DB1, and in the process setting the precedent on which the brand's current reputation is built, the DB2 had a twin-cam six-cylinder engine designed by none other than W.O. Bentley.

Available as a coupe or an extremely rare drophead convertible, the DB2 was beautifully built and perfectly finished, while it also had impressive performance.

The only real downside was the car's lack of practicality, as space inside the cabin was especially cramped. Aston Martin addressed this in 1953 with the launch of the larger DB2/4, which was essentially the same car but with 2+2 seating, a taller and slightly wider cabin, and opening rear windows. Again, a drophead was available to special order, but is extremely rare.

DB Mk III

For reasons best known to Aston Martin, there was never officially a DB3. This could partly be because, with no funds to develop brand-new models, Aston instead decided to rework the existing DB2/4. Visual differences aside, the DB Mk III (as it subsequently became known) was essentially the same car.

There were, however, some differences. Externally, the drooping nose, lower headlamps and smaller radiator grille gave the car a more aerodynamic appearance, although the car was not necessarily any more streamlined. Power was also up from 140bhp (104kW) to 162bhp (120kW) (or as much as 202bhp/150kW if you went for the optional triple carburettor set-up). The Mk III is a rare car, but the best derivative of the original DB chassis.

Specifications

Engine type: Inline six-cylinder		Length: 4.36m (171.5in)	
Displacement: 2,922cc (178.3ci)		Width: 1.65m (65.0in)	
Maximum power: 120.8kW (162bhp) at 5500rpm		Height: 1.36m (53.5in)	
Top speed: 193km/h (120mph)		Wheelbase: 2.51m (99.0in)	
0–96km/h (0–60mph): 9.4sec		Weight: 1334.5kg (2940lbs)	

▼ ▶ **Aston Martin DB2/4 and DB Mk III**

The DB2/4 and DB Mk III were essentially the same car save for a few minor detail changes. The DB Mk III, right, had a smaller, mesh-style radiator grille and a slightly more aerodynamic front end.

▲ **Aston Martin DB4**

The DB4 was the first Aston Martin to clearly show the 'coat hanger' radiator grille that became a trademark of the DB series over the years. Of all the DB series, it was the DB4 that had the most motorsport success.

DB4

No longer styled in-house by Aston Martin, the DB4 showed a shift towards more global designs in the car industry. It was styled by Touring of Milan to what was called the Superleggera principle, where light alloy panels were stretched and hand-beaten over a steel frame – a build method that would go on to become an Aston Martin trademark. The car was built, as ever, at the British Newport Pagnell factory, and Aston Martin was forced to expand its premises to make room for the new model, and built a new body shop across the road. Even today, it's common to see bodyshells holding up the traffic as they're wheeled across the road on dollies for final assembly.

The DB4 was a truly beautiful car, with an all-new, all-alloy engine to add to its appeal. The

An Aston Martin trademark, the 'struck-through' side air intake made its debut on the classic DB5. Initially, its purpose was purely functional and was to allow the effective through-flow of air into the car's cabin, but on later models it became a simple styling cue, and has featured on every Aston Martin model introduced since.

most desirable version is the drophead (only 32 were built), which is highly coveted today.

DB4GT/GT Zagato

Designed primarily for competition use, the GT version of the DB4 was a whole 12.5cm (5in) shorter than the standard car, and was therefore a strict two-seater. As well as the difference in length, the front end of the GT was modified, with the headlamps hidden beneath cowls to aid the car's aerodynamic efficiency.

Developing 302bhp (225kW) from a highly tuned derivative of the twin-cam engine, it was also immensely quick. Zagato of Italy also developed a body for the DB4 GT, which looked more muscular but was actually lighter than that of the 'ordinary' GT, making it even quicker. Only 19 Zagato models were ever made.

▲ **Aston Martin DB4 GT Zagato**

One of the rarest and most desirable Aston DBs, the DB4 GT Zagato was more aerodynamic than the standard car and featured special lightweight bodywork. This example is one of only 19 built.

◀ ▼ **Aston Martin DB4**

The DB4 was the first Vignale-styled Aston Martin, and was one of the prettiest and most appealing models of its era. It was also one of the most expensive, especially in highly desirable drophead form.

Specifications	
Engine type: Inline six-cylinder	Length: 4.5m (179.0in)
Displacement: 3670cc (224ci)	Width: 1.4m (55.5in)
Maximum power: 225kW (302bhp) at 6000rpm	Height: 1.3m (51.0in)
Top speed: 140km/h (149mph)	Wheelbase: 2.4m (93.0in)
0–96km/h (0–60mph): 6.4sec	Weight: 1270kg (2800lbs)

DB5

As the car made famous by none other than James Bond, 007, the Aston Martin DB5 needs no introduction. Launched in 1963, it was arguably the most stylish of all the standard DB cars, with a new, aerodynamic front end, standard headlamp cowls and miniature rear fins accentuating the lithe lines of its coupe bodywork. The engine from the DB4 was used, but was bored out to 4.0 litres (244ci) and came with three SU carburettors as standard, meaning in standard tune it was capable of emitting 282bhp (210kW), while the even more potent Vantage (from 1964) developed 314bhp (234kW). A drophead model was available, albeit in limited numbers, while a handful of DB5s were also made with automatic gearboxes. Despite their rarity, automatics are actually worth less than manuals, as they are considered less rewarding to drive.

DB6

A more mature version of the DB5, the DB6 was longer and wider on the outside and more spacious within, emphasizing the model's role as very much a Grand Tourer rather than a sports car. The DB6 was more powerful than the DB5, but despite this it was no faster, as its more luxurious interior and larger bodywork added to its overall weight. Drophead models were renamed Volante for the DB6 and were much more popular than soft-top Astons of yore, largely because the car was aimed more at the luxury car buyer than the out-and-out performance enthusiast. The DB6, then, was a bit of a sop to market demand, and wasn't as well loved as its predecessors. Despite that, it was still a highly desirable and well-made car.

DBS

After a succession of similarly styled, curvaceous cars, Aston Martin went radical for the 1970s

◀ ▼ **Aston Martin DB5**

Classically elegant and with simple yet flowing lines, the DB5 was the car that found fame in the hands of Ian Fleming's top secret agent, James Bond. In the earliest films, Bond's car was gold, but he is better remembered for driving a Silver Fox example such as this.

Specifications

Engine type: Inline six-cylinder	Length: 4.57m (180.0in)
Displacement: 3995cc (243.8ci)	Width: 1.69m (66.6in)
Maximum power: 210kW (282bhp) at 5500rpm	Height: 1.32m (52.0in)
Top speed: 230km/h (143mph)	Wheelbase: 2.49m (98.0in)
0–96km/h (0–60mph): 8.6sec	Weight: 1565kg (3450lbs)

▲ ▶ Aston Martin DB6

Seen in isolation, the DB6 looks very similar to the DB5 that preceded it, but it is actually a much larger car, with a lengthened wheelbase and wider bodywork. It was also more a grand tourer than a sports car, and was heavier and slower than its predecessor.

courtesy of the William Towns–designed DBS. Aimed at cracking the US market, the DBS was larger and more angular than any Aston before, while inside it had developed into a full four-seater, with all the luxury accoutrements imaginable, including air conditioning.

It kept the DB6 engine at first, but after two years gained a 5.3-litre (323ci) quad-cam V8, necessary not only for it to appeal to America, but also for it to carry the DBS's vastly inflated bulk. If the DBS was considered controversial, imagine the reaction when Aston unveiled William Towns's second design in 1976 – the infamous wedge-shaped Lagonda saloon.

Specifications	
Engine type: Inline six-cylinder	Length: 4.62m (182in)
Displacement: 3995cc (244ci)	Width: 1.68m (66in)
Maximum power: 242kW (325bhp) at 5750rpm	Height: 1.32m (52in)
Top speed: 241km/h (150mph)	Wheelbase: 2.59m (101.8in)
0–96km/h (0–60mph): 6.7sec	Weight: 1550kg (3418lbs)

V8

Critics were not especially kind to the DBS, so in a bid to make Aston Martin a bit more traditional the car was renamed simply 'V8' for 1972. The six-cylinder engine was dropped, and the front end of the car was restyled to once again wear the traditional Aston Martin 'Coat Hanger' grille.

Although nowhere near as agile or rewarding to drive as the earlier DB models, the V8 enjoyed a huge 18-year production run, riding the highs and lows of the company from liquidation in 1974 to its buy-out by Ford some 16 years later. As well as in coupe form, the V8 was offered as a convertible and, for a very short time, four-door Lagonda model, which is not to be mistaken with the later Wedge model.

DB7

After a 24-year absence, the DB name finally returned in 1994 aboard the all-new DB7. Based on the running gear and platform of the recently revised Jaguar XJ-S, the DB7 was nonetheless

▲ **Aston Martin DBS V8**

A 1972 restyle saw the DBS evolve into the Aston Martin V8, which remained the mainstay of the Aston Martin range for the next 20 years. Build volumes were always fairly low, and each car was finished by hand.

Model	0–96km/h (0–60mph)	Top Speed km/h (mph)
2-Litre (DB1)	N/A	161 (100)
DB2	11.2sec	187 (116)
DB2/4	12.6sec	177 (111)
DB Mk III	9.3sec	191 (119)
DB4	8.5sec	227 (141)
DB4 GT	6.4sec	245 (152)
DB4 GT Zagato	6.1sec	247 (153)
DB5	8.1sec	227 (141)
DB6	6.5sec	238 (148)
DBS	8.6sec	238 (148)
DBS V8	6.0sec	261 (162)
V8	6.0sec	261 (162)
DB7	5.8sec	253 (157)
DB9	4.7sec	300 (186)

faithful to the origins of the DB line, with a six-cylinder inline petrol engine (albeit of Jaguar design) and pretty two-door coupe bodywork. The car marked a sensational return to form for Aston because, despite an eye-watering £78,000 ($155,000) price tag, it quickly became the firm's fastest-ever seller. Performance was excellent, thanks in part to an Eaton supercharger that helped the Jaguar engine to develop in excess of 223kW (300bhp). Coupe and convertible models were offered, with a choice of manual or automatic transmission.

DB9

Aston's replacement for the successful DB7 came in 2004, in the shape of the DB9. Styled by Scotsman Ian Callum, it was also the first car to be built at the company's all-new factory in Gaydon, Warwickshire, UK – the final big investment that Ford would pour into Aston Martin before finally selling the brand off to racing company Prodrive in 2007.

Unlike any previous DB model, the DB9 comes with a potent 5.9-litre (360ci) V12 engine derived from that of the awesome Vanquish supercar. Beautifully built and agile to drive, the

Model	Years Built	Numbers Built
2-Litre (DB1)	1948–50	14
DB2	1949–53	411
DB2/4	1953–55	7764
DB Mk III	1957–59	551
DB4	1958–63	1110
DB4 GT	1959–66	375
DB4 GT Zagato	1960–66	319
DB5	1963–65	1021
DB6	1965–70	1782
DBS	1967–73	857
DBS V8	1969–72	405
V8	1972–90	2666
DB7	1994–2004	c.5000
DB9	2004–	In production

DB9 is an inspiring modern interpretation of the Aston Martin DB breed.

It was with a highly modified version of the DB9 that Aston Martin also made its illustrious return to the Le Mans 24 Hour Race, with the 2006 DB9R. The R model was designed exclusively for racing and so it came with light carbon fibre bodywork, a single driver's seat and a race-tuned V12 powerplant developing more than 600bhp (447kW).

▲ **Aston Martin DB7**

The DB7 was a much-needed modernization of the Aston Martin brand, although beneath the skin it was still a fairly basic vehicle, sharing its platform with the aged Jaguar XJ-S to keep costs to a minimum.

Specifications

Engine type: Inline six-cylinder	Length: 4.6m (182.3in)
Displacement: 3239cc (197.7ci)	Width: 1.8m (71.6in)
Maximum power: 250kW (335bhp) at 5750rpm	Height: 1.3m (49.8in)
Top speed: 253km/h (157mph)	Wheelbase: 2.6m (102in)
0–96km/h (0–60mph): 6.0sec	Weight: 1750kg (3858lbs)

▼ **Aston Martin DB9**

Finally blowing tradition into the water, the DB9 was the first thoroughly modern Aston Martin for over three decades when it was revealed in 2004. Beautifully finished and powered by a thumping V12 engine, it became an instant classic.

Audi Quattro
1979–91

The Quattro is the story of how a German maker renowned for sturdy but dull saloon cars changed its image, along with the face of rallying, for good.

Coupe

Based on the uninspring but dutiful Audi 80, the Coupe was the very first glimpse at what lay in store for the future of the German brand. Styled by British designer Martin Smith, the Audi Coupe took the floorpan of the 80 and added a two-door coupe body style, which looked like a hatchback but wasn't, as a rival to the likes of the Ford Capri and Opel Manta – both of which were especially popular in Europe.

The Coupe was a pretty car, if not especially dramatic to look at, and performance was subdued on smaller-engined models. It was a fairly heavy car, and the 90bhp (67kW) 1.8-litre (110ci) entry-level model was never going to set the pulses of performance car enthusiasts racing.

Other engine choices included a 115bhp (86kW) 1.9-litre (116ci) unit, which was equally staid, or some more interesting five-cylinder engines of 2.1 litres (128ci) or later 2.2 litres (134ci), both producing 136bhp (101kW). These lively engines hinted at the Quattro technology that was coming Audi's way, they sounded great and they bestowed the Coupe with excellent performance, although in front-wheel drive form the handling still wasn't brilliant. The

Quattro would sort all that, but for the moment the Coupe would set the precedent for quality build and reliability that are as much hallmarks of the Audi brand as the Quattro itself.

Quattro

Quite possibly the most sensational car of the 1980s, the Audi Quattro joined the ranks of the true legends when it made its debut in 1980.

Built to give Audi a presence in rallying, a feat that the Quattro achieved with undeniable success, winning the World Rally Championship for four seasons in succession, it was also the first passenger car since the Jensen FF to be offered with permanent four-wheel drive as standard. As well as the complicated but highly effective 4x4 system, which gave the car phenomenal grip, the Quattro came with a 2.1-litre (128ci) turbocharged five-cylinder engine developing a heady 200bhp (150kW), a figure that might not sound too mighty today, but in a mainstream performance coupe of its era this kind of power output was unheard of. Further technological developments included anti-lock brakes as standard, and a complicated all-digital instrument panel, which wasn't the car's best feature.

The Quattro wasn't perfect. Turbo lag was prominent, but once you got through it the car would pelt off towards the horizon with ligament-snapping aplomb, and, while it was a heavy and tiring machine to drive, it was also truly thrilling. There was nothing that could match it on road or on the rally tracks, and its shattering acceleration

◀ **Audi Coupe**
Here's where it all started – Audi's decision to build a two-door coupe version of the popular 80 saloon gave rise to one of the rally world's biggest performers. Yet even in standard two-wheel drive form, the Coupe was a smart-looking car.

 ▲ **Audi Quattro Sport**

The Quattro Sport was a thoroughbred racing machine, with Kevlar bodywork built on a shortened Coupe chassis. This example was rallied by Hannu Mikkola and Arnie Hertz, and still wears its battle scars with pride.

and totally dependable grip made it a much-revered machine among performance car enthusiasts, who even today speak of it in hushed tones. Although the car was initially available only in left-hand-drive, British and Australian fans of the Quattro finally got right-hand-drive versions in 1983.

Quattro Sport

Launched as a homologation special for a proposed Group B rally car, the Quattro Sport is the most desirable and collectable of the Audi Quattro models. It was far from pretty, with a short wheelbase giving it an oddly truncated appearance, while a huge rear wing (fender), fat wheelarches and bumper-free nose made it look even more ungainly. Other modifications over a standard Quattro included a bodyshell made entirely from Kevlar, and a much more steeply raked windscreen – by request of the Audi rallying team, as this improved outward visibility.

Power came from a 2.1-litre (126ci), five-cylinder engine with four valves per cylinder – a

Specifications	
Engine type: Inline five-cylinder	Length: 4.06m (160in)
Displacement: 2133cc (130ci)	Width: 1.78m (70.1in)
Maximum power: 228kW (306bhp) at 6700rpm	Height: 1.34m (52.9in)
Top speed: 248km/h (154mph)	Wheelbase: 2.22m (87.6in)
0–96km/h (0–60mph): 5.0sec	Weight: 1300kg (2867lbs)

▶ **Audi Quattro UR**

Prior to 1989, the Quattro used a 2.1-litre (128ci) five-cylinder engine with two valves per cylinder. These models are known to enthusiasts as UR Quattros, *Ur* being German for 'original'.

Model	Years Built	0–96km/h (0–60mph)	Top Speed km/h (mph)
Coupe	1979–88	9.9sec	182 (113)
Quattro	1980–89	6.5sec	223 (138)
Quattro Sport	1983–85	4.8sec	249 (154)
Quattro 20v	1989–91	6.3sec	228 (141)

▲ **Audi Quattro 10v**
Although a brilliant car in standard form, the Quattro was still modified by some owners, who liked to experiment with its handling. This late 10v example has aftermarket alloy wheels and lowered suspension.

feature that would later appear on the mainstream production model – and the eventual power output was 355bhp (257kW).

Rally cars were much more potent than the road-going homologation models, though. The Quattro Sport S1, sold exclusively to rally teams, developed an enormous 600bhp (447kW). Unsurprisingly, the S1 became a competition winner first time out at the San Remo Rally, in the hands of legendary Audi driver Walter Rohrl. A modified version of the S1, driven by French female driver Michelle Mouton, also famously won the Pike's Peak International Hillclimb in 1985.

Quattro 20V

The four-valves-per-cylinder version of the Quattro was the ultimate road-going model to go into full-scale production. Launched in 1989 and built for the final two years of Quattro production, it took its name from the engine layout, as with five cylinders it had 20 valves in total. The 2.2-litre (134ci) engine had twin overhead camshafts and an electronic engine management system, which boosted the power output to 220bhp (164kW) – but it was the engine's prodigious torque that made the most difference, almost eliminating turbo lag. Audi

used a torque-sensing Torsen differential to distribute the power between the front and rear axles as appropriate, depending on the engine speed and load, and this engineering approach gave the 20V far better road manners than the rather crude original, which was renowned for its turbo lag and frantic acceleration. Yet despite being a far more civilized companion from behind the wheel, the 20V was also a faster vehicle: 0–60mph (0-96km/h) from a standstill took only 6.3 seconds – a figure that is less than many performance cars of today – while the top speed of 228km/h (141mph) was perfectly respectable for a performance model.

Admittedly, the Quattro 20V was flawed. It still looked smart from the outside, but the styling was dated, the interior was especially ancient-looking by this stage and the small, awkward-to-access boot (trunk) was comprehensively outclassed by most rivals – but it didn't matter. The Quattro was always a car that was all about driving, and no car of the 1980s was quite as accomplished, exciting or as well made.

◄ **Audi Quattro 20V**
Later Quattros came with four valves per cylinder and were both more responsive and more reliable than the earlier cars. They were by far the best road car versions of the Quattro, although by the time the 20V was launched in 1989 the car's motorsport career was but a distant memory.

BMW 02 Series
1966–77

There was a time when BMW's future looked very shaky indeed. Then along came its new compact model, the 1600, the forerunner of the classic 02 series.

1600/1602

Back in the early 1960s, BMW was in trouble. It had a fine range of well-made cars, but they were expensive to build and buy, and as a result their popularity was limited. What the company needed was a car that would take traditional BMW virtues to a more widespread market, and in 1966 that car arrived in the form of the 1600 (later badged 1602). Only marginally bigger than a Ford Escort, the 1600 had a pretty two-door body style, complete with smart 'clamshell' bonnet (hood) and boot (trunk) panels. Although fairly sparsely equipped and not especially quick, the 1600 was beautifully constructed and felt very special indeed compared to its main rivals. What is more, the 1600 was a truly excellent car to drive. The rear-drive chassis was communicative and stable, and the steering had a rewarding feel to it – it was these traits that would become BMW trademarks over the next four decades. As the 1600 evolved into the 02 series, the dynamic abilities of its chassis would soon become apparent …

▼ **BMW 2002**

It was sturdy rather than dynamic, but the original 02 was the car that transformed BMW's fortunes. Here was a compact car that had a level of build quality never before seen from a European volume manufacturer.

2002

If the major criticism of the 1600 was that it was inadequate in terms of performance, then the answer came in the form of the 2002, launched in 1968. Powered by a larger 2.0-litre (121ci) version of the 1600's overhead cam engine, the 2002 was lively, had great handling and possessed the added attraction of an optional five-speed gearbox, making it the world's first compact executive car – an area of the market that is still a BMW speciality even today. Not only that, but the 2002 was reasonably economical and held its value extremely well second-hand, meaning it even made financial sense to own one. Undisputedly the car that saved BMW, the 2002 set the tone for the company's monumental growth over the next 40 years.

▲ BMW 2002 Touring

Touring versions of the 1602 and 2002 were introduced in 1972 and successfully combined the practicality of an estate car (station wagon) with the style of a hatchback. Here is a 1974 2002 Touring with optional sports road wheels.

◀ BMW 2002 Touring

From 1973 onwards, the 02 had a minor facelift, with more black plastic parts replacing the original chrome detailing of earlier cars. The most noticeable difference is on the radiator grille – this example has much less brightwork than the earlier car featured on the preceding page.

▶ ▲ **BMW 2002tii**

BMW's first real sports saloon (sedan) was the 2002ti, closely followed by the tii. The tii had a Kugelfischer fuel injection system and an impressive power output of around 130bhp (97kW), yet despite the power styling remained discreet.

Specifications

Engine type: Inline four cylinder	Length: 4.23m (166.5in)
Displacement: 1990cc (121ci)	Width: 1.59m (62.6in)
Maximum power: 120kW (160bhp) at 6700rpm	Height: 1.41m (55.5in)
Top speed: 204km/h (127mph)	Wheelbase: 2.50m (98.4in)
0–96km/h (0–60mph): 9.2sec	Weight: 943kg (2080lbs)

1600/2002 Convertible

One of the few true four-seater convertibles of the 1960s, the 1600 Cabriolet was a stylish, fully open-topped version of the 1600 saloon (sedan). The bodywork was constructed by coachbuilder Baur and had no rollover bar. It was replaced by a ragtop version of the 2002 in 1971, but this was built with a different roof mechanism and proper roll hoop. This modification made the car more practical but far less pretty.

1602/2002 Touring

BMW was good at confounding its critics. First, it had responded to suggestions that the 1600 was underpowered by introducing the punchier 2002, then it answered claims that the two-door saloon body style was impractical by launching the Touring in 1971. Half hatchback, half estate (station wagon), the Touring offered greater loadspace and more flexibility for rear passengers.

Its launch also coincided with a minor facelift for the 02 line-up, which received revised interior trim, new wheel trims and chrome coachlines. The 2002 Touring remained in production until 1976, alongside the E21 3-Series, which was launched to replace the 02 range, but was never offered with an estate or hatchback variant. Indeed, it would be 1988, and midway through the later E30 3-Series life-cycle, before a Touring BMW appeared again.

2002ti/tii

The first attempt at a performance variant of the 2002 came in 1968 with the launch of the 2002ti. Fitted with twin-choke dual Weber carburettors, the ti was lively and rewarding to drive, exploiting the 02's chassis. However, neither American nor British buyers could experience the ti, as it was sold in mainland

◀ ▲ **BMW 2002 Turbo**

If the 2002tii hid its light under a bushel, then the Turbo model was its polar opposite. Finished with garish side stripes and riveted-on bubble-shaped wheelarches, the ultimate performance version of the 02 was most definitely not a shrinking violet.

Specifications

Engine type: Inline four-cylinder	Length: 4.22m (166.1in)
Displacement: 1990cc (121ci)	Width: 1.62m (63.8in)
Maximum power: 127kW (170bhp) at 5800rpm	Height: 1.40m (55in)
Top speed: 209km/h (130mph)	Wheelbase: 2.50m (98.4in)
0–96km/h (0–60mph): 7.6sec	Weight: 1080lbs

Europe only. They did, however, get the tii, which did away with the Weber carbs and replaced them with Kugelfischer fuel injection, which gave the tii 130bhp (97kW) – about as much as the car's unmodified chassis could take. Loved by performance car fans, the tii was BMW's seminal performance model, and the

precursor of the highly desirable M-Sport series of cars that would follow.

2002 Turbo

Building on the reputation of the now much-admired 02 model range, BMW scored another impressive first in 1973 with the launch of the 2002 Turbo. Although turbo technology had been tried and tested by various manufacturers in the past, it was the Bavarian maker that would be the first to offer it on a mainstream production car. Unsubtle, with a deep front spoiler and garish side decals, the 2002 Turbo was nevertheless a great car, with 170bhp (127kW) and a top speed of 227km/h (140mph), while revisions to the chassis and suspension layout made it handle even better than the tii.

Model	Years Built	0–96km/h (0–60mph)	Top Speed km/h (mph)
1602	1966–72	11.8secs	159 (99)
2002	1968–76	10.6secs	173 107)
2002 Touring	1968–76	10.8secs	173(107)
2002ti/tii	1968–74	8.3secs	188(116)
2002 Turbo	1973–74	6.9secs	227(140)
1502	1974–77	12.9secs	155 (97)

BMW's only mistake was to launch the car at the height of a global oil crisis, a time when such an indulgent model appeared out of place.

1502

Such was the universal popularity of the '02 range that when BMW introduced the E21 3-Series in 1974, it was loath to drop the car completely. The Touring model remained for a while as a practical alternative, while the saloon soldiered on in one trim level only: the new 1502. With a detuned version of the 1602 engine offering just 75bhp (56Kw), it was BMW's attempt at an economy model (reflecting concerns about fuel costs), although even then it came with a quality of build not seen on rivals. Equipment levels were highly spartan, though, and the 1502 wasn't even especially cheap, which meant that its sales success was limited to say the least. Production of the 1502 finally ceased in 1977.

▲ **BMW 2002tii (2006)**

BMW is a manufacturer committed to its heritage, and to prove this it decided to build an entirely 'new' 2002tii to mark the model's fortieth anniversary in 2006. The orange car, which is housed at the company's Munich HQ, was built entirely from spare parts still produced by BMW.

▼ **BMW 1502**

The 1502 was a basic car built to satisfy the demands of those who wanted a quality vehicle at a low price, much in the mould of the VW Beetle. It remained in production after the rest of the 02 Series had ceased, but wasn't in keeping with BMW's new marquee image.

Cadillac Eldorado
1953–70

Complete with an exotic-sounding Latin name, the Eldorado was the flagship of the Cadillac model range for almost 20 years.

Eldorado 1953–55

The first of the Eldorado line-up appeared in 1953, and was based upon the Cadillac 62 – a car that had, in itself, garnered a reputation for being one of the most advanced and desirable luxury models of its era. Classically styled, with a bulbous, rounded nose, elaborate chrome overriders in the bumpers and low-slung rear wheel spats, the 62 lent itself well to the concept of being developed into a flagship for the Cadillac brand.

The standard equipment list was phenomenal, even by today's standards, and it is incredible to think that many of the Eldorado's features even existed in the early 1950s, as some have yet to become commonplace on modern models. For $7,750, which may not sound a lot in today's money but certainly was then, an Eldorado buyer got a power-folding roof, electrically adjustable seats, electric windows, automatic transmission, air conditioning, central door locking, self-levelling suspension and a beautifully ornate dashboard-mounted record player.

Admittedly, the Eldorado 62 was rather brash, but it somehow remained more tasteful than many of its rivals, largely thanks to its exclusivity – the high price meant that Cadillac sold only 532 cars in total. Power came from GM's ubiquitous V8, which gave the Eldorado enough power to cruise at 161km/h (100mph) – the only downside being frighteningly heavy fuel consumption.

Eldorado Brougham 1956–59

For 1956, the Eldorado morphed from large convertible into a more limousine-like, four-door saloon (sedan), aimed at an older, less ostentatious buyer.

Even so, the styling was still intricate. It was penned by legendary designer Harley Earl, renowned for numerous GM designs through the company's most elaborate period, and widely regarded as the inventor of the tailfin. Fins were certainly something of which the

▼ **Cadillac 62**
The Series 62 had an unmistakable front profile – its radiator grille and bumpers were the epitome of the US motor industry's 1950s chrome excess.

In the Eldorado, Cadillac looked at new-era styling as well as new technology, including headlamps that were concealed behind retractable hoods bearing the Cadillac script log.

Specifications

Engine type: V8	Length: 5.71m (224.8in)
Displacement: 6391cc (390ci)	Width: 2.03m (79.9in)
Maximum power: 242kW (325bhp) at 4800rpm	Height: 1.42m (55.9in)
Top speed: 195km/h (121mph)	Wheelbase: 3.30m (130.0in)
0–96km/h (0–60mph): 11.0sec	Weight: 2216kg (4885lbs)

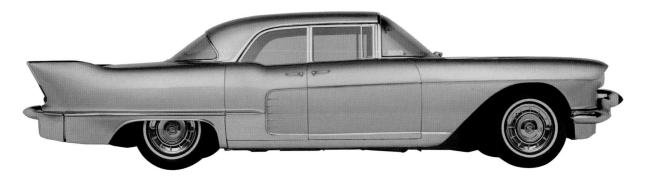

Eldorado Brougham could be proud. The trailing edge of the rear wings (fenders) rose prominently into blades at the rear to give the Brougham a look never before seen, but set to become one of the most well-known American styling cues of the 1950s and 1960s.

At the front, twin headlamps and distinctive 'cowhorn'-styled bumpers gave the Brougham an even more individual look, while from the side the styling was kept lean and low, with frameless doors and a coupe-height stainless-steel roof. Access to the rear was via reverse-opening doors, making access much simpler and more dignified for those who preferred to be driven, rather than drive themselves.

Like its predecessor, the Brougham featured numerous state-of-the-art features, including air suspension, which could be lowered at the push of a switch to make access easier from the pavements (sidewalks).

By 1959, the Brougham had been restyled by Pininfarina, and much of the appeal of Harley Earl's original was gone. These last cars were actually built in Italy and shipped to the United States, but were often criticized for their inferior build quality. While extremely rare, they are less collectable as a result.

▲ **Cadillac Eldorado Brougham**

Styled by Harley Earl, the Eldorado Brougham featured 'suicide' rear doors, which were designed to allow easier access to the rear seats and give the car a pillarless side profile.

Specifications

Engine type: V8	Length: 5.49m (216.3in)
Displacement: 5981cc (365ci)	Width: 1.99m (78.5in)
Maximum power: 242kW (325bhp) at 4800rpm	Height: 1.41m (55.5in)
Top speed: 177km/h (110mph)	Wheelbase: 3.20m (126.0in)
0–96km/h (0–60mph): 11.4sec	Weight: 2410kg (5315lbs)

▲ **Cadillac Eldorado Brougham**

Eldorado models stood out from lesser cars because the centre of the radiator grille was picked out in gold. The Brougham's 'Cowhorn' style bumper bars were very much a Cadillac trademark.

Eldorado/Coupe de Ville 1959

The 1959 Cadillac is one of the quintessential American classics – its flamboyant styling and sheer mass mean that it is instantly identifiable and can't be mistaken for anything else.

At almost 5.4m (225in) long, the replacement for the original Series 62 was nothing if not imposing, while it was also the widest car on the road at the time – a fact further emphasized by the menacing appearance of its quad headlamps and enormous 'cheese-grater' radiator grille.

Available as a coupe or a convertible, the '59 model continued the Eldorado line's reputation for innovation, introducing a feature called 'Twilight Sentinel', still used and so-named on GM cars today. Using light sensors inside the lamp lens, this would automatically sense dusk and switch the headlights on automatically, while it would also switch between dipped and full beam if another car came the other way.

▲ Cadillac Eldorado 1959 Coup de Ville

As with the original Series 62, the 1959 model had one of the most distinctive front ends of any car made in America. The car's eight-lamp front end is one of the United States' all-time design classics.

Specifications	
Engine type: V8	Length: 5.71m (224.8in)
Displacement: 6391cc (390ci)	Width: 2.03m (79.9in)
Maximum power: 242kW (325bhp) at 4800rpm	Height: 1.42m (55.9in)
Top speed: 195km/h (121mph)	Wheelbase: 3.30m (130.0in)
0–96km/h (0–60mph): 11.0sec	Weight: 2216kg (4885lbs)

Tailfins were all the rage in the 1950s, and Cadillac brought the decade to a close by taking them to their most impressive level yet. The 1959 Eldorado had huge fins that incorporated pointed tail lamps – the only car that could match the Cadillac's fins for height was the Plymouth Fury of the same year.

At the back, the Caddy got the biggest fins ever seen on a car, along with rear light clusters that were deliberately styled to look like jet engine afterburners.

You certainly couldn't criticize Cadillac for being unadventurous with its new generation of Series 62, but the car's immense size, high price and rather ostentatious appearance meant that it would appeal only to a certain type of buyer,

▼ Cadillac Eldorado FWD

It was all change as Cadillac moved towards the 1970s. Gone were the glitzy excesses of the Series 62 so beloved of stars such as Elvis Presley, to be replaced by a more sombre, square-edged front-wheel drive model.

especially when you looked at the available colour palette – more than one in five examples were finished in candy pink. The stalwart Cadillac for the early 1960s had a reputation for flamboyance all of its own, and, while it was successful in its own right, it did take Cadillac a while to shake off the image of the car's Hollywood-esque excesses.

Eldorado 1967–70

By the late 1960s, Cadillac's approach was a lot more discreet, and in styling terms the Eldorado of 1967 was an altogether more sober affair. It was still vast, but the fins and chrome were practically all gone, and the car had a much more subdued appearance as a result. It was still a big innovator, though, especially in light of Cadillac's traditional market. The Eldorado was front-wheel drive, which went against almost every rule in the book for an American luxury model, but it was always the brand's intention to shock.

Under the skin, it used the same separate chassis and 8.2-litre (455ci) engine as the even more oddball Oldsmobile Toronado – the only front-drive muscle car – while it was also offered as a coupe only. The mechanical layout and available power would have been too much for a roofless model to contend with, although the next-generation Eldorado FWD did come with the option of a folding soft-top. This was a big seller for Cadillac – almost 90,000 of the FWD vehicles were built, compared to the 532 of the very first Eldorado.

Model	Years	Number Built
1953 Eldorado	1953–55	532
1956 Eldorado Brougham	1956–59	904
1959 Eldorado/Coupe de Ville	1958–59	33,054
1967 Eldorado FWD	1966–70	89,633

Chevrolet Corvette
1953–

America's most legendary sports car, the Corvette is an enduring legend that transformed the way sports cars were built.

Corvette 1953–55

Given the legendary status of the Corvette today, those uninitiated in the car's history may be surprised to learn that the original incarnation was a bit of a commercial flop. The Corvette was an undeniably brilliant piece of design and engineering, but in sales terms fewer than 5,000 cars found homes in the first three years of production

The reasons behind this situation were threefold. First, the styling, penned by Harley

▶ ▲ **Chevrolet Corvette 1954**

As well as being the first car to bear the legendary name, the original Corvette was a design masterpiece, introducing a new method of construction to the car industry – the body was made entirely from fibreglass.

Specifications

Engine type: Inline six-cylinder	Length: 4.24m (167in)
Displacement: 3851cc (235ci)	Width: 1.83m (72.2in)
Maximum power: 112kW (150bhp) at 4200rpm	Height: 1.30m (51.3in)
Top speed: 172km/h (107mph)	Wheelbase: 2.59m (102in)
0–96km/h (0–60mph): 11.0sec	Weight: 1293kg (2851lbs)

The first-generation Corvette was a classic GM/Harley Earl design from the days when the company pretty much dictated the design themes for the entire US car industry. The Corvette's compact rear fins were definitely an Earl trademark, reminiscent of those seen on the back of the Cadillac Series 62 and Chevy Bel Air, but on a smaller, more rounded scale.

◀ **Chevrolet Corvette 1957**
More changes were afoot for the 1957 model year, with a leaner, less fussy body style penned by Bill Mitchell, one of Harley Earl's design team. A new grille, bigger air intakes and longer rear-deck panel were the car's most prominent features.

Corvette 1955

By 1955, the Chevrolet company was on the verge of dropping the Corvette altogether and writing it off as an expensive loss. But then along came Ford with the Thunderbird, and the 'Vette was given a stay of execution.

Earl, was considered somewhat strange in comparison to what American buyers were used to – the car was small, had a wraparound windscreen, detachable side windows and unusual curves. Second, the original six-cylinder engine was a bit weedy in terms of power, and third, it was made out of fibreglass, and the notion of a plastic car from the nation that invented steel was instantly unpopular.

It goes without saying that, thanks to its rarity, the first-generation Corvette is today highly sought-after, its plastic bodywork, ornate cabin and jukebox-style dash now revered by engineers and style fans alike. How times change …

The last of the 1953–55 cars had Chevy's famous small-block V8 under the bonnet (hood), carried over from the Bel Air saloon (sedan), and as a result were much more potent and beefier-sounding than the old straight-sixes. The lightweight bodywork also meant that the Corvette was faster than its Ford rival. A sudden upturn in interest led GM to commission an all-new car for 1956, instead of canning the project.

▶ ▼ **Chevrolet Corvette 1959 (Customized)**
The Corvette has always been popular with custom car fans. This particular example is a mild custom, with aftermarket wheels, lowered suspension and a chopped-down windscreen.

Specifications	
Engine type: V8	Length: 177.2in
Displacement: 6817cc (416ci)	Width: 4.5m (70.5in)
Maximum power: 339kW (454bhp) at 5,500rpm	Height: 1.2m (48.2in)
Top speed: 264km/h (164mph)	Wheelbase: 2.59m (102.0in)
0–96km/h (0–60mph): 4.6sec	Weight: 1188kg (2620lbs)

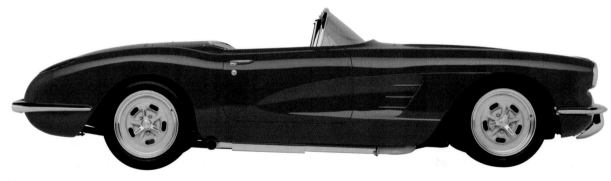

▶ **Chevrolet Corvette Sting Ray 1963**
The 1963 Sting Ray was a powerful beast, and its lightweight body and short rear-drive chassis also meant that it could be a real handful to drive in the wet. The Sting Ray's quad rear lamps remain a Corvette trademark to this day.

Corvette 1956–62

Based on the same chassis as the original Corvette, the second generation appeared midway through 1956 and had slightly less unusual body styling. This time, the shape came from the pen of Bill Mitchell, one of GM's senior stylists, but was still overseen by Harley Earl, and some of Earl's trademark touches were apparent, notable in the shape of the cabin tub and stylized grille and bumper arrangement.

The newcomer also saw the debut of one of Corvette's most enduring styling features in the form of its twin rear lamps – a cue seen on the latest models, along with every Corvette since the second generation.

Power for all of the new models came from a small-block V8, while from 1957 onwards a Rochester Ramjet fuel injection system was offered so that buyers could have even more power to play with, in turn making the Corvette a serious force to be reckoned with in performance terms – no other American car could match its acceleration. Finally, an interesting but little known Corvette fact – when

developing the car, Chevrolet evaluated the Jaguar XK120, which was renowned for its handling. Was it really a coincidence that, when the Corvette was launched, the two vehicles had an identical wheelbase?

Corvette Sting Ray

For its third generation, the Corvette morphed once again, this time into something really rather special. Styled by Bill Mitchell, the Sting Ray was the boldest-looking Corvette yet. In coupe form, the car had a distinctive split rear window, along with a distinctive, tapered rear-end profile that looked truly gorgeous.

But it wasn't just the back of the car that looked right. Up front, the previous car's fixed twin headlamps were replaced by pop-up versions, while in profile the car exhibited butch-looking swollen wheelarches.

The split-window models are the most collectable of the Sting Ray generation. Because the window was for there for style and style alone, GM insisted that it was replaced by a one-piece window for models from 1964 onwards on grounds of cost.

Inside, the Sting Ray was much more mature than earlier 'Vettes, with a multi-dial dashboard, three-spoke wood-rimmed steering wheel and full carpets and door cards – luxuries not previously familiar to all buyers.

Convertible models were arguably less pretty than the coupes because the convertibles lost much of the rear detailing, although the roof

Specifications

Engine type: V8	Length: 4.45m (175.3in)
Displacement: 5359cc (327ci)	Width: 1.77m (69.6in)
Maximum power: 224kW (300bhp) at 5000rpm	Height: 1.26m (49.8in)
Top speed: 190km/h (118mph)	Wheelbase: 2.49m (98.0in)
0–96km/h (0–60mph): 6.1sec	Weight: 1433kg (3160lbs)

◀ ▲ **Chevrolet Corvette Sting Ray 1963**

One of the boldest and most distinctive shapes in motoring history, the coupe-bodied Corvette Sting Ray was an instant hit, although GM cost-cutting meant that the original two-piece rear window was dropped after the first year.

could be folded away completely and stowed beneath a flush-fitting fibreglass panel to keep things neat and tidy.

1968–83

Replacing the Sting Ray was no mean feat. In its creation, GM had put the Corvette firmly on the map, and the car was considered a legend in its own lifetime. To come up with worthy successor was going to be a tricky task.

Yet at the 1966 Motorama, Chevy showed a concept car called the Mako Shark, styled by Larry Shinola. Taking its styling cues directly from a great white, the Shark had cooling fins on

its sides, a distinctly fish-like profile and was wider at the front than the rear. Two years later, and changed only in the detail, that car became the new Corvette.

Available as a coupe, complete with flying buttress-style rear pillars, or as an incredibly pretty convertible, the Corvette 'Sharknose' was an instant classic. Powertrains were all V8, although buyers could choose between the Chevy small-block V8 or the more potent big-block; enthusiasts preferred the smaller engines as they were better balanced and easier to handle. The Stingray name made a comeback in 1969, albeit as one word this time, to mark out the flagship versions, while the ultimate incarnation was the L88. Only 116 examples were built in 1969, with an estimated 530bhp (395Kw) on tap – making them incredibly quick.

Such was the purity of the Sharknose Corvette's shape that Chevrolet felt no need to replace it until 1983, after a 15-year production run. That said, it was the earlier cars that were by far the best, as those from the mid-1970s onwards fell victim to emissions regulations and the addition of safety equipment that detracted from the original styling.

1984 Corvette

Officially the 'Corvette that never was', the C4 generation, as it was known internally, was due to go on sale in 1983, but never actually made it to the showrooms. Thanks to various complications during the launch process, the launch was delayed on several occasions, and in the end there were no Corvettes built or sold in the 1984 model year, other than 43 pre-production prototypes. Of these, only one survives, and lives in the National Corvette Museum at Bowling Green, Kentucky. If you see a 1984 Corvette for sale, it's a fake …

Corvette C4 1985–96

Launched for the 1985 model year, the Corvette C4 was styled by Jerry Palmer under the guidance of GM's chief engineer Dave McLellan.

With the exception of the venerable small-block V8 – a stalwart component of any Corvette from 1955 onwards, the car was entirely new from the ground up, although it was still built on traditional Corvette principles of a fibreglass body encapsulating a separate chassis.

Given the longevity of the Sharknose model, Palmer had been briefed to create a car the wouldn't age too badly, the aim being to once again launch a 'Vette that could enjoy a life of

heady sales for well over a decade, thus saving GM the development costs of an all-new model.

Inside, the car was much more spacious and comfortable, while the car had a much lower drag coefficient (0.34) than its predecessor, making it more aerodynamic and significantly reducing wind noise.

Four body styles were offered – coupe, targa, soft-top and T-top, while a moderate facelift in 1993 saw the car receive more rounded nose and tail sections, plus a better quality interior.

Corvette ZR-1

The ultimate expression of the C4, the ZR-1 was one of a series of cars developed for GM by the British sports car maker Lotus. Developed alongside the Lotus Carlton/Omega super saloon designed for Europe, the ZR-1 had an exclusive six-speed manual gearbox coupled to a Lotus-developed quad-cam V8 based on the classic small-block unit. It came with a special fuel injection system and four valves per cylinder, and was capable of developing an incredible 375bhp (280kW).

▶ **Chevrolet Corvette 1969**

Known affectionately as the Sharknose, the 1969 Corvette enjoyed one of the longest production runs of any American car. Fifteen years after its debut, examples were still rolling off the production line in Bowling Green, Kentucky.

Specifications	
Engine type: V8	Length: 4.34m (171.0in)
Displacement: 6997cc (427ci)	Width: 1.72m (67.8in)
Maximum power: 324kW (435bhp) at 5600rpm	Height: 1.24m (48.9in)
Top speed: 217km/h (135mph)	Wheelbase: 2.49m (98.0in)
0–96km/h (0–60mph): 5.5sec	Weight: 1427kg (3145lbs)

◀ ▲ **Chevrolet Corvette ZR-1 1991**
Bigger and butcher than earlier models, the Corvette ZR-1 wasn't an especially laid-back affair. Yet despite its exterior excesses, this was a finely honed performance car that could rival most European supercars.

Specifications	
Engine type: LT5 V8	Length: 4.53m (178.5in)
Displacement: 5735cc (350ci)	Width: 1.86m (73.2in)
Maximum power: 280kW (375bhp) at 5800rpm	Height: 1.89m (46.7in)
Top speed: 290km/h (180mph)	Wheelbase: 2.44m (96.2in)
0–96km/h (0–60mph): 5.0sec	Weight: 1596kg (3519lbs)

Corvette C5 1997–2004

After 11 years of successful sales the C4 Corvette was eventually replaced in 1997, this time by a much more powerful yet also more civilized car. Available as a coupe or a convertible from the beginning, the Corvette C5 was designed from the outset to do battle with European sports models such as the Porsche 911 and TVR Cerbera, and this meant that as well as being true to the Corvette's legendary tradition (which effectively meant it had to have a small-block V8, a steel chassis and fibreglass bodywork), it also had to be well made, well equipped, comfortable and also accomplished to drive.

Performance-wise, the C5 was phenomenal. The design team had taken a lot of weight out of the car's chassis, and the new, lighter car was able to accelerate from 0 to 60mph (96km/h) in a mere 5.8 seconds, then on to a top speed of 272km/h (168mph).

Yet despite the great performance, the C5 was still luxurious, with leather trim, air conditioning and a well-equipped cabin.

The handling was entertaining, and grip was excellent despite the fact that Chevrolet still insisted on using leaf springs for the rear suspension set-up, although in the eyes of some enthusiasts this added to the car's tail-happy

▶ **Chevrolet Corvette C5 1998**
Softer and rounder than the C4, the Corvette C5 was a much more forgiving car to drive. It was also sensationally quick and well equipped.

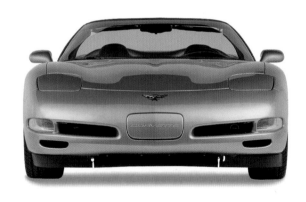

cornering characteristics and was actually part of the C5's appeal.

The days of a production car lasting for more than 10 years were well and truly over by this stage, however, and by the time the 2005 Geneva Motor Show came around, it was time for Chevrolet to launch a replacement …

Corvette C6 2005

Replacing the C5 wasn't easy – it had been the first Corvette to really take the fight to some of Europe's top performance models, where American models had traditionally fared badly, and it had done wonders for the car's reputation as a result.

But in the C6, Chevrolet unveiled the most technically advanced Corvette yet. True, it still had leaf springs at the back and still used the traditional pushrod V8 engine beloved of generations of hot GM models, but it also came with features such as a computer-aided gearshift, traction control and a clever head-up display, which projects the car's speed onto the windscreen ahead of the driver so he needn't look away from the road at his instruments.

The C6 was also the first Corvette since 1962 to have exposed headlamps. This configuration was a side effect of tight global safety legislation, which banned pop-up lamps from any car

developed from 2000 onwards on the grounds of pedestrian safety.

In 2006, Chevy unveiled the Corvette Z-06. With a 7.0-litre (428ci) V8 engine, the Z06 is the fastest Corvette ever, hitting 60mph (96km/h) from rest in just 3.9 seconds during a road test by US magazine *Car and Driver*.

In 2007, Chevrolet announced even more power for the Corvette by increasing the capacity of the LS2 engine to 6.2 litres (378ci) in a special performance model called the Z07.

Model	0–96km/h (0–60mph)	Top speed km/h (mph)
53–55	9.8sec	202 (125)
56–59	8.8sec	210 (130)
59–62	8.8sec	210 (130)
Sting Ray	6.5sec	235 (145)
68–83	6.7sec	243 (150)
85–96	7.2sec	259 (160)
96–04	6.4sec	286 (177)
05–date	6.3sec	291 (180)

Model	Years Built	Number Built
53–55	1953–55	4,640
56–59	1955–59	28,644
59–62	1959–62	35,731
Sting Ray	1962–67	117,964
68–83	1967–83	566,683
85–96	1984–96	366,267
96–04	1996–2004	248,715
05–date	2004–on	N/A

Specifications

Engine type: V8	Length: 4.56m (179.7in)
Displacement: 5686cc (347ci)	Width: 1.87m (73.6in)
Maximum power: 257kW (345bhp) at 5400rpm	Height: 1.21m (47.7in)
Top speed: 282km/h (175mph)	Wheelbase: 2.64m (104.5in)
0–96km/h (0–60mph): 4.7sec	Weight: 1461kg (3220lbs)

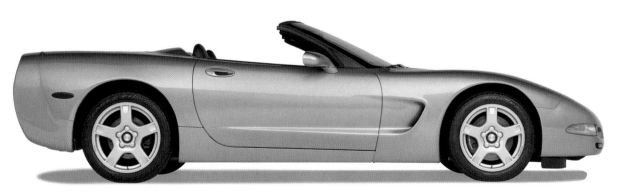

Citroën 2CV
1948–90

A legend for more than 40 years, France's 'Tin Snail' was conceived in the most unlikely circumstances, but became a symbol of French ingenuity and charm.

2CV 1948–60

Having already pioneered front-wheel drive in the Traction Avant, Citroën wanted to develop a car that would have the versatility and popularity of the Ford Model T, based on front-wheel drive technology and very simple construction methods and techniques.

As such, Andre Citroën set the 2CV chief designer, Pierre Boulanger, a rather unusual mission – to create a car that could be driven across a rough ploughed field, without losing any of its traction, and do it with a box of eggs sitting on the passenger seat without breaking a single one of them.

Work started in earnest in 1938, but then came the disruption of World War II, and the first ungainly prototypes (which looked much like corrugated-iron chicken sheds) were put into hiding for safekeeping until the war was finally over in 1945.

It would be another 10 years before the first 2CVs appeared, but when they did they wormed their way firmly into the French consciousness. They were cheap, fun to drive and equipped with a folding canvas roof so that you could store your baguettes on the back seat without having to

Specifications	
Engine type: Horizontally opposed rwo-cylinder	Length: 3.78m (149in)
Displacement: 375cc (22.9ci)	Width: 1.47m (58in)
Maximum power: 6.71kW (9bhp) at 3500rpm	Height: 1.60m (63in)
Top speed: 66km/h (41mph)	Wheelbase: 2.40m (94.4in)
0–96km/h (0–60mph): n/a	Weight: 499kg (1100lbs)

▶ ▼ **Citroën 2CV**
The original 2CV was an object lesson in keeping costs to a minimum. It featured flimsy tin body panels, basic steel seat frames and a cheap fabric roof, yet also spacious and easy to drive.

break them. The car was just what the French people were looking for. It was rugged and utilitarian in rural areas, yet chic and easy to drive in urban landscapes, and rewardingly cheap to buy and run in either environment. The original 'Deux Chevaux' (meaning 'two horses' – the suggestion being that the 2CV could do the farm work of both) became such a phenomenal success story that Citroën had to open factories in the United Kingdom, Spain and Portugal to cope with the pan-European demand.

2CV/2CV6 1960–90

The one and only major facelift in the 2CV's life came in 1960, when the original car's corrugated body panels were smoothed off and the interior was redesigned so that the seats could be removed and used as outdoor furniture where necessary.

The original 425cc (25.9ci) engine was supplemented by a more potent 602cc (36.7ci) unit from 1963, which proved to be a popular option and was made standard in 1970 when the range was rechristened 2CV6.

▲ **Citroën 2CV Sahara**
Sahara models employed a bizarre yet effective four-wheel drive system. The conventional front-mounted engine drove the front wheels, and a second engine was hidden in the boot (trunk) to drive the back axle.

Over the years, there was a myriad of special editions. The luxury Charleston, for example, had classic colour schemes and buttons on the seats, while the 1970s Spot had garish orange body graphics and denim interior trim, and the ubiquitous Dolly came in various bright colour schemes and was pretty much the standard model in the car's later years, outselling the non-limited edition Special.

Cars built from 1982 onwards had disc brakes as standard, which made a huge difference, although the very last cars, built from 1988 to 1990, were made in Portugal only and suffered from poor build quality and corrosion problems. Regardless, the inimitable 2CV is one of the world's most incredible cars, with a timeless and classic appeal.

2CV Sahara

North Africa was an important market for Citroën, so the decision to introduce the Sahara made a lot of sense, even if the concept of the car was a little unusual. Rather than go to the expense of a complicated four-wheel drive

fashion to turn them into unique cars in their own right. Using a fibreglass coupe shell, the Bijou (meaning 'jewel') was based on the 2CV running gear, but much of the interior came from the DS model. The Bijou was an interesting anomaly, but was also a slow, crude and unpleasantly cramped car.

system for the 2CV, Citroën instead decided to simply use two engines, one at the front of the vehicle and one at the back. Each drove a separate axle, while in normal driving mode the rear engine could be switched off to save fuel. Although a seemingly demented idea, the Sahara actually remained in production for eight years and, thanks to its simple yet effective suspension and good ground clearance, was a far better off-road machine than most people gave it credit for.

Mehari

A classical example of Citroën having fun with the 2CV theme, the Mehari was introduced in 1968 as a bargain-priced alternative to a Jeep. The bodywork was almost completely open to the elements, with a canvas tilt to keep the worst of the weather at bay and a one-piece body tub, moulded out of ABS plastic, to keep costs to an absolute minimum.

Bijou

The only 2CV variant never to be built in France, the Bijou was the idea of Citroën's UK operation, which was building cars in Slough, Berkshire, from 1953 to 1960. When it stopped making 2CVs in 1959, the Slough factory was left with several incomplete chassis, and rather than break them up it decided in enterprising

▶ **Citroën Mehari**

One of the more entertaining 2CV variants, the Citroën Mehari was a much less expensive alternative to a Jeep. It was really only useful in warm climates, however, as the canvas top wasn't very weatherproof.

▲ Citroën Ami
With its rear sloping back window and strange headlight 'eyebrows', the Ami 6 wasn't much of a looker – but it was a fun, cheap and practical family car.

The specification was as basic as you could possibly imagine – seats, a speedometer and a fuel gauge were about as much as you got. The Mehari proved especially popular in French (and some other European) holiday resorts, however, where it became an especially funky and inexpensive hire car for many a holidaymaker. Indeed, in some resorts you still see them plying their trade. The Mehari was great fun to drive, but the biggest concern was its safety – the plastic bodyshell wasn't flame-retardant, while it also offered very little in the way of protection in the event of an accident.

Ami 6

Citroën's attempt at building an upmarket version of the 2CV, the Ami 6 was much more of a family-orientated model, with bodywork that looked more modern than the 2CV, albeit fabulously ugly.

The first Amis had a reverse-raked rear windscreen that was reminiscent of the British Ford Anglia, while at the front odd-shaped stainless-steel cowlings housed headlamps that were completely the wrong shape for the car. It was reasonably comfortable, however – although the conventional boot (trunk) did little for the car's practicality. This issue was addressed with the Ami 8.

Ami 8

Not quite as ungainly as the Ami 6, the Ami 8 not only looked more palatable, but was also more practical than its predecessor. It had a full-length tailgate at the rear, giving it load-lugging capacity similar to an estate (station wagon) and proving surprisingly popular as a result. Thanks to low running costs, a cheap purchase price in the first place and ease of maintenance, almost two million Ami models were shifted by Citroën, and they remained in production for 18 years.

Ami Super

In response to people who liked the concept of the Ami, but weren't convinced by its two-cylinder engine, Citroën offered the Super. The flagship of the range came with a flat-four unit from the recently launched GS, and, although 61bhp (45kW) of power might not sound a huge amount on paper, it was more than enough for the Ami with its lightweight 2CV chassis. Skinny tyres, roly-poly cornering characteristics and the 2CV's weird push-pull gearchange made it quite a dramatic machine to drive – thoroughly entertaining in the right hands, but truly big box-like rear end, crudely finished in corrugated metal, but beloved of the French postal service for years.

An unusual tax law in France meant that Citroën offered a rear bench seat and side windows that buyers could fit to the vans themselves, thus avoiding having to pay purchase tax or passenger car road tax rates. Needless to say, take-up on the option proved very popular.

Today, a network of specialists exists, dedicated to the long-term survival of the 2CV and its many variants. Indeed, the 2CV Centre in Frome, Somerset, in the United Kingdom, has started building 'new' 2CV6s to order, using brand-new galvanized steel chassis and new panels made from the original pressings. Judging by the number of cars it either sells or restores (currently more than 20 a year), there is still sufficient demand out there from a devout band of enthusiasts to guarantee the 2CV a healthy future. Ironically, nearly half of the rebuilt 2CVs that the company supplies are owned or commissioned by customers in France.

▲ Citroën 2CV van

The 2CV's versatility knew no boundaries – the panel van variant being a simple yet effective way of transporting goods or, indeed, family members.

frightening in the wrong ones. Whatever the case, the Ami Super undoubtedly had character.

Dyane

By 1967, Citroën had decided the 2CV was ripe for replacement. It was, apparently, too much like a vintage car, and customers wanted something that was a little more practical, without separate wings (fenders) and with a more luxurious cabin. That car would be the Dyane, and it would also introduce the innovation of a hatchback at a price level that wouldn't scare traditional 2CV fans off. The price, though, had nothing to do with it. To call a car that sold almost 1.5 million a failure would be a little harsh, but, while it was a good seller for Citroën and enjoyed an 18-year production run, the Dyane did fail in its original aim. The car it was supposed to replace outlived it by five years …

2CV Van/Acadiane

As well as its many uses in standard form, the 2CV (and even Dyane) were converted into commercial vehicles, the former coming with a

Model	Years Built	0–96km/h (0-60mph)	Top Speed km/h (mph)
48–60	1948–60	N/A	65 (43)
60–90	1960–90	32.8	107 (67)
Sahara	1958–66	N/A	104 (65)
Bijou	1959–64	N/A	96 (60)
Mehari	1968–86	25.4	107 (67)
Ami 6	1961–69	44.0	108 (68)
Ami 8	1969–79	31.7	114 (72)
Ami Super	1972–76	17.1	134 (88)
Dyane	1967–85	30.8	109 (69)
Acadiane/Van	1955–90	N/A	96 (60)

Citroën DS
1955

Pronounced Déesse, meaning 'goddess', Citroën's first big saloon (sedan) introduced a pack of historically significant features – and was beautiful, too.

DS

Technologically, stylistically and aerodynamically astonishing, the Citroën DS probably brought more to the market in one package than any other car. Launched in 1955, the DS had unique hydro-pneumatic self-levelling suspension, headlamps that swivelled with the steering to help the driver see round corners, a clever unitary construction bodyshell, with bolt-on external panels for ease of repair, hydraulic brakes and the option of a semi-automatic gearbox. Not only that, but also the car's styling was avant-garde, yet remained beautiful at the same time. After 20 years in production and sales of almost 1.5 million, the DS was taken out of production – but even then it was still far more advanced than many of its contemporaries, such was its importance when new.

ID

ID, or Idée, meaning 'idea', was a more basic version of the DS and had far fewer pneumatic features. The suspension still did the whole Citroën levitation thing for which the DS was

Specifications

Engine type: Inline four-cylinder	Length: 4.80m (189in)
Displacement: 2175cc (133ci)	Width: 1.79m (70.5in)
Maximum power: 81kW (108bhp) at 5500rpm	Height: 1.6m (63in)
Top speed: 153km/h (95mph)	Wheelbase: 3.12m (123in)
0–96km/h (0–60mph): 18.4sec	Weight: 1324kg (2919lbs)

▶ ▼ **Citroen DS**

Even today, it's hard to believe that the DS's shark-shaped styling originated in the first part of the 1950s. And that's even before you look at the car's many other technical innovations.

▶ **Citroen DS Pallas**

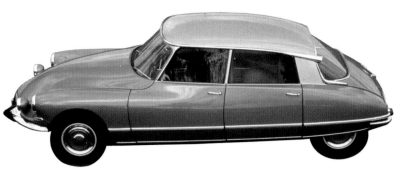

On more luxurious DS variants, supplementary front llamps were fitted that swivelled with the car's steering wheel to help the driver see round corners – an innovation seen on many cars of today.

famous, but it had conventional brakes, headlamps and steering, and was less of a challenge to maintain as a result. It was as attractively styled as a DS, but compared to its more accomplished sister you do feel you're missing out on something if you drive one.

Décapotable

The Décap is the most desirable DS variant, with an elegant two-door body and a full foldaway hood. Mechanically identical to the DS, the car was offered for two years only and a total of just 1365 were officially built – although French coachbuilder Chapron, which finished the 'official' cars for Citroën, went on to build several more …

Safari/Familiale

Here was a truly massive estate car (station wagon) that did away with some of the styling appeal of the DS, but was nonetheless intriguing. It came with unusual round rear lamps, a split

Model	Years Built	0–96km/h (0–60mph)	Top Speed km/h (mph)
DS	1955–75	18.4secs	148 (92)
ID	1957–75	21.1secs	140 (87)
Decaptoable	1961–71	14.1secs	173 (107)
Safari/Familiale	1958–75	15.6secs	157 (97)
Pallas	1971–75	10.4secs	194 (120)

tailgate and no wheel spats, giving it a rather weird appearance, but for carrying loads the estate version of the DS was hard to beat. The Safari was a seven-seater with inward-facing rear seats, but the Familiale would seat eight in three rows.

Pallas

The flagship of the DS range is a truly beautiful machine. Fitted with every option imaginable, the Pallas looks best in a dark metallic colour, with traditional yellow headlamps. Leather, fuel injection, unique wheel trims and chrome rubbing strips distinguish the government ministers' favourite from lesser DS variants.

▼ **Citroën DS Safari**

If you wanted space, the DS Safari had more than enough on offer, as well as a level of comfort and ride quality that the family would love. The only downside was that you lost the saloon model's glorious looks.

Datsun Z-Cars
1969–

America's big three weren't ready for Datsun's first Z-Car – it even made a dent in sales of the Ford Mustang.

Part of the original 240Z's appeal was the smoothness of its six-cylinder engine. This had a double advantage for Datsun, which was aiming to conquer the American market. To a start, it matched the cylinder capacity of entry-level versions of the Ford Mustang and Chevrolet Corvair, which were considered direct competitors, while at the same time it offered two more cylinders than most of its European rivals, which had small and noisy four-cylinder units. The only exception was the Triumph GT6.

240Z

For years, the affordable sports car market had been dominated by British and American makers, so the Datsun 240Z's arrival came as quite a surprise – not least to the likes of America's muscle car makers, and Britain's MG, Jaguar and Triumph. Here was a cheap, affordable sports car with a stunning body, styled by none other than Count Albrecht Goertz – the man behind the legendary BMW 507. With a big six-cylinder engine, rear-wheel drive and a level of reliability that the Japanese soon became renowned for, the 240Z quickly

▼ **Datsun 240Z**

A classic case of a manufacturer getting it right first time, the Datsun 240Z was a difficult car to beat. Its handsome looks, agile handling, lively performance and luxurious equipment levels made it irresistible.

became the world's fastest selling sports car. Indeed, initial sales in the United States were so strong that Datsun didn't export them anywhere else for the first two years of production, as it couldn't build enough 240Zs to satisfy demand.

The earliest cars are definitely the prettiest, with matt black hubcaps, slim bumpers and opening rear quarterlights.

260Z

After five years, the 240Z was adapted to comply with tight new emissions legislation, meaning that the engine size was increased to compensate for the inevitable effects of detuning. In reality, the 2.6-litre (159ci) 260Z had comparable performance to the 240Z and was a decent car, but it wasn't the original, and minor styling changes such as larger rear lamps, thicker bumpers and a much fussier interior took away some of the sportiness.

That said, 260Zs were generally better equipped than 240Zs, and, although the visual differences are relatively slight, the 260 is a much cheaper buy for the enthusiast looking for classic Z-Car style without the extra cost.

From 1975 onwards, even tougher emissions laws led Datsun to increase the size of the engine in US-specification cars to once again compensate for strangulation of the car's air intake system, and thus the 2.8-litre (171ci) 280Z

was born. The particular version was sold only in the United States, though, as other markets continued with the 260Z.

260Z 2+2

One problem that Datsun faced with the 260Z was a general decline in sales of two-seater cars. By the mid-1970s, British sports cars were becoming fewer, and America's breed of Pony cars, launched off the back of the Mustang, were generally four-seaters, making it an unwritten rule that, if you didn't have a four-seater, you were missing out on something.

Whether it was worth gaining a couple of seats for the sacrifice faced by 260Z buyers was a different matter, though – although the appeal of a 2+2 version of a Datsun Z was obvious, the execution wasn't brilliant. The car's wheelbase was increased by 30.5cm (12in), and the roofline was raised so that back-seat passengers had more headroom. The doors and rear quarter panel were lengthened to try to disguise the changes, but much of the original Z-Car's design harmony was lost, and today the 2+2 is very much the poor relation in the Z-Car line-up.

280ZX 1978–83

By the third incarnation, Datsun's Z-Car had morphed from being a proper, hairy-chested sports car into a flabby, tired-looking and over-decorated cruising car. It was much larger, heavier and wider than before, and, while this meant that the four-seater cabin had much more space for its occupants, it also meant that the original lithe appeal of the 240Z was well and truly gone. Add in the 280Z's ability to rot badly, and the fact that the power steering was far too heavily assisted, and you can see why fans of the original were disappointed. Its two saving graces were its smooth straight-six engine and the option of a targa roof.

300ZX 1984–89

Replacing the 280ZX in 1984, Nissan (as Datsun was now known) introduced what was really the final expression of the original Z concept. Like the 280ZX, it was too heavy and cumbersome to

This is a UK-specification 260Z interior, and it clearly illustrates what British buyers found alluring about the car. Specification levels were significantly better than those found on most rival models, with a radio, heated rear window, rev counter and heater as standard. On most British cars of the era, each of these luxuries had to be paid for separately.

▶ ▼ **Datsun 260Z 2+2**

This is a 2+2 version of the 260Z, identifiable by its longer wheelbase and slightly awkward-looking rear side window. Although not as pure-looking as the two-seater, it proved popular with families who wanted a sexy second car.

Specifications

Engine type: Inline six-cylinder	Length: 4.40m (173.2in)
Displacement: 2565cc (156.5ci)	Width: 1.65m (65.0in)
Maximum power: 121kW (162bhp) at 5200rpm	Height: 1.29m (50.6in)
Top speed: 182km/h (113mph)	Wheelbase: 2.61m (102.6in)
0–96km/h (0–60mph): 10sec	Weight: 1211kg (2669lbs)

really call itself a sports car, but in its defence it was incredibly smooth and comfortable to drive. That, of course, made it quite a good car, especially when you factored in Nissan's legendary dependability, but it also meant it was a dreadful sports car, with very little to stir the soul. A turbo version (from 1987) raised an eyebrow, but wasn't accomplished enough to really get things going. It was a steady seller for Nissan, but not one of its best efforts.

300ZX 1989-95

If the 1980s 300ZX was a damp squib, then the 1990s incarnation offered a glimmer of hope. Powered by a twin-turbo engine, the newcomer looked fabulous compared to the two most recent ZX models. It was also devilishly quick and had the ability to excite, even if its handling wasn't the most accomplished for a sports car. Its downfall was its reliance on a fairly old powerplant, revised from that of the previous car, as this failed to meet post-1996 emissions legislation, and the cost of reengineering it to accept a newer unit was prohibitive. The Z-Car was finally killed off … or was it?

350Z 2003–

Come 2003, and enter the 350Z – Nissan's revival of one of its most famous model lines, and this time minus the X part of the badge to prove that the company really was not looking towards past glory to promote its new car. And not without good reason. Powered by a 3.5-litre (213ci) V6, the 350Z made an incredible debut. It had a mind-blowing performance in terms of both acceleration and its top speed. It also had a great chassis and a superb smooth gearshift. Into the bargain, the 350Z was also fabulous value for money, so much so that there was a waiting list in operation as soon as the car went on sale. Here was a sure-fire case of a little bit of history repeating itself …

◀ ▼ **Datsun 280ZX**

Instantly identifiable as a member of the Z-Car family, but nowhere near as neatly styled or delicately detailed, the 280ZX was nonetheless a popular car for Datsun.

Specifications

Engine type: Inline six-cylinder	Length: 4.32m (174.0in)
Displacement: 2753cc (168ci)	Width: 1.69m (66.5in)
Maximum power: 101kW (135bhp) at 5200rpm	Height: 1.30m (51.0in)
Top speed: 195km/h (121mph)	Wheelbase: 2.32m (91.3in)
0–96km/h (0–60mph): 9.2sec	Weight: 1281kg (2825lbs)

Specifications

Engine type: V6	Length: 4.52m (178.2in)
Displacement: 2960cc (180ci)	Width: 1.8m (70.9in)
Maximum power: 223kW (300bhp) at 6400rpm	Height: 1.25m (49.4in)
Top speed: 249km/h (155mph)	Wheelbase: 2.57m (101.2in)
0–96km/h (0–60mph): 5.8sec	Weight: 1580kg (3485lbs)

350Z Convertible

A year after the 350Z caused a stir, Nissan added to the model's appeal by introducing a ragtop variant. The 350Z convertible had the same 3.5-litre (213ci) V6 engine as the coupe, along with its superb six-speed manual gearbox or automatic option, but with the advantage of a power folding fabric roof. Although criticized by some for being a car designed primarily for posing in, the 350Z cabriolet was still a well thought-out driver's machine, with a stiff chassis and excellent steering feedback – the only downside was the relatively high cost compared to that of the hardtop model.

▲ **Nissan 300ZX Turbo**

Now badged as a Nissan, the 300ZX Turbo was quick, but crude. Unsurprisingly, it still sold in great numbers to buyers who loved the car's reputation for reliability, but unlike the 240Z it will never be remembered as one of the all-time greats.

▼ **Nissan 350Z**

It was a long time coming, but the car that reignited the spirit of the original 240Z finally came along in 2003 in the shape of the 350Z. It offered fine handling and great value for money, the two things that set its legendary forebear apart.

Model	Years Built	0–96km/h (0–60mph)	Top Speed km/h (mph)
240Z	1969–74	8.0secs	202 (125)
260Z	1974–79	9.9secs	194 (120)
260Z 2+2	1974–77	10.1secs	186 (115)
280ZX	1978–83	9.8secs	181 (112)
300ZX	1984–89	7.0secs	231 (143)
300ZX	1989–95	5.6secs	250 (155)
350Z	2003–	5.4secs	248 (154)

Ferrari 200 Series
1951–67

Picking a finest hour in Ferrari's history is tricky, but the 200 series cars of the 1950s and 1960s were perhaps the company's most beautiful models.

212

The first Ferrari to bear a 200 series badge was the 212, although this was in effect a race-bred version of the earlier 195 – a car that was designed primarily to compete in long-distance endurance and touring events. It used a V12 engine developed by former racing driver Enzo Ferrari, whose company had been set up in 1948 and, when the 212 appeared in 1951, was still in its infancy. The unit was relatively small for a V12, being only 2.6 litres (159ci) in capacity, yet it was still capable of developing as much as 170bhp (127kW).

A choice of different bodies were offered by Ghia, Vignale and Pininfarina, as by this stage Ferrari had yet to establish his long-standing (and still continuing) relationship with Pininfarina for body styling.

The most common 212 was actually the Export model, designed for and sold primarily to buyers in the United States. It had basically the same chassis as other models, but the 212 Inter (also offered for export) had a longer wheelbase and was more suited to those buyers wanting a Ferrari for road use.

250 Europa

Undisputedly a pretty vehicle, the 250 Europa was the very first Ferrari to be developed solely for road use. The Europa went on sale in 1953, with a Pininfarina-designed coupe body. Note, however, that other coachbuilders were still supplying alternative bodywork according to customer preferences.

As with the 212, the Europa was based on the chassis of the original 212 and had a new derivative of the Aurelio Lampredi–designed V12 engine, this time with a displacement of 2963cc (181ci) and twin overhead camshafts.

▼ **Ferrari 212**

With a long chassis and bulky bodywork, the 212 is not necessarily what you would expect of a Ferrari. Despite its size, however, the car was still fast and surprisingly agile during manoeuvres.

In standard tune, the engine developed 200bhp (150kW), and this was more than enough for most, although some drivers who insisted on using their 250 Europas for motor racing had them tuned to develop as much as 250bhp (162kW), and sometimes beyond.

The Europa is widely regarded as one of the most usable Ferraris ever, even compared to those of modern times, thanks to its modest power output, all-syncromesh gearbox and relatively reasonable fuel consumption. Indeed, only its rarity (17 examples were built) and subsequent high value would put you off using one on a daily basis.

250 GT

The Europa might have been the first Ferrari to be engineered for the road, but it was the GT that was the first of the breed to be built in any kind of volume. Again produced on the original Ferrari chassis, the 250 GT had a long nose and truncated rear end, yet thanks to the influences of the great Pinifarina (which by 1958 was the sole supplier of Ferrari's coachwork) it managed to look both purposeful and harmonious at the same time. It also had a more advanced suspension system, with coil springs at the front and a beam axle at the rear, which meant that it could be enjoyed with a little more power.

▲ **Ferrari 250 Europa**

Developed specifically for road and not competition use, the Europa was Ferrari's first car built purely for commercial purposes. Its beguiling style no doubt made it well worth saving up for.

In standard tune, the well-established V12 developed 200bhp (150kW), but the engine could be tuned up to 280bhp (1210kW) without too much trouble. Indeed, Ferrari offered tuned versions to customers itself.

The 250 GT Tour de France was a limited run of 84 cars to mark the company's success in the famous race of the same name, and came with an all-alloy body built by coachbuilder Scaglietti from Modena, Italy. The Tour de France was, however, a road-legal special car, built primarily for racing. Far more usable were the Scaglietti-built Cabriolet and California models, introduced in 1957 with a choice of long and short wheelbase. While still eligible for racing and built to the same lightweight principles, they had more in the way of luxury accoutrements and were among the most refined road-going Ferraris ever.

250 GT Berlinetta Lusso

Initially called the 250 GT/L, Ferrari's Berlinetta Lusso was effectively a racing car converted for road use. Do not be fooled by the Lusso tag

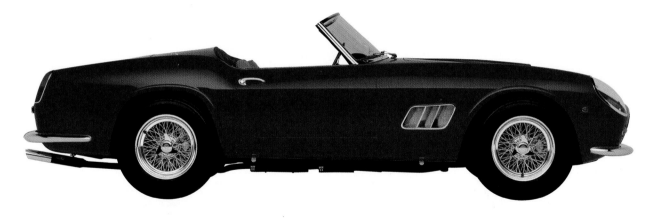

◀ ▲ Ferrari 250 GT

This is a rare soft-top version of the 250 GT – a car that is hugely coveted in collectors' circles today. With leather trim and extra chrome, it was more of a grand tourer than a sports car.

Specifications

Engine type: V12	Length: 4.20m (165.4in)
Displacement: 2953cc (181ci)	Width: 1.72m (67.7in)
Maximum power: 208kW (280bhp) at 7000rpm	Height: 1.37m (53.9in)
Top speed: 241km/h (150mph)	Wheelbase: 2.40m (94.5in)
0–96km/h (0–60mph): 7.0sec	Weight: 1050kg (2315lbs)

('lusso' is Italian for 'luxury'), as everything is relative – you got two seats and a full complement of dials, along with wind-down windows, but there was nothing in the way of a glovebox or provision to install a radio, while the lightweight alloy body, again built by Scaglietti, did little to suppress the robust noise of the frantic 140bhp (105kW) V12 engine.

One thing the Berlinetta Lusso did have going for it, though, was its looks. The smart Kamm-tail and AC Cobra-esque front-end styling were utterly beguiling and it is regarded today as one of the all-time classic Ferrari models.

250 GT SWB

Arguably the prettiest of the 200 series Ferraris, the GT SWB was effectively a Berlinetta Lusso built onto a racing chassis, the wheelbase

▼ ▶ Ferrari 250 GT Berlinetta Lusso

With closed coupe bodywork and a front end not dissimilar to the AC Cobra, the 250 GT Berlinetta Lusso was a hardcore driving machine, the elegance of its Scaglietti-designed body disguising some of its more brutal characteristics.

Specifications

Engine type: V12	Length: 4.41m (173.5in)
Displacement: 2953cc (180ci)	Width: 1.65m (65.0in)
Maximum power: 186kW (250bhp) at 7500rpm	Height: 1.29m (50.8in)
Top speed: 233km/h (145mph)	Wheelbase: 2.44m (94.5in)
0–96km/h (0–60mph): 8.1sec	Weight: 1359kg (2995lbs)

▲ Ferrari 250 GT California 1961

The 250 GT found fame on the silver screen in the movie *Ferris Bueller's Day Off*, more than 20 years after it first appeared. A fake car had to be made so it could be written off at the end of the movie, as the real thing was far too valuable.

reduced from 2560cm (102.3in) to 2435cm (94.5in), which made the shell significantly stiffer and as a result made it handle in a much more assured manner.

With racing in mind, the GT SWB also came with four-wheel disc brakes, and a variety of different axle ratios were offered depending on whether the car was to be used for circuit racing, road racing or hillclimbs.

The GT SWB looked especially attractive in road-going form, with standard fit centre-locking Borrani wire wheels, fog lamps set into the grille and slim quarter bumpers. Unlike some Scaglietti-

built models, which had all-alloy bodywork, the GT SWB used a combination of metals, with alloy doors, bonnet (hood) and boot (trunk), but a steel bodyshell. As such they were prone to corrosion, especially if used for competition and exposed to the risk of paint damage.

Although not the most valuable of the 200-era Ferraris, the 250 GT SWB is among the examples most prized by collectors, especially if you can find one of the 35 originally built as road cars and never campaigned.

250 GTO

Perhaps the most famous Ferrari of all time, the 250 GTO was a legendary road-going race car, with a lightweight body on the 250 GT SWB chassis, the engine from a Ferrari Testarossa and a five-speed gearbox. Styled by Bizzarini, rather

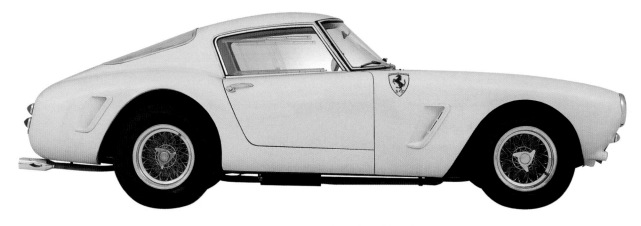

◀ ▲ **Ferrari 250 GT SWB**

It wasn't Ferrari's intention to create one of its prettiest cars ever in the form of the 250 GT SWB – the car's handsome good looks turned out to be both a lucky and a happy coincidence.

Specifications	
Engine type: V12	Length: 4.17m (164in)
Displacement: 2953cc (180ci)	Width: 1.50m (59.1in)
Maximum power: 208kW (280bhp) at 7000rpm	Height: 1.25m (49.4in)
Top speed: 225km/h (140mph)	Wheelbase: 2.40m (94.5in)
0–96km/h (0–60mph): 6.7sec	Weight: 1272kg (2805lbs)

than Pininfarina, the GTO developed 300bhp (225kW) and was incredibly reliable, making it perfect for endurance racing, while its slippery shape gave it unrivalled aerodynamics. In total, only 39 GTOs were ever made, making it an incredibly rare and prized possession among the world's many Ferrari collectors.

Indeed, one example is known to have sold for as much as $15 million in a private sale, while in 1997 another GTO set the highest ever bid received at a car auction by Bonhams in Gstaad, Switzerland, of $9 million – but failed to meet its reserve. These prices have resulted in many fakes, though, and identifying them can be tricky as some are so well done.

The English peer Lord Brocket was jailed for insurance fraud in 1996 after passing off his replica GTO as a genuine example, then destroying it to raise money. His actions led the well-known British motoring pundit Quentin Willson to comment: 'of the 3000 or so Ferrari GTOs that have ever been built, all 39 are still running!'

◀ **Ferrari 250 GTO**

The most expensive car ever sold at auction, the 250 GTO is an all-time classic. But that doesn't stop some of the model's more committed owners from still campaigning them.

Model	Years Built (0–60mph)	0–96km/h km/h (mph)	Top speed
212	1951–53	7.5secs	227 (140)
250 Europa	1953–55	8.0secs	194 (120)
250 GT	1954–62	6.6secs	194 (120)
250 GT Berlinetta	1962–64	8.0secs	218 (135)
250 GT SWB	1959–63	6.0secs	227 (140)
250 GTO	1962–64	5.4secs	250 (155)
275 GTB	1964–67	6.9secs	235 (145)

▲ **Ferrari 275 GTB**

More luxurious and easier to drive than most of its forebears, the 275 GTB was designed much more as a road car than a racer. It was still quick, though.

275 GTB

The successor to the 250 GT Berlinetta Lusso, the 275 GTB was a much more mature package, with more in the way of passenger comfort, physical space and road manners. But despite this, it was still a lively performance car. The mandatory V12 engine produced a healthy 280bhp (210kW), which was more than enough for light competition use, while later GTB 4 models came with quad-cam heads and triple carbs, delivering 300bhp (225kW). Of these, a handful were made available with an all-alloy bodywork, making them ideal for those who wanted a competitive race car.

The GTB had a far more supple ride than its predecessors, thanks to fully independent suspension all-round, while the standard-fit five-speed gearbox was also lighter and more positive to use than on earlier models.

Ferrari also built a convertible version of the 275, called the GTS. This was less powerful, with 260bhp (195kW), and had softer suspension settings because it was aimed entirely at road users. The car is regarded with sorrow and a certain amount of regret by some enthusiasts, who say that it was the first Ferrari to be built purely for commercial purposes and does not truly reflect the marque's impressive motorsport pedigree. As such, they are worth less today.

Specifications

Engine type: V12	Length: 4.47m (176in)
Displacement: 3286cc (201ci)	Width: 1.69m (66.5in)
Maximum power: 224kW (300bhp) at 8000rpm	Height: 1.35m (53in)
Top speed: 265.5km/h (165mph)	Wheelbase: 2.40m (94.4in)
0–96km/h (0–60mph): 7.0sec	Weight: 1100kg (2426lbs)

▼ **Ferrari 275GTB**

Styled by Pininfarina, the 275 GTB was arguably far less pretty than the Scaglietti cars that had gone before it, but that did not stand in the way of the styling house's long and fruitful affair with Ferrari.

Fiat 500
1936–

Small but perfectly formed, the Fiat 500 showed the world how to make a city car.

500 Topolino

The first car to bear the immortal '500' badge was the 1936 'Topolino', meaning 'little mouse'. The car was styled by Dante Giacosa and was built to cope with Italy's already congested cities, its aim being to offer minimalist, austere but highly affordable motoring. This was a brief that the 500 filled perfectly, and the range quickly expanded to include soft-top and estate (station wagon) variants, all powered by a side-valve two-cylinder engine developing only 13bhp (8kW) – although the Italian driving style dictated that each of these 13 horses be flogged almost to

A full-length folding roof was always a trademark of the Fiat 500 range, from the earliest Topolino right through to the model's 2008 reincarnation. Its original purpose was not for comfort, but to allow large loads to be carried on the back seat.

death. The engine was replaced by an overhead-valve unit in 1948, while the following year the Topolino evolved into the 500C, with a more streamlined front end, integrated grille and headlamps, and a mighty 16.5bhp (9.5kW) from its 569cc (36ci) engine. Despite the modest power output, the 500 was great fun to drive, with a superb chassis.

600

A sign of what was to come from Fiat, the 600 went on sale in 1955 to replace the 500C – but the 500 name wasn't dead and, even at the launch of the 600, Fiat said there was something even smaller still to come.

Back to the 600, though, where Fiat had listened to criticisms of the 500C and responded accordingly. The ride was smoother, there were four seats instead of two and, despite being smaller than the Topolino, the 600 was well packaged and was also entertaining to drive. Popular options included a rollback roof, while the 600D from 1960 had such luxuries as wind-down windows and a fuel gauge. The car's

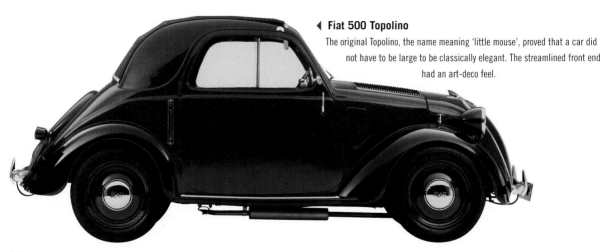

◄ **Fiat 500 Topolino**
The original Topolino, the name meaning 'little mouse', proved that a car did not have to be large to be classically elegant. The streamlined front end had an art-deco feel.

▶ **Fiat 600**

Contrary to popular belief, the Fiat 600 appeared before the Nuova 500 and consequently enjoyed a longer production run. It was neatly styled, but somehow didn't work its way into the consciousness of Italians as much as the 500 did.

power came from a rear-mounted water-cooled 633cc (38.5ci) engine, giving the 600 just enough power to cruise at just over 100km/h (60mph). Production ceased in Italy in 1969; however, the 600 remained on sale in Spain as a SEAT until 1973, and in the former Yugoslavia as a Zastava until the late 1980s.

600 Multipla

Sometimes a car arrives that's ahead of its time – and the 600 Multipla is a case in point. If you think that the current predilection across the motor industry towards minivans and multi-purpose vehicles (MPVs) is a relatively recent development, you would be wrong – the people carrier was invented by Fiat as early as 1955. Based on a lengthened 600 platform, the Multipla offered three rows of seats and could carry up to six passengers, despite its diminutive dimensions. Not easy to drive, and not pleasant to travel in, the Multipla was nonetheless a true innovator. It was also cheap to build – from the rear, it looked identical to a normal 600, as it used the same body pressings, but at the front it was more blunt-looking. Viewed in profile, its evident aerodynamic disadvantage going forwards made the car look as if it was the wrong way round.

Nuova 500

Two years after the Topolino disappeared, Fiat revived the 500 name with its smallest car yet. Powered by an air-cooled twin-cylinder engine in the rear, and initially with only two seats and a non-syncromesh gearbox, the Nuova 500 was as basic as motoring got – a fact that was

reflected in its price. But it was also brilliantly packaged, with a compact all-independent suspension set-up, suicide doors, a luggage area at the front and a standard roll-top roof.

There were numerous changes through the years – front-hinged doors came in 1965, the engine was gradually increased in size and output, and there was even a luxury model called the 500L, which came with an upgraded interior and extra dials, along with rear seats that were next to useless. One of the more charming 500s was the 'Jolly', an open-topped version with no weather protection whatsoever, and unusual wicker panels; it had limited appeal when new, but is highly prized today.

The 500 was a huge hit, with sales of more than 3.5 million in an 18-year production run. Even today, it is a regular sight in some Italian cities, where the residents have yet to find a better means of city transport.

500 Giardiniera

Answering criticisms of the 500's limited passenger space, Fiat introduced the Giardiniera in 1960, based on a wheelbase lengthened by 10cm (4in). This stretching allowed Fiat to develop an estate- (station wagon–) style body for the 500, but this didn't solve the problem of what to do about the engine, as it was in the rear of the car. To get round this complication, Fiat turned the vertically mounted twin-cylinder unit sideways to it lay flat, then built a false floor into the estate car's boot (trunk) to overcome the problem – a simple, effective idea. Popular with families thanks to its rear seats and better legroom, the Giardiniera was quite pricey in comparison to the standard 500, but more than 300,000 buyers evidently thought the extra space was worth it. Fiat officially stopped building Giardinieras in 1968, but it was constructed from then on by Autobianchi and badged as such, eventually bowing out in 1977, two years after the saloon (sedan) car.

126

Replacing a legend is never easy, as Fiat found out with the 126. Cleaner and more modern-looking for the 1970s, the 500's successor actually went on sale in 1972 and was sold alongside the 500 for three years. In traditional style, it had a rear-mounted air-cooled twin-cylinder engine and independent suspension, while the clever packaging allowed it to have four usable seats from the outset, along with rock-bottom prices.

Overall, the 126 was a car that fitted the brief of the 500 perfectly, yet somehow managed to lose much of the original car's character. That said, more than two million examples were sold and it enjoyed more than 30 years in production, so Fiat must have got something right.

500 2008

There's nothing like heritage to sell a new car – you have only to look at BMW's success with the reborn Mini to see that a car which has appealed to millions over the years will appeal again if you get the marketing just right. For that reason, Fiat pulled the wraps off its all-new 500 at the 2007

Specifications

Engine type: Inline two-cylinder	Length: 2.97m (116.9in)
Displacement: 499cc (30.5ci)	Width: 1.32m (51.9in)
Maximum power: 13.4kW (18bhp) at 4600rpm	Height: 1.33m (52.2in)
Top speed: 95km/h (59mph)	Wheelbase: 1.84m (72.5in)
0–96km/h (0–60mph): n/a	Weight: 470kg (1036lbs)

◀ ▲ **Fiat Nuova 500L**
So neat was the styling and packaging of the Nuova 500 that it remained in production virtually unchanged for more than 20 years, during which time almost three and a half million were sold.

▶ Fiat 126

With the 126, Fiat tried to modernize the concept of the 500. But while the fundamental ideas behind the newcomer were sound, it failed to demonstrate the same flair or character with which its predecessor had won the hearts and minds of the Italian public.

Specifications

Engine type: V8	Length: 2.97m (117.0in)
Displacement: 5735cc (350ci)	Width: 1.37m (54.0in)
Maximum power: 224kW (300bhp) at 4800rpm	Height: 1.46m (57.5in)
Top speed: 222km/h (138mph)	Wheelbase: 1.84m (72.5in)
0–96km/h (0–60mph): 4.3sec	Weight: 532kg (1173lbs)

Model	Years Built	Number Built
500 Topolino	1936–55	520,207
600	1955–69	2,452,107
600 Multipla	1955–66	160,260
Nuova 500	1957–75	3,427,648
500 Giardiniera	1960–77	327,000
126	1972–92	1,970,000
2008 500	2008–	N/A

Geneva Motor Show, three years after its Trepiuno concept had hinted that a revival of the 500 was in the offing. That car hit showrooms in 2008, based on the platform of the existing Fiat Panda and with a choice of Panda-based mechanical layouts.

Despite its being front-engined, water-cooled and also significantly more expensive than the original, Fiat's reincarnated 500 possesses styling that is more than enough to charm those buyers who found the original 500 adorable.

▶ Fiat 500 2008

A legend returns! Having experimented with small cars of all shapes and sizes over the years, Fiat finally settled on a near replica of the original 500 when it came to proving it could still build small cars as well as ever…

Ford Mustang
1964–

The fastest-selling car of all time, the Mustang introduced America to a new concept in motoring.

Mustang Mk 1 64–68

Nobody was more surprised than the Ford Motor Company itself when the Mustang made its debut in 1964. Word had got round a few months earlier that Ford was planning to introduce a compact model that would take the sporty appeal of the Thunderbird and mix it with the utilitarian practicality of the Falcon and Fairlane sedan ranges. But the 'pony car' concept was ultimately much more successful than anyone had anticipated, and the initial rush expected by Ford dealers never died down, leading to waiting lists of over seven months for

▼ **Ford Mustang GT 1965**

The original, and by far the best. Ford's 'pony car' was an instant hit, and for all the right reasons it quickly became the best-selling new model of all time, holding a record yet to be beaten.

Specifications

Engine type: V8	Length: 4.61m (181.6in)
Displacement: 4736cc (289ci)	Width: 1.73m (68.2in)
Maximum power: 202kW (271bhp) at 6000rpm	Height: 1.30m (51.0in)
Top speed: 198km/h (123mph)	Wheelbase: 2.74m (108.0in)
0–96km/h (0–60mph): 7.3sec	Weight: 1406kg (3100lbs)

Ford managed to create a car that was almost a brand in its own right, with its galloping mustang on the badge. Indeed, on the back of the Mustang's success, the new breed of performance-oriented personal coupes built on the success of Ford's value-for-money offering became known generically as 'pony cars'.

▲ ▶ Shelby Mustang GT350

The ultimate early Mustangs were those that received the tune-up treatment from legendary race engineer Carroll Shelby – the man behind the AC Cobra. This is the smaller-engined GT350 variant.

Specifications	
Engine type: V8	Length: 4.61m (181.6in)
Displacement: 2898cc (177ci)	Width: 1.73m (68.2in)
Maximum power: 228kW (306bhp) at 6000rpm	Height: 1.40m (55in)
Top speed: 217km/h (135mph)	Wheelbase: 2.74m (108.0in)
0–96km/h (0–60mph): 5.7sec	Weight: 1266kg (2792lbs)

a new car and sales in the first year of more than 400,000, with Mustang passing the million mark before it celebrated its second birthday.

Much of its success, of course, could be attributed to chief stylist Lee Iacocca, who had endowed the 'Stang with wonderfully well-balanced proportions – be it a notchback coupe, convertible or 2+2 fastback (from 1965). On top of that, there was a myriad of different engine and trim combinations, from weedy six-cylinder units for nipping round town or cruising, through to mighty V8s with enough power to seriously threaten the rapidly expanding muscle car posse. In 1965, there were more than 250 different Mustang variants available, and options included disc brakes, air conditioning, automatic transmission, sports suspension and racing body stripes, to name but a few. The Mustang's nose was altered slightly in 1967 to accommodate bigger V8 engines, while a hatchback-bodied coupe appeared at the same time. The Mustang was one of America's all-time classics, and a

folklore legend to boot. Everyone in the United States, if not having actually owned a Mustang, at least holds memories of one.

Shelby GT350

With Mustang being such a well-known vehicle already, it's no surprise that Ford wanted the car to achieve competition success to match its performance in the showrooms – and who better to promote the new model than folk hero, chicken farmer and AC Cobra creator Carroll Shelby? Complete Mustang fastback shells were shipped straight to Shelby's works in Los Angeles from the factory, where the legendary racer's team matched them up with 306bhp (227kW) 4.7-litre (289ci) small-block V8s, complete with high-lift manifolds, four-barrel carbs and free-flow straight-through exhausts. Tougher axles and differentials completed the Shelby Mustang mechanical package, while to keep weight to a minimum all Shelbys came

▲ **Ford Mustang 1969**

Later-style performance Mustangs were bigger and wider than the original model, but came with a more purposeful look, with modifications including magnesium alloy wheels, rear deck louvers and tail spoilers.

with a fibreglass bonnet (hood) and stripped-out interior. It was a Shelby GT350 that famously came to prominence as the car named 'Eleanor' in the movie *Gone in 60 Seconds*.

Shelby GT500

The ultimate expression of the Shelby Mustang, the GT 500 appeared in 1967 and took the GT350's performance appeal to another level. Typically painted white with blue stripes, it came with a 7.0-litre (428ci) engine, which Shelby advertised as being capable of producing 355bhp

(238kW), although it is widely rumoured that this stated figure was for political reasons, and that the true power output was in fact much closer to 400bhp (300kW).

For the final year, there was also an even faster, more butch-looking variant called the GT500KR (for 'King of the Road'), along with a handful of factory-built convertibles, although these officially number fewer than 10. There are, however, a number of fakes, and because factory records of Shelby chassis numbers are vague,

▼ ▶ **Shelby Mustang GT500**

This is a late model GT500 – the very last of the breed were badged GT500KR, with the 'KR standing for 'King of the Road', and came with the later, wider-style Mustang bodywork.

▶ ▲ **Ford Mustang Mach 1**

After the tie-up with Shelby ended, Ford developed its own performance Mustangs, badged Mach 1. Although they were great cars, they failed to build up the same legendary status as the GT-badged originals.

Specifications	
Engine type: V8	Length: 4.75m (187.0in)
Displacement: 7014cc (428ci)	Width: 1.82m (71.8in)
Maximum power: 250kW (335bhp) at 5200rpm	Height: 1.28m (50.3in)
Top speed: 195km/h (121mph)	Wheelbase: 2.74m (108.0in)
0–96km/h (0–60mph): 5.3sec	Weight: 1551kg (3420lbs)

without the correct provenance it's very difficult to judge which ones are genuine and which are actually impostors.

Like the GT350, the 500 has a fibreglass bonnet and uprated axles, while a four-speed automatic option was also on offer.

Mustang 69–73

Although not officially a Mk 2 version of the original (it would be another four years before

Ford completely ruined the Mustang …), the 1969 model represented a significant restyle of the original, and purists argue that the next-generation car was nowhere near as pretty as the landmark 1964 car.

Some 10cm (4in) longer, all in the bodywork and not in the wheelbase, the new-look Mustang was also wider and more plain to look at, with no side scallops and a front end that incorporated an extra pair of incongruous rectangular headlamps. It still looked fairly beefy, however, and the changes did at least provide more room for passengers front and rear, and extra space for

Specifications	
Engine type: V8	Length: 5.00m (197.0in)
Displacement: 7014cc (428ci)	Width: 1.82m (71.8in)
Maximum power: 250kW (335bhp) at 5200rpm	Height: 1.28m (50.3in)
Top speed: 209km/h (130mph)	Wheelbase: 2.74m (108.0in)
0–96km/h (0–60mph): 5.5sec	Weight: 1406kg (3100lbs)

▼ ▲ **Ford Mustang Boss 302 1970**

For 1969, the Mustang had a flatter, more angular bodywork, a wider track, longer wheelbase and fewer different body styles. This is the Boss 302 version – one of the most collectable Mustangs ever, and definitely one of the best looking.

Specifications	
Engine type: V8	Length: 4.76m (187.4in)
Displacement: 4949cc (302ci)	Width: 1.83m (71.9in)
Maximum power: 216kW (290bhp) at 5800rpm	Height: 1.36m (53.5in)
Top speed: 206km/h (128mph)	Wheelbase: 2.74m (108.0in)
0–96km/h (0–60mph): 6.5sec	Weight: 1464kg (3227lbs)

luggage in the car's boot (trunk). The different body styles on offer remained consistent with the earlier car, meaning you could have a notchback, a convertible or a 2+2 coupe, now christened SportRoof.

A few changes came again in 1970, with the welcome return to single headlamps and recessed tail lamps, while for 1971 the Mustang grew again, becoming longer, wider and much heavier – its appeal diminishing in line with its growth in bulk. By 1972, Mustang sales had plummeted to 125,000 a year, compared to more than 600,000 in its best year of 1965.

Mach 1

Its tie-in with Shelby coming to an end, Ford decided to save money by developing its own high-performance version of the Mustang in 1969. The Mach 1 was a SportsRoof coupe with a standard 250bhp (163kW) 5.7-litre (351ci) V8 and revised sports suspension. In order to add visual clues to the car's sportiness, Ford also fitted magnesium alloy wheels, sign-written

tyres and a matt black bonnet, with integrated air scoops. At the front, it got extra fog lamps and a black-coloured radiator grille, while a variety of garish body colours were offered, taking the Mach 1's appeal firmly into muscle car territory, but without the conviction of rival Chrysler-Dodge and GM products. Despite Ford's best efforts to market it as such, the Mach 1 was not even close to the Shelby-tuned models in terms of its appeal.

Boss 302/429/351

One step up from the Mach 1, and infinitely more convincing as a performance car, the Boss 302 was inspired by Ford's racer in the Trans American (TransAm) race series. Although equipped with a smaller powerplant than the Mach 1, with a 4.9-litre (302ci) unit, the Boss 302 had a power output of at least 290bhp (218kW) and came with a far more expressive collection of styling bits, including a chin spoiler, a rear wing (fender), side stripes and a louvred rear window. It was also a much sharper drive, with uprated

Specifications

Engine type: V8	Length: 4.81m (189.5in)
Displacement: 5752cc (351ci)	Width: 1.88m (74.1in)
Maximum power: 246kW (330bhp) at 5400rpm	Height: 1.27m (50.1in)
Top speed: 187km/h (116mph)	Wheelbase: 2.77m (109.0in)
0–96km/h (0–60mph): 5.8sec	Weight: 1610kg (3550lbs)

▶ **Ford Mustang Boss 351 1971**

Boss 351 versions of the Mustang Mach 1 came with a matt black painted hood, which was designed to stop reflections from the car's paintwork from blinding the driver in bright sunlight.

race-bred brakes and suspension making it a far more composed and driveable package.

The 4.9-litre (302ci) variant was built for homologation purposes, as TransAm rulings meant a restriction in engine size; however, for road-going use Ford also introduced two other variants. The Boss 429, with its 7.0-litre (429ci) Cobra Jet big-block alloy-head engine, developed 375bhp (280kW) and was capable of sprinting to 96km/h (60mph) from a standstill in six seconds, while the 5.7-litre (351ci) Boss 351 of 1971 only

was slightly less powerful, offering 330bhp (246kW) of thrust.

Mustang II

It's hard to believe that the Mustang II was created by the same man, Lee Iacocca, as the original – for it was so different in so many ways, most of them regrettable. You can see the reasoning behind the Mustang II quite clearly – by 1973, the muscle car era was completely dead,

Specifications

Engine type: V8	Length: 4.75m (187in)
Displacement: 7030cc (429ci)	Width: 1.83m (72in)
Maximum power: 280kW (375bhp) at 5200rpm	Height: 1.24m (49in)
Top speed: 190km/h (118mph)	Wheelbase: 2.74m (108.0in)
0–96km/h (0–60mph): 6.8sec	Weight: 1755kg (3870lbs)

▶ ▼ **Ford Mustang Boss 429 1969**

Built as road-going versions of Ford's TransAm racing models, the Boss variants of the Mustang were performance icons in their own right. This is the ultimate 429 version, with the biggest engine ever fitted to a 'Stang.

▲ Ford Mustang II

In the 1970s, it all went horribly wrong for Ford, and the Mustang II was a damp squib in comparison to the heroic Mustangs of the past. The drab styling and limp power outputs did little to stir the enthusiast's soul.

shut down in its prime by oil crises and a new environmental awareness in the United States that led buyers away from big gas guzzlers, and into more compact, more fuel-efficient cars. This had hit Mustang sales hard, and had seen them in freefall for the past four years; Lee Iacocca's brief was to create a car that would offer the same sporty looks, variety and spirit as the original Mustang, but in a more politically correct package. Sadly, the Mustang II was too

much of a sop to political requirements. It was advanced in so far as it had unitary construction and a hatchback, but these were its only saving graces. The styling looked muddled, the cabin was cheaply finished and the engine choice was miserable – a four-cylinder or a European-sourced V6 were the options, and neither delivered anything vaguely reminiscent of Mustang's performance heyday. V8s were offered from 1975, but these were pared down by tight emissions legislation and offered an emaciated power output as a result. A truly miserable car from the US auto industry's darkest hour, and one that many enthusiasts today consider as not worthy of such an enigmatic name.

Mustang III

While not an icon like the original, the Mustang III was a welcome return to form for Ford. Proper V8s with respectable power outputs were embraced with open arms by Mustang fans, while for those in favour of smaller engines, Ford offered turbocharged fours with surprisingly lively performance. The Mustang III was also a decent car to drive, with entertaining, tail-happy handling and good brakes, while the ride comfort was acceptable and it built on the traditional Mustang virtue of excellent value for money. It wasn't perfect by any stretch of the

Model	0–96km/h (0–60mph)	Top Speed km/h (mph)
64–68	12.2sec	178 (110)
Shelby GT350	7.3sec	194 (120)
Shelby GT500	6.1sec	222 (137)
69–73	11.5sec	191 (118)
Mach 1	6.8sec	194 (120)
Boss 302/429/351	17.0sec	194 (120)
Mustang II	12.5sec	176 (109)
Mustang III	11.8sec	194 (120)
2004	6.4sec	250 (155)

imagination, and it couldn't encapsulate the same legendary following as its seminal forbear, but the Mustang III did enjoy a 15-year production run and over two million sales. It was also sold as the Mercury Capri.

Mustang 2004

Finally, the genuine return to form that Mustang fans had all been waiting for …

In 2004, Ford pulled the wraps off the third of its 'American Retro' concept cars, the brainchild of chief designer J. Mays. Following the Thunderbird and the GT, both of which made it into production, the retro-styled Mustang used the exact dimensions of the car launched 40 years previously, but in a more modern package. True to Mustang tradition, the car came with leaf springs at the rear, a live rear axle and a small-block V8.

When sales began of a production model later that year, it came as no surprise that Mustangs

Model	Years Built	Number Built
64–68	1964–68	2,204,038
Shelby GT350	1965–70	7403
Shelby GT500	1967–70	7000
69–73	1968–73	675,000
Mach 1	1968–73	213,042
Boss 302/429/351	1968–71	13,609
Mustang II	1973–78	1,107,718
Mustang III	1978–93	2,305,000
Mustang 2004	2004–	N/A

once again started flying out of showrooms, leaving huge waiting lists in their wake. This was proof, if you like, that the original ideas are always the best. Indeed, it was proof that was quickly picked up on by two of Ford's main rivals. It's no coincidence that since the retro-Mustang's arrival, GM has announced a similarly old-school Chevy Camaro and Chrysler Group a modernized replica of the original Dodge Challenger.

▼ **Ford Mustang III**

Although not as stylish as the first-generation cars, the Mustang III and its variants were at least dynamically able cars and were more in keeping with the spirit of the Mustang.

Jaguar E-Type/XKE
1961–75

Voted the most beautiful model of all-time, Jaguar's E-Type was *the* classic sports car.

Series 1

Launched at the 1961 Geneva Auto Salon, the original E-Type was undoubtedly the star of the show. Building on a reputation for fine sports cars, which Jaguar had carefully honed for itself with the XK120, XK140 and XK150, the E-Type was the next step towards completely redefining the sports car as a breed.

For a start, the car looked truly fabulous. Whether you opted for the roadster or for the unusual coupe, with its side-hinged tailgate, there was no denying that the E-Type had one of the most distinctive yet beautiful profiles of any car ever made. But the looks were functional, too – the faired-in headlamps helped to improve the car's aerodynamic efficiency. The interior was as much of a work of art as the exterior, with the dashboard effectively wrapping around the driver's lower limbs, decorated with beautifully intricate instrumentation. Power came from the 3.8-litre (232ci) XK engine, as found in the Mk 2,

▲ ▼ Jaguar E-Type S1

Although the convertible model is more collectable, there are many fans who prefer the slippery lines of the E-Type Coupe. From this angle, it is easy to see why. The interior and dash were suitably appealing, too.

and gave shattering performance. With 265bhp (198kW) on tap, it could easily reach 240km/h (150mph), yet despite this the E-Type was incredibly affordable. An Aston Martin DB5, which was only just about able to keep up, would cost you four times as much to buy. It's hardly surprising, then, that the original E-Types are considered legendary, and are highly collectable today. As well as through the 3.8-litre (232ci) engine, you can identify one of the pre-1964 cars by virtue of its 'flat' floorpan pressing. Later models had ridged metal.

Series 1.5

Although this car is not officially recognized as a new generation, Jaguar made some significant changes to the E-Type in 1964. While it doesn't have quite the same collector cachet as the original flat-floor models, the so-called Series 1.5 is arguably the better car.

The most significant change was under the bonnet (hood), where the original 3.8-litre

(232ci) engine was superseded by a new 4.2-litre (256ci) derivative. Still based on the XK powerplant, it had better mid-range torque and made the E-Type more pleasant to drive in town, although there was no real difference in the car's overall performance.

Further improvements included the addition of a syncromesh to the car's first gear, again missing from the first examples, along with a bigger servo for the brakes. This latter addition was hugely welcome, as one of the fiercest criticisms of the earliest E-Types was pointed at its braking system, which although effective required a very strong foot to produce the best effect. The modifications made the Series 1.5 the most enjoyable of E-Types, as they enabled you to more freely enjoy the car's wonderful handling, performance and touring ability.

Lightweight E-Type

Shortly after the introduction of the E-Type, Jaguar's management wanted to investigate the possibility of building a car more in the spirit of

the D-Type racer from which elements of the E-Type's styling and design were derived. As a result, a one-off, called the Low Drag Coupe, was developed by Jaguar's aerodynamicist Malcolm Sayer.

It evolved into the so-called 'Lightweight E-Type' of 1963–64, built solely for motorsport and which made extensive use of aluminium alloy in the body panels and other components in order to reduce its weight significantly. However, with at least one exception, it remained an open-top car in the spirit of the D-Type to which it was arguably a more direct successor than the production E-Type. The cars used a tuned version of the production 3.8-litre (232ci) Jaguar XK engine with 300bhp (225kW) output rather than the 265bhp (198kW) produced by road-going cars. While Lightweights won various competitions, they never earned victories in classic endurance races such as Le Mans and Sebring, unlike their illustrious predecessors.

Specifications

Engine type: Inline six-cylinder	Length: 4.45m (175.3in)
Displacement: 3781cc (230.7ci)	Width: 1.66m (65.2in)
Maximum power: 257kW (344bhp) at 6500rpm	Height: 1.22m (48.0in)
Top speed: 253km/h (157mph)	Wheelbase: 2.44m (96.0in)
0–96km/h (0–60mph): 5.0sec	Weight: 1007kg (2220lbs)

▶ ▼ **Jaguar Lightweight E-Type**

Built purely for endurance racing, the Lightweight E-Type was available with either closed or open bodywork. It never lived up to the legend of the C- and D-Type models, though.

▶ **Jaguar E-Type 2+2**

The longer doors and extended glass areas mark this out as a 2+2 version of the E-Type coupe. The car's ungainly looks make it the least collectable version today.

2+2

One of the biggest criticisms faced by the E-Type at launch was that it could seat only two people, and this was finally addressed in 1966 with the introduction of a 2+2 variant. In order to incorporate the extra rear seats, the 2+2 had a wheelbase that was 23cm (9in) longer than that of the standard car, while the roofline was also raised by 5cm (2in) to give the rear seat passengers a token amount of headroom.

The 2+2 was an agreeable concept, but in reality wasn't that much more practical than a standard car. The back seats were suitable only for small children, and the effect that the extra length and height had on the bodywork easily outweighed any space benefit for those without the need to carry offspring. A necessity, rather than a desirable addition to the E-Type line, this is the variant most overlooked by collectors today.

Series 2

For 1968, Jaguar was forced into making several changes to the E-Type if the car was to continue to be such a sales success in the United States, although to the purist many of these changes did little to benefit the car. Most noticeable was the change from cowled headlamps to upright sealed beam items, set inside scallops on the wings (fenders). This change did little to aid aerodynamic efficiency or maintain the lithe looks of the car, but was an essential modification to comply with new US safety legislation, which dictated that the headlamps on any car had to be at a certain minimum height – annoyingly 5cm (2in) higher than on the Series 1. The bumpers also had to be raised, which meant the original E-Type's pretty rear lamp clusters were relocated to below the bumper at the back, while up front the centre bar now sat towards the top of the car's intake, rather than symmetrically across the middle as before. Finally, the car's ride height was increased slightly.

▼ **Jaguar E-Type S2**

Although little changed from the first-generation car, the biggest difference between S1 and S2 E-Types was the headlamps. Later models had to have the lamps raised to suit US safety legislation, so they were no longer covered by fairings.

The result may have been to partially detract from the E-Type's handsome lines, but at least the changes didn't affect the way in which the car drove, as similar changes did to the MGB. Non-US cars didn't have to meet new emissions criteria, either, and kept three carburettors. American fans of the marque, where the car was called the XKE, will know that owners were forced to endure twin instead of triple Stromberg carburettors, the net result being a drop from 265bhp (198kW) to 171bhp (128kW).

Series 3

The E-Type's final incarnation managed to once again inject some of the desirability that had been lost with the Series 2 styling changes, although this time it was not the car's looks that would be the key to its appeal. Far from it, in fact, as all of the Series 3 cars, including the roadster, were based on the long-wheelbase platform of the 2+2, and two-seater coupes, which had traditionally been the most attractive E-Type variants, were dropped altogether.

To add to the oddball styling, Series 3s received an unusual 'egg-crate' radiator grille, while the wheelarches were flared out and fattened all round. But the Series 3 had one significant saving grace, and it lived under the bonnet. In place of the six-cylinder XK engine lived an all-new 5.3-litre (323ci) V12 that had prodigious amounts of torque and phenomenal acceleration, yet also had unbeatable levels of refinement. Series 3 E-Types were, as a result, seriously rapid cars, with a 0–60mph (0–96km/h) time of 6.4 seconds and a top speed of more than 236km/h (146mph). Automatic models outsold manuals for the first time, and over 80 per cent of sales went to the United States, where the V12's unquenchable thirst for fuel wasn't such a financial disincentive.

One of the most desirable E-Types of all-time is the run-out Jubilee model of 1975. The last 50 cars off the line, all right-hand-drive and painted black, came with a special plaque to mark the passing of one of the greatest classic cars in history. The E-Type's replacement, the XJ-S, was a good car in its own right, but it never matched its predecessor's appeal.

Model	Years Built (0–60mph)	0–96km/h km/h (mph)	Top Speed
Series 1	1961–64	7.1sec	241 (149)
Series 1.5	1964–68	7.4sec	241 (149)
Lightweight	1964	6.0sec	250 (155)
2+2	1966–70	7.4sec	225 (139)
Series 2	1968–70	7.4sec	241 (149)
Series 3	1970–75	6.4sec	236 (146)

▶ Jaguar E-Type V12

The last E-Types came with the V12 engine from the XJ12 saloon (sedan), and are easily identifiable by their more prominent oval radiator grille, needed to help cool the now-cramped engine bay.

Specifications

Engine type: V12	Length: 4.61m (184.4in)
Displacement: 5343cc (326ci)	Width: 1.68m (66.1in)
Maximum power: 186kW (250bhp) at 6000rpm	Height: 1.30m (51.0in)
Top speed: 241km/h (150mph)	Wheelbase: 2.67m (105.0in)
0–96km/h (0–60mph): 6.8sec	Weight: 1538kg (3390lbs)

One of the E-Type coupe's more unusual features was its side-hinged rear tailgate, which allowed plenty of luggage storage space and gave it a distinct advantage over many of its European rivals. The idea was copied by the car's cheaper rivals, namely the MGB GT and Triumph GT6.

Jaguar Mk 2
1955–69

Jaguar's mantra was one of 'Grace, Space and Pace'. The Mk 2 had all three and became one of the marque's most celebrated models.

2.4-Litre/3.4-Litre

Unofficially known as the Mk 1, the 2.4- and 3.4-Litre models were the very first Jaguars to make their presence felt in the small luxury car market. Instantly identifiable as the precursor to Jaguar's most legendary small saloon (sedan) ever, the 1955 2.4 (and later 1957 3.4) had unitary construction and a short-stroke version of Jaguar's twin-cam six-cylinder XK engine. While nowhere near as quick as the cars that succeeded it, the Mk 1 was a fairly lively performer, and its coil-sprung independent front suspension made for reassured handling characteristics. A choice of gearboxes was offered, including a standard four-speed, a four-speed manual with overdrive and a three-speed auto, although the self-shifter was unpleasant and lacked refinement at speed. The 3.4-Litre looked even more like the Mk 2 eventually would, as the distinctive rear wheel spats were cut away to expose the back wheels. Although it was the original, the Mk 1 isn't as highly valued or as well loved as the Mk 2.

Mk 2

Probably the archetypal classic Jag, the Mk 2 was much admired not only for its harmonious looks, but also for the way it drove. Based largely on the outgoing 2.4-/3.4-Litre (Mk 1), the Mk 2 was wider and lower, which gave it even better roadholding, while four-wheel disc brakes, power steering and, on later models, an all-syncromesh gearbox meant that it was a

▼ **Jaguar Mk 1**

The most obvious difference between a Jaguar Mk 1 and Mk 2 is the presence of rear wheel spats – on the earlier car they more or less completely covered the back wheels.

Specifications

Engine type: Inline six-cylinder	Length: 4.59m (180.8in)
Displacement: 3781cc (230.7ci)	Width: 1.70m (66.75in)
Maximum power: (164kW) 220bhp at 5500rpm	Height: 1.46m (57.5in)
Top speed: 201km/h (125mph)	Wheelbase: 2.73m (107.4in)
0–96km/h (0–60mph): 9.2sec	Weight: 1542kg (3400lbs)

▲ ▶ **Jaguar Mk 2 3.8-Litre**

In 3.8-litre (183ci) form, the Mk 2 Jaguar was a sports saloon par excellence. It was agile, incredibly fast and beautifully styled, making it a big hit with bank managers and bank robbers alike.

pleasure to drive as well. Three engines were offered – the 2.4-litre (146ci) and 3.4-litre (207ci) were carryovers from the Mk 1, but the 3.8-litre (232ci) was entirely new and was developed for the forthcoming E-Type. In standard tune, it produced an impressive 220bhp (165kW), which made it the most powerful production saloon of its day. It was also the fastest, with a top speed of more than 200km/h (125mph). Those figures make the 3.8 the most collectable Mk 2 variant, and mean it commands a significant premium over the smaller-engined models today, despite being the most common variant in terms of build numbers. Those who want the style and image of the Mk 2 but aren't overly concerned about the performance would do better to seek out a well-preserved or restored 2.4- or 3.4-Litre model.

Of these, it's actually the smaller-engined model that makes the most sense, as apart from a torque deficit there's little to choose between

the two models in terms of performance and the 2.4 is more economical.

That said, a large number of 2.4s were very basically trimmed, and many exist with either manual gearboxes or non-power-assisted steering, both of which are big no-nos unless you want a car that's unnecessarily difficult to drive. The majority of 3.4-Litre models were more luxuriously appointed and should have leather, auto and power steering as standard. Last-of-the-line models, built in 1966, had much of the luxury trim taken out to reduce their price and distinguish them from the S-Type.

S-Type

With the Mk 2, Jaguar had the compact luxury car market sewn up, but there was no middle ground between it and the gargantuan Mark X, leaving an obvious gap in Jaguar's product line-

73

The 3.4-Litre is the least-loved member of the Mk 2 family, as it offered little performance advantage over the cheaper 2.4-Litre, but used more fuel. That fact, however, does make it more affordable as a collector's car.

up. But the numbers in this mid-sized executive market were too small to justify producing a brand-new car from the ground up, so instead, Jaguar's engineers decided to develop the Mk 2 and make it bigger all round.

Enter the S-Type, launched in 1963 and incredibly similar to the Mk 2 in appearance. It used the platform, engines and chassis of the smaller car, coupled to its centre hull, so it could also make use of the same doors, windows and roof panel. The front end was different, though, with wraparound indicators and a deeper grille, while at the rear the car was lengthened to incorporate a Mk X-style sloping tailgate, in turn creating space for independent rear suspension and inboard rear disc brakes, which actually made for a better handling car despite the S-Type's relative lack of collector value compared to the Mk 2. The S-Type was generally more luxurious than the smaller car, and almost half of all S-Types sold were automatics.

Daimler 2½-Litre

Snubbed by Daimler purists, as it was the first car to wear the illustrious Daimler badge but was based on a Jaguar, the 2½-Litre is often sadly overlooked as a result.

Ironically, it was actually one of the best variants of the Mk 2 family, the compact Edward Turner–designed V8 from the SP250 sports car being the perfect companion for the compact Jaguar bodyshell, with 140bhp (105kW) on tap and the ability to cruise comfortably at three-figure speeds. Generally more luxurious than Jaguar models, Daimlers had leather trim, darker stained wood and a standard automatic gearbox, although a manual with overdrive was offered as a cost-free option from 1967. A 2½-Litre does look very similar to a Jaguar Mk 2, but is identifiable by its fluted Daimler radiator grille and discreet 'D' insignia.

240/340

The late 1960s and the threat of an imminent takeover from the British Leyland Corporation saw Jaguar indulge in some serious cost-cutting with the Mk 2's replacement, although it was essentially the same car.

With the 3.8-litre (232ci) engine inexplicably dropped, the 2.4- and 3.4-Litre variants of the compact luxury car were renamed 240 and 340 accordingly, and specification levels were somewhat denuded to reduce their overall cost. Leather trim was replaced by faux-leather 'Ambla', the front fog lamps were replaced by

▼ **Jaguar Mk 2 240 1968**

Later 240 and 340 models were easy to distinguish from earlier Mk 2s because the front and rear bumpers were much slimmer. The interior was also trimmed in fake rather than real leather. This 1968 example is an entry-level 240.

▲ **Jaguar Mascot**

The famous 'Growler' mascot has adorned the hood of many a classic Jaguar, but the Mk 2 is where Jaguar's traditional adage of 'Grace, Space and Pace' was perhaps best applied.

Model	Years Built	0–96km/h (0–60mph)	Top Speed km/h (mph)
Mk 1	1955–59	14.4sec	165 (102)
Mk 2 3.8	1959–67	8.5sec	202 (125)
Mk 2 3.4	1959–67	11.9sec	194 (120)
Mk 2 2.4	1959–67	17.3sec	155 (96)
S-type	1962–65	8.8sec	186 (115)
2½-Litre	1965–69	13.8sec	181 (122)
Daimler 250 V8	1962–69	13.8sec	181 (122)
240	1967–69	12.5sec	171 (106)
340	1967–69	8.8sec	186 (115)

Specifications

Engine type: V8	Length: 4.59m (180.8in)
Displacement: 2548cc (155.5ci)	Width: 1.70m (66.8in)
Maximum power: 104kW (140bhp) at 5800rpm	Height: 1.47m (57.8in)
Top speed: 180km/h (112mph)	Wheelbase: 2.73m (107.4in)
0–96km/h (0–60mph): 13.8 sec	Weight: 1.474kg (3250lbs)

chrome grilles and the chunky Mk 2 bumpers were dropped in favour of slimline S-Type-style items. Some enthusiasts argue that the slimmer bumpers were actually prettier than those originally fitted to the Mk 2, but, unless you can find one fitted with optional leather and fog lamps, they're not enough to make up the difference against the decreased specification. The only saving grace was an increase in power for the entry-level car, up from 120bhp (90kW) to 133bhp (99kW).

Daimler 250 V8

A similar set of cost-cutting measures was introduced for the Daimler, which was renamed 250 V8 in keeping with the 240 and 340 monikers dished out to Jaguar models. But for the 250, they had less of an impact on the car's overall desirability. In order to keep Daimler specification levels at a more luxurious level than those of the Jaguar cars, the leather trim survived the cull, and this meant that the 250 V8 was still an attractive and well-equipped car. If you're a fan of the slimline bumpers, which somehow looked more congruent with the Daimler grille, then the 250 V8 is an appealing and massively undervalued classic car.

◀ ▼ **Daimler 250 V8**

Identical to the Mk 2 in terms of its panels, the Daimler 250 V8 was the first 'badge-engineered' Daimler model. But it retained a unique powerplant in the form of its compact Edward Turner-developed V8.

Jensen Interceptor
1966–75

British soul, American power and Italian design conspired to create a design masterpiece, even if it was a little fragile.

Mk 1

Although Jensen had been building cars for 20 years, it wasn't until the Interceptor made its debut in 1966 that the company really hit the headlines. Not to be confused with the streamlined drophead coupe of the early 1950s, which shared its name, the later Interceptor was conceived on a budget, yet at the same time managed to feel incredibly special.

Styled and built by Italian design house Vignale, the hefty grand tourer body managed to be imposing, yet at the same time alluringly pretty, while the curved glass tailgate was an especially distinctive styling feature that went on to grace numerous coupes in the 1970s and 1980s. Not content with going to Italy for the bodywork and styling, Jensen went Stateside for the Interceptor's

▲ **Jensen Interceptor I SP**

The SP was the performance version of the Interceptor, with firmer suspension, more power and a faster steering response.

Specifications

Engine type: V8	Length: 4.78m (188in)
Displacement: 6276cc (383ci)	Width: 1.79m (70in)
Maximum power: 246kW (330bhp) at 4600rpm	Height: 2.40m (53in)
Top speed: 221km/h (137mph)	Wheelbase: 2.68m (105in)
0–96km/h 0–60mph): 6.4sec	Weight: 1677kg (3696lbs)

oily bits, with power coming from a 6.3-litre (384ci) Chrysler V8, mated to a three-speed Torqueflite gearbox. Manual transmission was officially offered as an option, although only 24 such models were ever officially built. These

Jensen was a uniquely British company, with a small workshop in West Bromwich, near Birmingham, building luxurious hand-built cars to order. Its existence was always something of a struggle, but throughout the 1960s the company fought off bankruptcy to build a range of cars with a truly unique character and a committed following. Sadly, Jensen went under in the mid-1970s and attempts  to revive the name in the 1980s and early 2000s were unsuccessful.

Italian influence, but, despite being assembled in West Bromwich, the Mk 2 Interceptor did develop a Mediterranean propensity towards severe body corrosion, the likes of which were equalled only by contemporary Fiats and Lancias.

FF

By far the most curious of the Interceptor variants, and an impressive first for such a small manufacturer, the Interceptor FF pre-empted the trend towards four-wheel drive road cars by developing an all-wheel drive system that was, quite literally, years ahead of its time. Longer than the Interceptor to incorporate the four-wheel drive mechanism, the FF nonetheless looked almost identical to the standard Interceptor, and could be told apart only by its discreet FF badging and twin air vents in the front wings, where the standard car had only one on each side. The 4x4 set up was developed by Ferguson ('FF' stood for 'Ferguson Formula'), better known for tractor manufacturing, while the FF was also the first car to be sold with anti-

have curiosity value, but are worth no more than autos by virtue of the fact that they're a real handful to drive.

Mk 2

After three years of steady sales, the Interceptor was revised for 1969 with some changes to the front-end styling and interior. The quad headlamps remained, but the grille was altered to line up with the edge of the car's front panel, while the front bumper was made deeper and larger. New optional alloy road wheels were fitted and different side strakes were incorporated into the front wings (fenders), while inside the Mk 2 received high-back leather seats and additional dials on the dashboard. It may have been the

▼ **Jensen Interceptor II**

With bulky GT bodywork designed in Italy, the Jensen Interceptor was one of the most imposing GTs of the 1960s and 1970s.

lock brakes as standard, its Dunlop Maxaret system usually being found on aircraft as part of their landing gear.

A true technological tour de force, the FF had great grip and forceful acceleration, and was a significantly more rewarding car to drive than the standard Interceptor, which could be a handful on even the driest of roads. The FF's downfall was more its hefty purchase price, which was almost twice that of a two-wheel drive model and seemed a lot to pay for a car with unproven reliability.

Mk 3

The last Interceptor arrived at the wrong time for the market. Planned as a luxurious flagship for the Jensen brand, the 1971 Mk 3 had the biggest engine fitted to any post-war British production car. The 7.3-litre (433ci) Chrysler V8 was considered a little excessive for British tastes, and despite its incredible performance, excellent motorway refinement and smooth-shifting automatic transmission, the Mk 3's ability to plunder the earth's oil resources at such an alarming rate – as little as 3km/L (9mpg) round

▲ **Jensen Interceptor I**

This has to be one of the Interceptor's best angles, its low, wide and purposeful stance showing off the Vignale-styled bodywork to its best effect.

town – meant that it found little favour with British buyers, especially in the austerity immediately after the fuel crises of 1973 and 1974. It may have seemed rather pointless at the time, but with hindsight the Mk 3 is the pinnacle of the Jensen brand – politically incorrect, and proud of it. As a footnote, the Interceptor was briefly revived by private investors in the 1980s,

Model	Years Built (0–60mph)	0–96km/h km/h (mph)	Top Speed
Mk 1	1966–69	7.3sec	215 (133)
Mk 2	1969–71	7.3sec	215 (133)
FF	1966–71	8.4sec	210 (130)
Mk 3	1971–76	7.6sec	209 (129)
SP	1971–73	6.9sec	231 (143)
Convertible	1974–75	7.7sec	204 (127)

but only a handful of cars were completed. All Mk 3s had alloy wheels as standard fitment.

SP

If the 7.3-litre (433ci) Mk 3 wasn't scary enough, with its skinny high-profile tyres and 300bhp (224kW) V8 powerplant, you could always opt for the SP. Identifiable by its louvred bonnet panel, the ultimate performance variant of the Interceptor had 330bhp (246kW) and a black vinyl roof to distinguish it from lesser variants. It was awesomely quick and had a certain appeal

Luxury was the byword of the Interceptor's cabin, with supple cream leather, walnut dashboard and door cappings, and thick pile carpets fitted. But despite this, Jensen's low budget was still very much in evidence. Many of the switches used were taken from mainstream British saloon cars, while the Interceptor's steering wheel was lifted directly from an Austin Maxi, not exactly the most elegant source.

to those who really did want their car to be the biggest and the best, but it was killed off in 1973 when energy crises made a complete mockery of its format. The SP is rare today – they rusted badly, and only 232 were made in the first place.

Convertible/Coupe

The most unusual Interceptor variants ever built were launched late in the car's life, perhaps in a bid to reinvigorate sales after the well-documented 1970s energy crises had practically ground them to a halt.

The pretty convertible had a slightly restyled rear end and came with a smart power-operated soft-top, and for those who could afford it this was a truly beautiful touring car, let down only by its wayward handling in wet conditions. A total of 267 was built. Even rarer is the oddball coupe, which was based on the convertible, but had a fixed bubble roof and just two seats. It was difficult to see the point of this car, and buyers obviously thought the same thing, as Jensen finished only 54 of them before financial pressure forced the company to close in 1976.

◀ ▼ **Jensen Interceptor FF**

The FF was technologically incredible, with permanent four-wheel drive and an anti-lock braking system developed from that used in aircraft.

Specifications

Engine type: V8	Length: 4.85m (191.0in)
Displacement: 6276cc (383ci)	Width: 1.78m (70.0in)
Maximum power: 246kW (330bhp) at 5000rpm	Height: 2.40m (53.0in)
Top speed: 220km/h (137mph)	Wheelbase: 2.74m (108.0in)
0–96km/h (0–60mph): 8.1sec	Weight: 1919kg (4230lbs)

Lamborghini Countach
1973–90

'Countach' is an exclamation used by men of Italy's Piedmont region at the sight of a beautiful woman. While untranslatable, it is the equivalent of a wolf whistle – a reaction common on sight of Lamborghini's icon.

▲ **Lamborghini Countach**

Even today, the Countach is a car that causes you to look twice. It could never be described as classically elegant, but there's no denying its wedge-shaped lines have real impact.

LP400

Styled by Marcelo Gandini as a replacement to the seductive and alluring Miura, the aluminium-bodied Countach was certainly a striking car to look at, with flat, angular lines and distinctive side ducts. The Countach was first seen as the LP500 prototype at the 1971 Geneva Motor Show, with a 5.0-litre (305ci) V12 engine; however, this was one of the few features that didn't make it through to final production.

When it appeared as a production car almost three years later, the LP400 (now with a 4.0-litre/244ci V12 under the engine cover) was almost identical in appearance to Gandini's original concept, and was equally shocking as a result. The odd scissor-style doors, futuristic light clusters and weird trapezoid profile remained, while the surprisingly skinny tyres meant that the Countach had very little in the way of drag –

Specifications	
Engine type: V12	Length: 4.14m (163.0in)
Displacement: 3929cc (240ci)	Width: 1.89m (74.4in)
Maximum power: 280kW (375bhp) at 8000rpm	Height: 1.07m (42.1in)
Top speed: 290km/h (180mph)	Wheelbase: 2.45m (96.5in)
0–96km/h (0–60mph): 5.5sec	Weight: 1370kg (3020lbs)

and made the car incredibly difficult to steer at speed, especially if you were driving it straight into a headwind.

Regardless, the Countach was still a stunning and marvellously fast car, capable of speeds of up to 282km/h (175mph) if you were brave enough to do battle with the steering. It was also well balanced, the weight distribution at lower speeds making the handling incredible providing you didn't provoke the aerodynamic issues by driving too quickly in a straight line. For better weight distribution, the engine was mounted 'backwards'; the output shaft at the front, and the gearbox in front of the engine, with the driveshaft running back through the engine's sump to a differential at the rear. This was a complicated layout, but one which gave the car near perfect front/rear balance.

Those doors were functional, too. True, the front-hinged design may have seemed gimmicky, but it provided three advantages. The first was that it kept the car low, as there was no need for a conventional hinge mechanism; the second was that rear visibility was so bad that, when reversing, you could drive with the doors open and look out while manoeuvring; and the third was that the Countach was so wide, it was the only way you could be sure of getting the doors open in a tight parking space.

LP400S

In 1979, the original Countach was replaced by the new LP400S, which was primarily aimed at strengthening the model's appeal in the hotly contested American market. Although the engine was slightly upgraded from the LP400 model, the most radical changes were to the exterior, where the tyres were replaced with much wider Pirelli P7 rubber, and fibreglass wheelarch extensions were added, giving the car the fundamental look it kept until the end of its

helping it cut through the air with little rolling resistance. Even so, it wasn't especially well thought-out aerodynamically, and it suffered from some of the problems that had marred the performance of its predecessor, the Miura. The body was so low that it generated very little in the way of downforce, and this meant that the front could suffer from aerodynamic lift, which effectively sucked it upwards away from the road

◄ ► ▲ **Lamborghini Countach LP400 1976**
One of the Countach's more unusual features was its scissor-style doors. They compensated for the car's gargantuan width by opening directly upwards, meaning you could still get in and out of the car if you were parked in a car park. Assuming, of course, there wasn't a low ceiling above.

production run. The wheelarch extensions made the Countach even wider, though, and this meant that it couldn't be parked in many bays, especially in Europe, where cars were generally much smaller than those available in the United States. Other styling cues included an optional V-shaped spoiler over the rear deck, which, while improving high-speed stability, reduced the top speed by at least 16km/h (10mph). Most owners ordered the wing, not least because it helped to reduce the symptoms of aerodynamic lift experienced by those who had ordered an earlier LP400.

Dynamically, the LP400S was a much better car than the LP400, the wider tyres giving it better cornering grip. Aesthetically, some prefer the slick lines of the original, but there are others who prefer the more aggressive lines of the later vehicles, beginning with the LP400S. Whichever you choose, though, you get a car that knows how to make an entrance.

LP500S/5000QV

Further tweaks came about in 1982, with the introduction of the LP500, which finally received the larger engine first seen in Gandini's concept car a decade earlier. The unit was actually 5.1 litres (311ci) in capacity, but LP500 had much more resonance as a name than LP510, so the extra few cc were often forgotten about.

Model	Years Built (0–60mph)	0–96km/h km/h (mph)	Top Speed
LP400	1973–79	5.9sec	282 (175)
LP400S	1979–82	5.5sec	282 (175)
LP500S/5000QV	1982–90	4.9sec	286 (178)

◀ **Lamborghini Countach LP500S**
One of the main styling differences between the LP500S and previous Countach models was the adoption of larger tail lamps, which were fitted to satisfy new European legislation to incorporate reflectors of a certain size.

legislation that meant the bumpers had to be raised and made thicker, which some purists said ruined the look of the car. Others thought that the more butch-looking bumpers simply made the car look more aggressive, especially when equipped with the enormous rear wing. QV models also got a more powerful engine sporting four valves per cylinder, hence the name (which stood for 'quattrovalvole').

Body changes came about in 1985 with the launch of the 5000QV, in line with US safety

1988 Anniversary

The ultimate evolution of the Countach was the 1988 Anniversary model, which was created to commemorate Lamborghini's twenty-fifth year. It received big 'air boxes' on the roof to aid cooling, narrower rear lights and what were, at the time, the widest tyres ever to be fitted to a production car, with 345/35R15s. Try finding those at your local fast–fit centre …

The enormous rear wing on the Countach 5000QV was an option, and it was there strictly for show, just in case an owner didn't think his Countach was imposing enough without it. In reality, the car's shape was such that it possessed natural aerodynamic downforce,  a large amount of which was supplied through the pods mounted on the car's rear quarter pillars. These pods sucked air back down to the rear of the car.

◀ ▼ **Lamborghini Countach 1998 Anniversary**
Later Countachs lost some of the design purity of the original – the flared wheel arches, deep side strakes and chunky rear bumper did little for the car's original, angular lines.

Specifications

Engine type: V12	Length: 4.14m (162.9in)
Displacement: 5167cc (315ci)	Width: 2.0m (78.7in)
Maximum power: 339kW (455bhp) at 7000rpm	Height: 1.07m (42.1in)
Top speed: 286km/h (178mph)	Wheelbase: 2.45m (96.5in)
0–96km/h (0–60mph): 5.2sec	Weight: 1446kg (3188lbs)

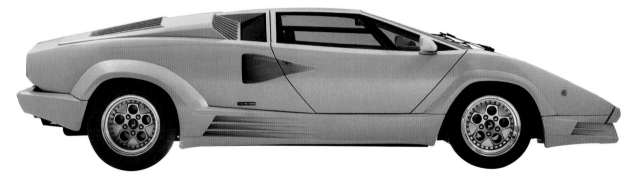

Land Rover
1948–

Ever since 1948 Land Rover has been proud of building, in the words of its advertisements, 'the best 4x4 by far'.

Series 1

Originally a product of the Rover Group, the Land Rover was produced as an answer to the American Willys Jeep. The brainchild of Rover's chief engineer Maurice Wilks, the very first prototypes were built by him for use on his farmland on the Welsh island of Anglesey, and these even consisted of a number of Jeep components in their running gear. So successful was Wilks's experimentation that he approached the company with a view to selling such a model as an agricultural vehicle, and the Land Rover was born. Initially, it used the 1.6-litre (98ci) petrol engine from the Rover 60 saloon (sedan),

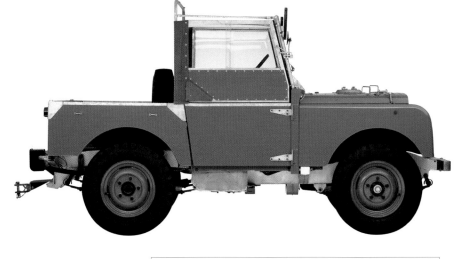

Specifications

Engine type: Inline four-cylinder	Length: 3.58m (140.8in)
Displacement: 1997cc (121.9ci)	Width: 1.59m (62.5in)
Maximum power: 39kW (52bhp) at 4000rpm	Height: 1.93m (76.0in)
Top speed: 96.6km/h (60mph)	Wheelbase: 2.18m (86.0in)
0–96km/h (0–60mph): Not quoted	Weight: 1346kg (2968lbs)

▶ ▲ **Land Rover Series I**
The original Series I Land Rover was simple but effective, with the bodywork either bolted or riveted to a separate chassis and only one basic body style.

Inside, the original Land Rover was spartan. It was very much a Land Rover belief that only the essential controls stayed within the cabin, although from Series III models onwards there were at least some concessions to modernity with a standard heater, radio wiring and dials moved ahead of the driver. True luxuries such as air conditioning and electric windows, however, did not become common until the late 1990s.

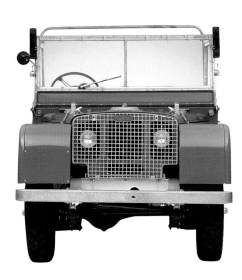

mounted in a steel chassis attached to which was a body entirely crafted from alloy panels. Estate (station wagon) versions of the Land Rover soon followed and were marketed as passenger cars, kicking off a model, called Station Wagon, that would remain a mainstay of the Land Rover launch for years to come.

Extra versatility came in 1953 with the introduction of a long-wheelbase model, which stretched the original Land Rover's 2.03m (80in) wheelbase to 2.71m (107in), and allowed several more body styles to join the range, along with a more powerful 2.0-litre (121ci) engine. Finally, in 1957, Land Rover introduced its first diesel engine – a 2.0-litre (121ci) unit that offered little in the way of performance, but was so low revving that it was practically indestructible.

Series II

Replacing the Series I shortly after the launch of the diesel engine was the Series II, which saw a relatively short production run from 1956 to 1959. It came in 2.24m (88in) and 2.77m (109in) wheelbases – measurements that would become familiar to Land Rover fans over the coming

▲ **Land Rover Series II**

The front radiator grille of the Series 2 was T-shaped for a reason. It was also always left unpainted so it could be easily detached and used as a makeshift barbecue grill for those who liked a more adventurous lifestyle.

years. From 1959, all models received 2.25-litre (139ci) engines in both petrol or diesel form, while on petrol versions an optional overdrive unit manufactured by Fairey was offered, which gave them fuel consumption comparable to the diesels plus much improved cruising ability.

The Series II set the basic shape of the Land Rover for the next 27 years, such was the simplicity of its design.

Series IIA

The Series IIA is considered by many to be the most durable of all leaf-sprung Land Rovers, and is certainly the most popular option among collectors who want a vehicle that's as usable as it is historically important.

It was certainly a success story, with over 60,000 sales a year in its home market, and many more worldwide. As well as succeeding in the United Kingdom, the Land Rover dominated in Australia, where it accounted for 90 per cent of 4x4 sales in the 1960s, as well as many countries in Africa and the Middle East, where it introduced mobility to those who would never have dreamed of driving a car in the past.

Produced between 1959 and 1971, the IIA was distinguishable from the Series II in only a handful of ways, most notably in the layout of the dashboard and the opening front ventilation flaps. From 1967, an inlet-over-exhaust valve 2.6-litre (159ci) straight-six engine was offered with extra torque, which was ideal for use as a tow truck or similar, but certainly gave no performance benefit.

From February 1969, the headlamps moved into the wings (fenders) on all models, after

criticism from safety campaigners, who said that the inset headlamps on earlier Land Rovers made the vehicles look narrower than they were when driven at night, and therefore more likely to cause accidents.

Lightweight/Airportable

In 1970, Land Rover launched a model designed specifically for military applications. Based on the standard 2.23m (88in) chassis, the Airportable, known among enthusiasts more simply as 'Lightweight', came with the absolute minimum amount of bodywork and a canvas tilt roof. It was designed to be carried by a helicopter in a sling, so that it could then be deployed by troops in areas that would usually be inaccessible by vehicles.

A good number of the Lightweight Land Rovers were lost, but those that have survived the rigours of time are now mostly used as leisure vehicles by their owners, as they're especially competent off-road.

▼ **Land Rover Series III**

As an estate (station wagon), even the short-wheelbase version of the Series 3 had room to seat up to seven people, although space on the rear bench seats was a little cramped for fully grown occupants.

Model	Years Built	0–96km/h (0–60mph)	Top Speed km/h (mph)
Series I	1948–56	N/A	89 (55)
Series II	1956–59	N/A	97 (60)
Series IIA	1959–71	36.1secs	108 (67)
Lightweight	1970–85	29.0secs	118 (73)
Series III	1971–85	29.1secs	110 (68)
Stage One V8	1979–83	26.1secs	131 (81)
90/110	1983–	22.3secs	136 (85)

Series III

Replacing the popular Series IIA, the Series III was in itself more of a facelift than a complete rework. Mechanically identical to the earlier models, and using the same suspension layout and 2.23m (88in) or 2.77m (109in) wheelbases, the Series III introduced a more luxurious cabin, with the option of 'Deluxe' seats and an all-syncromesh gearbox. The dials were moved from the centre into a pod ahead of the driver, and a more sophisticated (and hugely welcome) windscreen wiper motor replaced the original Lucas item.

As competent as all its predecessors, the Series III was further improved in 1979 with the introduction of a new engine with five main bearings instead of three, offered in both petrol and diesel variants, which essentially used the same block. The newer engine was tougher and less prone to camshaft rattle than its predecessors, as well as being slightly higher-revving and more economical. These are the most desirable of the Series Land Rovers today for those who want a vehicle that is still capable of working hard for a living.

Also of interest was the 'County', launched in 1982. Intended much more as a family vehicle than one designed to work its life off-road, it was more comfortable and luxurious than earlier estate cars. The concept was so popular that the County name is still used today.

Stage One V8

In 1979, a V8 was installed in the Series III for the first time. Called the Stage One, the 3.5-litre (215ci) model used the engine from the Range Rover and had a new, flattened-off front end that indicated the styling direction that Land Rover would follow with the new Defender that replaced it.

Incredibly thirsty on fuel, the Stage One was nonetheless a much more viable proposition for road use than a standard Land Rover, which by now felt as though it would struggle to keep up with modern traffic. But all that was about to change …

90/110/Defender

Perhaps the most significant change since the Series II replaced the

▼ **Land Rover Stage One V8**
Identifiable by its flat front and longer bonnet (hood), the Stage One V8 was powered by the 3.5-litre (215ci) powerplant from the Range Rover, but with more torque and less power.

▶ ▼ Land Rover Defender

Although different in every respect, the DNA of the original Land Rover is instantly identifiable in the Defender – an icon that continues to this day.

Series I in 1956, the 90 and 110 brought new levels of refinement and flexibility to Land Rover at their launch in 1983. With new coil springs all-round for a more supple ride, plus a completely redesigned cab, the new models were much more usable, while a choice of 2.25-litre (139ci) petrol or 2.5-litre (152ci) diesel engines offered slightly more in the way of performance than before.

A turbo diesel added even more in the way of power in 1985, by which time sales of petrol models had all but dried up.

More changes came in 1990, when the 90 and 110 names (which reflected the length of the short- and long-wheelbase models, in inches) were renamed 'Defender'. The turbo diesel engine, which had proved troublesome, was replaced by a new direct-injection unit called the 200TDI and which was co-developed with Freight Rover for use in delivery vans. This gave the Defender a new burst of performance, with a top speed in excess of 129km/h (80mph). This powerplant was superseded itself by a revised (and more powerful) 300TDI unit in 1993, which is still used today in developing markets where modern electronic engine technology is yet to be fully understood.

The TDI was replaced again in 1998 by a new five-cylinder engine called the TD5, while at the same time a range of special metallic blue fiftieth Anniversary models was produced to mark Land Rover's biggest milestone yet.

But the story of the Land Rover does not end there. Despite many threats to kill off the Defender in light of advanced emissions and safety legislation, the vehicle survived European law changes to receive yet another facelift in 2007, complete with an all-new Ford/Peugeot-derived 2.2-litre (134ci) diesel engine. The new

Specifications

Engine type: Inline four-cylinder turbodiesel	Length: 3.99m (157.1in)
Displacement: 2500cc (153ci)	Width: 1.79m (70.5in)
Maximum power: 84kW (113bhp) at 4000rpm	Height: 2.04m (80.2in)
Top speed: 140km/h (87mph)	Wheelbase: 2.36m (92.9in)
0–96km/h (0–60mph): 13.5sec	Weight: 1695kg (3737lbs)

unit delivered excellent refinement and economy by comparison with earlier models, yet the rest of the vehicle remained true to the Land Rover's original and as yet not-bettered concept.

Although the latest version looks very similar to the original Series One, the only surviving component common to both the new Defender and the Series One is the hook for securing the canvas tilt on pick-up models …

Lotus Elan
1962–94

Developed by a race car maker, the gorgeously pretty Elan set new standards for handling and performance.

S1

Launched to replace the pretty but incredibly expensive Elite, the Lotus Elan made its debut at the 1962 Earls Court Motor Show in London, England.

The brainchild of Lotus founder and legendary race car designer, Colin Chapman, the car was developed with the assistance of an engineer called Ron Hickman. His brief was to make the

Elan, known in Lotus parlance as the Type 23, handle like no other car, which required something of a lateral approach to its method of construction.

Rather than build the car on a separate chassis, Hickman (who was better known for designing the Black & Decker Workmate portable workbench), developed a strong but compact steel backbone, onto which an entire bodyshell made out of fibreglass could then be mounted. At the front, it used twin wishbone suspension with coil springs and dampers, while at the rear the car had the 'Chapman Strut' – a form of rear suspension developed by Colin Chapman for Lotus's race cars, and a

▼ **Lotus Elan**

Lotus founder Colin Chapman always argued that the Elan's faultlessly pretty styling was coincidental. His main concern was to create a car that was exceptional to drive, and that was certainly something that the company achieved.

system already proven on race circuits with great effect.

As a result, the Elan caused quite a sensation. With its light weight, coming it at under 800kg (1500lb), the car had independent suspension all-round and four-wheel disc brakes, while the Elan's incredible chassis and near-perfect weight distribution meant that it was one of the finest-handling cars around.

Initially, power came from a Lotus-tuned version of Ford's five-bearing 1500cc (93ci) engine with a unique twin-cam cylinder head, although within a year this was substituted with Lotus's own 1558cc (96ci) twin-cam overhead-cam engine. These later models were known as the Elan 1600, until the S2 appeared in 1964.

▲ **Lotus Elan Powerplant**
Power for all but the earliest Elans came from a twin-cam overhead-cam powerplant designed in house by Lotus itself, and later supplied to Ford for use in the Lotus Cortina.

Much loved and praised for being such a great car to drive, the Elan received its main criticisms centred on poor build quality and rather spartan trim levels, although those who valued driver appeal above all else were happy to put up with these minor misgivings.

S2

Lotus's policy was one of gradual improvement, rather than replacement – and so it was with the Elan S2. Mechanically identical, although for some peculiar reason S2 models had a much better reputation for reliability, the revised version of the Elan S1 had improvements that focused mainly on the interior. The only external differences were new wheel centres, with a small centre cap replacing the chrome hubcaps of earlier cars, and a new set of tail lights, this time borrowed from the Vauxhall Victor, with curved edges that looked fairly harmonious with the Lotus's lithe and adorable lines.

Inside, though, there were more significant changes. The original black vinyl dash was substituted for a full-length wood veneer item, while further practicality and security came in the form of a lockable glovebox.

As with the S1, the S2 was among the world's greatest sports cars to drive, and this was further emphasized in 1964 with the introduction of a lightweight version of the Elan developed for competition. Known as the Type 26R, only 43 examples were built, despite a production run of more than two years.

S3

For its third incarnation, which was unveiled in 1965, the Elan had grown up into a more luxurious and practical sports car, with prices raised accordingly.

Unusually, Lotus also took the opportunity to launch the car as a coupe only – the new fixed-head body style being something that had been under consideration since the Elan's launch four years earlier. It wasn't long, however, before enthusiasts complained and the S3 was made available as a drophead convertible as well, this being by far the most popular and desirable body style for an Elan then, as it is now.

Mechanical changes were limited to a change in the car's final drive ratio to give it more refined cruising manners on motorways, and in US-market cars the twin Weber carburettors were replaced by twin Strombergs for emissions reasons, although the Elan didn't suffer a significant drop in power like many of its rivals.

Specifications

Engine type: Inline four-cylinder	Length: 4.28m (168.0in)
Displacement: 1558cc (95.08ci)	Width: 1.61m (63.5in)
Maximum power: 88kW (118bhp) at 6000rpm	Height: 1.19m (47.0in)
Top speed: 190km/h (118mph)	Wheelbase: 2.44m (96.0in)
0–96km/h (0–60mph): 9.0sec	Weight: 878kg (1935lbs)

▼ **Lotus Elan +2 1968**

The Elan +2 had little of the lithe appeal of the convertible in its styling, but the important fact was that it still drove as well as an Elan should.

Luxury touches included full-size window frames for the first time, standard electric windows and head restraints, while the Elan S3 SE (for Special Equipment) was introduced in time for the 1967 model year, with a slight horsepower increase from 105 to 110bhp (78 to 83kW), and knock-on 33cm (13in) wheels with chrome centre spinners.

Elan +2

Never one to react to market demand, Colin Chapman was instead responding to his own needs with the Elan +2. With a new addition to his family making life with two-seater Elans rather difficult, he designed a 2+2 variant himself, with an extra 30cm (12in) of length added to the chassis and a slight increase in the width of the body to boot.

The modifications gave the Elan +2 a reasonable increase in cabin space, although any pretensions that this was a proper four-seater were lost as soon as you tried to squeeze anyone

The Elan +2 came into being only because Colin Chapman wanted a company car with room for his offspring, yet it was designed with the same engineering precision as any other Lotus. Although the rear seats were cramped and ended ahead of the rear axle, the window and C-pillar extended further backwards than necessary, not to create extra space but to even up the car's weight distribution between front and rear.

▶ ▲ **Lotus Elan Sprint 1971**
The best of the early Elans was the Sprint, identifiable by its gold bumpers and black road wheels – both of which were copied directly from the Team Lotus Formula One cars.

bigger than a small child in the back. The odd looks were also criticized in some quarters, especially when you consider how pretty the standard Elan was.

Regardless, the +2 was still a fabulous sports car, with typically assured Lotus handling and a lively choice of twin-cam engines, which were improved in line with those in the rest of the Elan line-up over the following few years. The best cars were those from the last two years of production, which not only were the most powerful, but also benefited from the addition of a five-speed gearbox.

S4/Sprint
More changes came in 1969, with the introduction of the Elan S4. Again benefiting from the same leech-like roadholding and superb steering of its predecessors, the S4 moved things even further on, with revised (and much more logically laid out) switchgear and revised seats inside.

External changes were more notable, too, with flared wheelarches introduced to both the coupe and convertible models, along with bigger knock-on wheels and low-profile tyres.

Changes under the bonnet (hood) included the standardization of Stromberg carburettors (first seen on US-spec S3s) on all Elan variants and for all markets, plus the welcome addition of servo-assisted brakes, which made the Elan's

Specifications

Engine type: Inline four-cylinder	Length: 3.68m (145.0in)
Displacement: 1558cc (95.08ci)	Width: 1.42m (56.0in)
Maximum power: 94kW (126bhp) at 6500rpm	Height: 1.15m (45.2in)
Top speed: 190km/h (118mph)	Wheelbase: 2.13m (84.0in)
0–96km/h (0–60mph): 7.0sec	Weight: 687kg (1515lbs)

already reassuring stopping power even more impressive. Incredibly usable, even today, the S4 is the most practical and therefore desirable of all mainstream Elan models.

It isn't, however, the ultimate Elan. That honour falls to the Sprint, launched in 1971 to celebrate Lotus's Formula One world championship victory. Initially available only in red over white with a gold pinstripe, like Lotus's race cars, it was later offered in a broader colour spectrum. It also came with a 126bhp (94kW) 'Big Valve' version of the standard Elan engine, which gave it the ability to top 194km/h

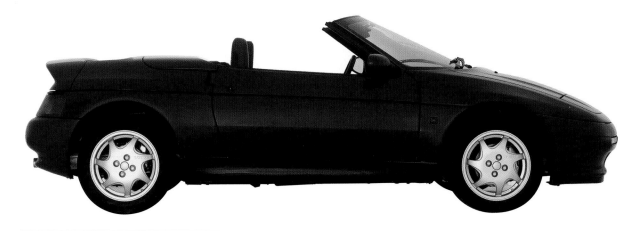

Specifications

Engine type: Turbocharged inline four	Length: 3.8m (149.7in)
Displacement: 1588cc (95.08ci)	Width: 1.73m (68.2in)
Maximum power: 123kW (165bhp) at 6600rpm	Height: 1.25m (49.3in)
Top speed: 219km/h (136mph)	Wheelbase: 2.25m (88.6in)
0–96km/h (0–60mph): 6.5sec	Weight: 1022kg (2254lbs)

▶ ▲ **Lotus Elan SE 1991**

The Elan's return in 1989 wasn't what fans of the marque would have expected from such a historic name – with front-wheel drive and a Japanese engine, the car's launch was controversial.

(120mph) flat out. A great, great car, and one that was much lamented when production finally ceased in 1974.

Elan FWD

The original Elan was not replaced in 1974, which meant that fans of the model were left feeling somewhat unfulfilled, especially when the closest equivalent cars were the likes of the MG Midget and Triumph Spitfire, both of which were woefully underpowered in comparison to the potency of the Elan. So when Lotus announced it was set to revive the Elan concept 15 years later, the new car was awaited with much anticipation.

Model	0–96km/h (0–60mph)	Top Speed km/h (mph)
S1	9.1sec	178 (110)
S2	8.7sec	184 (114)
S3	8.7sec	184 (114)
Plus 2	8.2sec	199 (123)
S4	6.7sec	196 (121)
FWD	6.5sec	220 (136)

Ironically, the new car debuted in the same year as the Mazda MX-5, a car that shamelessly took its styling cues and driving characteristics from the original Elan, so it came as quite a surprise when Lotus announced that its new Elan would come with front-wheel drive and a Japanese engine.

That would certainly have put some purists off, but aside from its unusual (for Lotus) mechanical layout, the Elan had a lot going for it. The Peter Stevens–designed two-seater body was unusual yet pretty, while under the skin it used a steel backbone chassis, built along the same principles as the original.

Under the bonnet, the 1.6-litre (98ci) engine came courtesy of Isuzu and developed 130bhp (97kW) in normally aspirated form, or 165bhp (123kW) in the turbocharged SE model, while the brilliant design of the chassis bestowed it with superb handling that made the front-wheel drive layout immaterial.

Yet despite being phenomenally good to drive, the new-generation Elan was a complete sales flop. First, it was snubbed by purists for its chassis layout. Secondly, it was affected commercially by the recession in the United Kingdom. Finally, it was never well received in the United States. Hence this new Elan was dead in the water within three years. Yet the story was by no means over.

Model	Years	Numbers built
S1	1962–64	900
S2	1964–66	1250
S3	1965–69	2650
Plus 2	1967–74	3300
S4	1969–74	4350
FWD	1989–94	4555

Lotus had a turbulent time in the 1990s, during which ownership of the company changed a total of four times. The Elan FWD was relaunched as a 'Series 2' in 1994, when Lotus was owned by Bugatti, and a further 800 were built while under the Kia company's stewardship. Four years later it was relaunched one more time, this time as labelled as the Kia Elan for the South Korean domestic market. The story doesn't end there, though. The design for the Elan is now owned by Malaysian manufacturer Proton, which bought out Lotus for its engineering and design expertise, and rumours abound that a derivative of the car will emerge as a sporting flagship for the brand – at least in its domestic market – in years to come.

▼ Lotus Elan FWD

The good news with the FWD was that the Elan still drove like a Lotus, while the Peter Stevens – designed two-door soft-top bodywork was undeniably pretty.

Mazda RX Series
1967–

Proud to be a maker that persisted where others failed, Mazda perfected the art of rotary power in its sports coupes.

Cosmo 110S

While it is the NSU Ro80 that is widely regarded as the first ever car to be sold with a rotary engine, it was actually Mazda that was first to market with Felix Wankel's revolutionary type of motor. The Cosmo 110S first appeared in the summer of 1967, a whole six months before the Car of the Year–winning Ro80 claimed to be the pioneer of such technology.

Using two 491cc (30ci) Wankel rotary powerplants, the admirably weird Cosmo 110S was one of the most oddball cars ever made, with curious fish-like styling features and a peculiar cabin layout doing little to reassure potential buyers that this was a rival to more mainstream GTs.

Nor, indeed, was it. Less powerful, less fuel-efficient and significantly less reliable than rivals, the Cosmo was a car you would buy only for its for its talking-point curiosity value, and after five years Mazda had managed to sell a paltry 1176 examples across the globe. That would have been enough to put most people off, but not Mazda – the company would persist with its use of rotary power for the next four decades and beyond …

RX-7

Unperturbed by the Cosmo's mediocre sales performance, Mazda spent the first half of the 1970s slowly building up confidence in its rotary technology, offering Wankel engines in its Capella, 818 and 929 ranges as the RX-2, RX-3 and RX-4, respectively, but it would be 1978 before it felt brave enough to once again offer the drivetrain in another sports car. That car was the RX-7, and it was by far the most successful application of

▼ Mazda Cosmo 110S 1968

It wasn't just the Cosmo's rotary-engine power source that was unusual – the car had utterly oddball styling, which critics of the time likened to a platypus, and inside the cabin layout was equally strange.

Specifications

Engine type: Twin-rotor Wankel rotary	Length: 4.14m (163.0in)
Displacement: 982cc (56.6ci)	Width: 1.54m (62.0in)
Maximum power: 95.5kW (128bhp) at 7000rpm	Height: 1.56m (45.5in)
Top speed: 201km/h (125mph)	Wheelbase: 2.18m (86.0in)
0–96km/h (0–60mph): 9.8sec	Weight: 957kg (2110lbs)

Mazda is one of the keenest and most committed exponents of the rotary engine, and always has been. Instead of using pistons, rotary engines use two combustion chambers, each of which contains a rotor similar in shape to a guitar plectrum to generate compression. The rotors spin more quickly than a traditional engine and offer smoother running. In the past, however, they were prone to failure as the the tips of the rotors wore out and allowed compression to drop.

the rotary engine ever. Using two 573cc (35ci) units, the RX-7 was much more reliable than any previous incarnation of rotary power, and was also an excellent machine to drive. As with all rotary engines, power delivery was unbelievably smooth, while the firm-shifting manual gearbox gave the car a proper sports car feel. Admittedly, the power output might not have been huge at just 120bhp (90kW), but the way in which the power was delivered meant that the RX-7 still felt fairly lively. Its only major failing was poor rust protection, which led to many an RX-7 suffering a premature death well before the engine's rotor tips had worn out.

Post-1983 cars were given a facelift, and had a much rounder nose and better-equipped cabins. Compared to the Cosmo, sales of almost half a million proved that Mazda's persistence was starting to pay off.

RX-7 Turbo

With the power output of the RX-7 being modest at the best of times, quite a few independent companies experimented with forced induction systems to try to give them a bit more force.

One of the most successful was British company TWR, which developed a turbocharger for the car primarily for motorsport purposes, but offered the modification to owners if they wanted to up the power output of their car to 160bhp (119kW).

So successful was the conversion, and with no detrimental effect on reliability, that Mazda adopted it as an official conversion for the car's final year of production, primarily for the American market, although European-spec turbo versions do exist.

RX-7 Mk 2

Smaller, softer and rounder, the second-generation RX-7 had obviously looked to Europe

Specifications

Engine type: Twin-rotary	0–96km/h (0–60mph): 9.2sec
Displacement: 1146cc (70ci)	Length: 4.28m (168.7in)
(equivalent to 2292cc (140ci) in a	Width: 1.67m (65.9in)
conventional gasoline engine)	Height: 1.26m (49.6in)
Maximum power: 75kW (100bhp) at 6000rpm	Wheelbase: 2.42m (95.3in)
Top speed: 193km/h (120mph)	Weight: 1300kg (2933lbs)

▼ **Mazda RX-7 1980**

The original RX-7 followed traditional sports car design principles in its exterior detailing at least – although there was nothing conventional about its engine with its smooth delivery of power.

Specifications

Engine type: Twin-rotor Wankel	Length: 4.29m (168.9in)
Displacement: 1308cc (79.82ci)	Width: 1.69m (66.5in)
Maximum power: 149kW (200bhp) at 6500rpm	Height: 1.26m (49.8in)
Top speed: 241km/h (150mph)	Wheelbase: 2.43m (95.7in)
0–96km/h (0–60mph): 6.7sec	Weight: 1300kg (2933lbs)

▲ **Mazda RX-7 Turbo II 1989**

For the second generation of RX-7, Mazda introduced two new versions – a turbo and a convertible. This version has the turbo engine and convertible body, making it the most desirable of Gen 2 cars.

for its styling cues – the effect being a car that looked not dissimilar to a Porsche 944.

The second-generation RX-7 was closer to the Porsche in performance terms than its predecessor, too, with a healthy 148bhp (110kW) available from Mazda's new 13B rotary engine. A new rear suspension system was introduced to give much better handling than the original RX-7, while from 1988 onwards buyers could opt for a pretty convertible version of the car.

A turbo also became a standard addition to the range, and was blisteringly quick – 0–60mph (0–96km/h) took just 6.7 seconds, although the power delivery was rather brutal and not in keeping with the rotary engine's trademark smoothness. Still, with 200bhp (150kW) on tap,

the turbo version had a power output up there with some of the fastest cars of its era, and at a highly affordable price.

RX-7 Mk 3

The final car to wear the RX-7 badge was also to enjoy the longest production run, going on sale in 1991 and remaining on the market for a full decade before finally being withdrawn from most markets because of its exhaust emissions.

When it debuted, the RX-7 Mk 3 had a lot to live up to, with its arch rival the Nissan 300ZX Turbo having established itself as the best Japanese sports coupe ever. The RX-7 took the fight to Nissan, however, and gave a very solid account of itself, with stunning good looks and impressive power from its turbocharged twin-rotor engine of 255bhp (190kW) – enough to give it a top speed well in excess of 240km/h (150mph), to which it was electronically limited in most markets. Unlike the first- and second-generation RX-7s, the Mk 3 was a real handful to drive, as it had a very light rear end and limited grip. But it was also incredibly exciting from behind the wheel.

By this stage, any fears over the reliability of rotary engines were gone for good.

RX-8

After a two-year absence, Mazda made a welcome return to the rotary fold with the RX-8, launched in 2003. Even though Mazda was the only manufacturer to offer such technology, the RX-8 proved that the Japanese maker was right to persist with the unusual layout by virtue of its incredible performance. Whether you opted for the low 197bhp (147kW) or high 231bhp (172kW) output version of its engine, you ended up with a car that was startlingly quick by comparison to its purchase price, while the oddball looks, fabulous handling and unusual 'suicide' rear doors were further selling points.

The RX-8's biggest problem was the smoothness with which it delivered its power because for the ham-fisted driver this presented a challenge of its own ...

On a less than perfectly dry road, over-enthusiastic use of the accelerator pedal by the driver could cause the RX-8 to lose rear traction and slew across the road, and the quietness of the power unit made it difficult to tell how much gas was too much.

Model	Years Built (0–60mph)	0–96km/h km/h (mph)	Top Speed
Cosmo 110S	1967–72	10.2sec	186 (115)
RX-7 Mk 1	1978–86	9.9sec	189 (117)
RX-7 Mk 2	1985–91	8.5sec	217 (134)
RX-7 Turbo	1985–91	6.7sec	239 (148)
RX-7 Mk 3	1991–97	6.0sec	254 (157)
RX-8	2003–	6.4sec	236 (146)

Widely respected across Europe, the United States and Australia, the RX-8 proves that rotary engines are great tools for delivering smooth power if fully developed, although the biggest criticism of the RX-8 is that despite its inherent reliability, fuel and oil consumption are still higher than most petrol engines.

▼ **Mazda RX-8**

Mazda's rotary return came in 2003 with the RX-8 – a four-seater sports car with a pair of cunningly concealed rear doors, hinged against the rear quarter panel.

Mercedes-Benz SL Models
1954–2001

Two letters steeped in history – Mercedes' SL ('Sports Lightweight') models found instant fame, and garnered a reputation for stunning looks and great performance.

300SL Gullwing

An instant classic, and one of the most famous cars ever built, Mercedes' 300SL Gullwing grew out of the 1952 Le Mans–winning race car to become a road-going flagship two years later.

Built on a spaceframe chassis and powered by a dry-sumped 3.0-litre (183ci) engine which developed a colossal 240bhp (179kW) – a huge amount of power for its day – the 300SL is widely attributed as being the world's first ever supercar. It's perhaps best remembered, though, for its roof-hinged doors, which existed for two reasons. The first was to maintain the aerodynamic efficiency of the car, which would have been disturbed by fitting hinges on the side, and the second was to allow the sills to be

▲ **Mercedes-Benz 300SL Gullwing**
A rare sight today, but the Gullwing's natural environment was on the racetrack. It was originally built to win Le Mans.

thicker and wider, giving the car greater torsional rigidity. Regardless of this attention to detail, the Gullwing was still a real handful to drive, with drum brakes all round and a lively tail-happy chassis. Of the 1400 cars built, 29 were built with a hand-finished alloy body. These examples are considered priceless today.

190SL

The 'poor man's' version of the Gullwing, the 190SL was similar to look at, but had little else in common with its bigger sister.

Aimed more at cruising than racing, it was based on a truncated version of the standard Ponton-bodied Mercedes saloon (sedan), and used a twin-carb version of the standard 190 saloon's four-cylinder engine, producing a moderate 105bhp (78kW). The heavy steel body meant that the car wasn't especially quick, while the old-fashioned underpinnings meant it wasn't rewarding to drive quickly either, but despite these shortcomings it was beautifully finished inside and out, and earned itself a well-deserved reputation for longevity. It was also undeniably pretty.

300SL Roadster

Replacing the Gullwing was no mean feat, but, in doing so with the 300SL Roadster in 1957, Mercedes created a car that more than satisfactorily filled the brief. Based on a stronger version of the Gullwing's chassis and using many of its forward panels, the Roadster was open-topped and far less claustrophobic as a

result, while conventional doors also made it easier for passengers to get in and out.

The body was mostly steel, but with alloy doors, bonnet (hood) and boot (trunk) lid, while from 1961 onwards disc brakes were fitted to all four wheels, making the car much safer to handle as a result. Although still a popular collectors' car, the 300SL Roadster doesn't have the same cachet as the Gullwing and is therefore nowhere near as valuable, despite it being indisputably the better car.

SL 'Pagoda Roof'

Known colloquially as the 'Pagoda Roof' because of its inversely sloping roofline, the 1963–71 generation of SL was styled by Paul Bracq and was based on a shortened version of the 220 Fintail saloon chassis, complete with its rudimentary

▶ ▼ Mercedes-Benz 300SL Gullwing

The Gullwing doors were not just a gimmick – they existed for two reasons. The first was to give the car better lateral stability, the second was to avoid any aerodynamic interference the door handles might cause.

Specifications

Engine type: Straight-six	Length: 4.52m (178in)
Displacement: 2.99cc (0.18ci)	Width: 1.78m (70in)
Maximum power: 179kW (240bhp) at 6100rpm	Height: 1.26m (49.7in)
Top speed: 266km/h (165mph)	Wheelbase: 2.39m (94in)
0–96km/h (0–60mph): 8.5 secs	Weight: 1293kg (2850lbs)

▶ **Mercedes-Benz 190SL**
Although nowhere near the performance model the original Gullwing was, the
190SL was a pretty car that shared the most beguiling elements of its styling.

swing-axle rear end and double wishbone front suspension. Three different engines were offered. The 2.3-litre (140ci) 230SL was the base model, and the only one available at launch, but in 1965 it was supplemented with the 250SL, with a 2.5-litre (152ci) engine, and in 1968 with the 280SL, which was 2.8 litres (171ci) in capacity. All of the engines were smooth six-cylinder units and were both lively and refined. All but the 230SL came with disc brakes all round, and despite the basic rear suspension set-up they were considerably better to drive than the previous-generation 190SL model. They were also the prettiest of the affordable SLs.

W107 SL

Enjoying the longest production run of any Mercedes model ever, the W107 SL Series was introduced in 1971 and remained on sale until 1990, by which time it had already established itself as a classic icon. Unfussy styling, with

sharp, slab-sided lines and an imposing radiator grille, meant that the SL aged brilliantly, still looking classy right up to its final incarnation.

Larger than the Pagoda models, the W107 also received more power in the form of a 3.5-litre

▼ **Mercedes-Benz 190SL 'Pagoda Roof'**
When the 190SL was in soft-top form, its 'Pagoda Roof' nickname lost much of its meaning, but these cars are still known as such by collectors. Convertible versions are the most cherished today.

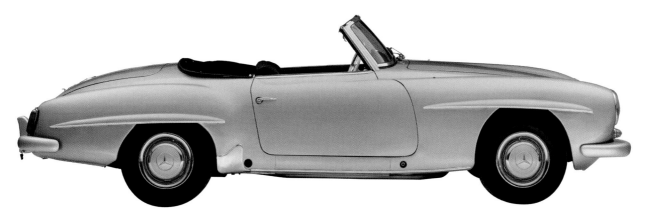

Specifications

Engine type: Inline four-cylinder	Length: 4.22m (166.1in)
Displacement: 1897cc (115.8ci)	Width: 1.74m (68.5in)
Maximum power: 89.5kW (120bhp) at 5700rpm	Height: 1.32m (52in)
Top speed: 171km/h (106mph)	Wheelbase: 2.40m (94.5in)
0–96km/h (0–60mph): 11.2sec	Weight: 1157kg (2550lbs)

ever-increasing engine capacities being the name of the game.

The fastest SL yet, but also the heaviest, the W107 remained much more of a touring car than a sports model; its weight and character had little to do with the original meaning of the SL nomenclature. Regardless, this was a Mercedes in the most classic of moulds.

(215ci) V8 engine (350SL), shortly followed by an even bigger 4.5-litre (274ci) unit (450SL). These were just two of a whole host of different engines that were used in the W107, however, including two six-cylinders (280SL and 380SL) and a myriad of V8s (500SL, 550SL, 600SL), with

▼ Mercedes-Benz 190SL

The 190SL drophead looked beautiful – but it was just a cruiser and the 1.9-litre (116ci) engine wasn't really powerful enough to give it any kind of sporting prowess on the road.

▲ **Mercedes-Benz SLC**
From the front, the SLC looked identical to the W107 SL, but the doors and
wheelbase were longer to accommodate its luxurious four-seater cabin.

SLC

SL style, but for families, the SLC was one of the most practical coupes on the market and was much more than just a 2+2 – it had good access to the rear bench and room for two adults to travel there in relative comfort.

Mechanically identical to the W107 SL and using mostly the same panels, the SLC had an extra 35cm (14in) added to its wheelbase, which, coupled to a stiffer shell, actually made it a better-balanced and nicer-handling car. Its downfall, though, was that the roof didn't come off, and with the roof fixed in place it was nowhere near as pretty as the car on which it was based.

SL 1989–2001

Not the last incarnation of the SL, but certainly the ultimate model to be built along Mercedes' traditional principles, the 1989 SL was long, low, wide and flat, with a thumping V8 engine in its nose and an incredible turn of pace. In V8 500SL form, it could top a heady 259km/h (160mph).

All this speed was partly kept in check by the addition of modern safety equipment, including standard ABS, airbags and a clever pop-up rollover hoop, which would instantly be activated if it sensed the car was about to roll over.

The less elaborate six-cylinder 300SL was nowhere near the car the 500SL was, but was significantly cheaper and had just as much style. For the ultimate in poseur value, however, you really needed the V12-engined SL600, which was for a long time the fastest Mercedes ever. Its barge-like proportions disguised what was actually quite an agile sports car underneath.

Model	Years Built	Number Built
190SL	1954–63	25,881
300SL Gullwing	1945–57	1400
300SL Roadster	1957–63	1858
SL Pagoda	1963–71	48,902
W107 SL	1971–89	300,175
SLC	1972–81	40,963
1989 SL	1989–2001	N/A

MG Sports Cars
1955–

Although there were MG cars built much earlier, it was the MGA that really fired up MG's appeal as a maker of popular sports cars. Its appeal was as easy as A,B,C.

MGA

Amazingly, the MGA almost didn't exist. As part of the newly formed British Motor Corporation, company boss Leonard Lord was looking to rationalize, and he preferred the handsome, macho lines of the Austin-Healey 100/6 to Syd Enever's classically curvaceous MGA.

Nonetheless, MG was given a stay of execution, its brief being to make sure the MGA, launched in 1955, was a sales success – an achievement that wasn't difficult given the car's many and obvious charms. Throw in an affordable asking

The MGA featured no fewer than three different types of tail-light design during its life. The first cars had simple red lamps. These were followed by this design, with a separate indicator lens mounted on a pod, while the last of the line cars had lower mounted lamp units fixed directly to the car's rear deck. These were larger, to meet with tougher US safety legislation require.

▲ ▼ **MGA Mk1 1959**

Despite being built on old-fashioned principles, the MGA had fresh and modern-looking lines – it was one of the most aerodynamic cars of the 1950s.

Specifications

Engine type: Inline four-cylinder	Length: 3.96m (156in)
Displacement: 1588cc (96.9ci)	Width: 1.47m (58in)
Maximum power: 60kW (80bhp) at 5600rpm	Height: 1.27m (50in)
Top speed: 166km/h (103mph)	Wheelbase: 2.39m (94in)
0–96km/h (0–60mph): 13.7sec	Weight: 900kg (1985lbs)

◀ ▲ **MGB Roadster 1962**
Britain's best-selling sports car, and not without good reason, the MGB enjoyed
a 20-year production run during which more than 600,000 were built.

the most desirable of all MGAs was the Twin
Cam. Using a Harry Weslake–designed cylinder
head, the Twin Cam was homologated for
motorsport and had a 28bhp (21kW) power
benefit over standard models, although the
sophisticated engine was renowned for
overheating and burning pistons if not given the
thoughtful maintenance it so richly deserved.

MGB 1962–74

Flying in the face of MG's traditional values, and
upsetting lots of purists along the way, the 1962
MGB did away with a separate chassis and brought
in such luxuries as elbow room, wind-up
windows and a standard heater – commodities
that were almost considered heresy to the
brand's traditional enthusiasts.

Specifications	
Engine type: Inline four-cylinder	Length: 3.89m (153.2in)
Displacement: 1796cc (110ci)	Width: 1.52m (59.9in)
Maximum power: 71kW (95bhp) at 5500rpm	Height: 1.24m (49.4in)
Top speed: 169km/h (105mph)	Wheelbase: 2.31m (91.0in)
0–96 km/h (0–60mph): 12.5sec	Weight: 943kg (2080lbs)

price, and it's hardly a surprise to learn that the
MGA significantly outsold the Big Healeys in
every single sales year, forcing Lord to eat his
words. It didn't matter that the 1.5-litre (91ci) B-
Series engine wasn't especially powerful, nor
that the car was cramped and unrefined. It was
beautiful to look at, and had impressive road
manners thanks to independent front suspension,
disc brakes and rack-and-pinion steering.

A fixed-head coupe model joined the standard
roadster in 1956, followed by an increase in
engine size to 1.6 litres (98ci) in 1959, complete
with a welcome if modest power increase. But

But what the MGB did best was to extend the appeal of the MG badge to new markets, specifically in the United States, where sales snowballed overnight.

Almost as pretty as the MGA and infinitely more practical, faster and better made, the B had plenty going for it, while the added practicality of the MGB GT, launched in 1965, meant that you could almost pretend you were at the wheel of a miniaturized Jaguar E-Type.

Handling on all models was excellent, while those from 1966 had the added benefit of a front anti-roll bar, an all-syncromesh gearbox and a revised rear axle, which made the car far quieter when cruising at speed. From 1969, the cabin was revised and the original 'crackle-painted' surfaces were replaced with padded vinyl items as MG moved into the 1970s.

Obviously effective, the MGB quickly notched up over a quarter of a million sales, and today is the world's most popular classic car, with a whole industry built up around its long-term survival. As such, it's an extremely inexpensive yet enjoyable classic to own and restore.

MGC

The proof that MG had ousted Austin-Healey came in 1968, with the death of the 'Big' Austin-Healey 3000. But there was still demand from some quarters for a large-engined, six-cylinder sports car at an affordable price, and so the MGC came into being.

The car was widely believed to have the Healey 3000's C-Series powerplant under its bonnet (hood), but the truth was slightly different. Although sharing much in common with the Healey engine, the powerplant in the MGC was actually a new seven-bearing engine that was shared only with the obscure and unloved Austin 3-Litre saloon (sedan), meaning that some spares were tricky to source as soon as the early 1980s. Don't be too surprised to find a five-bearing Healey engine under the bonnet of a restored car as a result.

Identifiable by its distinctive square-edged power bulge, the MGC had revised front suspension with torsion bars, larger 38.1cm (15in) wheels and servo brakes as standard, while automatic and overdrive gearboxes were offered as options. Regardless of transmission, or whether you opted for a soft-top or a GT, all MGCs were a complete handful to drive, with too much power and weight for the MG's body to handle. The C was dropped in 1969, after less than three years on sale.

◀ ▼ MGC 1969

Similar to the MGB from most angles, the MGC was easily identifiable by its larger-diameter wheel and distinctive square-edged bonnet hump to accommodate the six-cylinder engine.

Specifications	
Engine type: Inline six-cylinder	Length: 3.89m (153.2in)
Displacement: 2912cc (177.7ci)	Width: 1.52m (59.9in)
Maximum power: 108kW (145bhp) at 5250rpm	Height: 1.26m (49.8in)
Top speed: 190km/h (118mph)	Wheelbase: 2.31m (91.0in)
0–96km/h (0–60mph): 10.1sec	Weight: 1179kg (2600lbs)

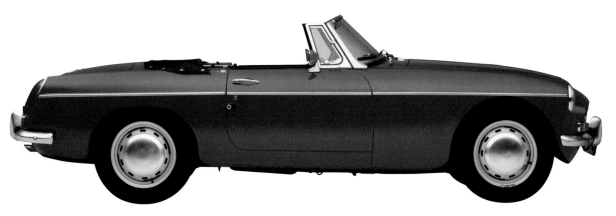

MG GT V8

In 1973, MG did what it should have done instead of the MGC, and modified the MGB GT's inner wing (fender) panels to accept the V8 engine used in the Rover P6 and P5B.

Although officially offered only as a GT (several roadster conversions exist), the V8 was a much better conceived car than that which it spiritually succeeded. The lightweight V8 was made entirely out of alloy, making it only marginally heavier

than the four-cylinder B-Series fitted to the common MGB models and far less nose-heavy, giving the car far better handling than the MGC. That said, the extra power to the back wheels still took some getting used to in wet weather.

Identifiable by its unique alloy wheels and Rover-sourced V8 wing badges, the GT V8 was a case of too little too soon, as strict emissions controls meant that it couldn't be sold in the United States, where such a model would have stood the best chance of becoming a big seller.

MGB 1974–81

It's all too easy to blame American safety legislation for finishing off the MGB. There were plenty of other reasons, however, why the so-called 'Rubber Bumper' models were pretty dismal in comparison to the earlier chrome-

Specifications	
Engine type: V8	Length: 3.93m (154.7in)
Displacement: 3528cc (215ci)	Width: 1.52m (60.0in)
Maximum power: 102kW (137bhp) at 5000rpm	Height: 1.27m (50.0in)
Top speed: 201km/h (125mph)	Wheelbase: 2.31m (91.0in)
0–96km/h (0–60mph): 8.6sec	Weight: 1083kg (2387lbs)

◄ ▼ **MGB GT V8 1973**

In 1973, the MGB finally got the engine it deserved in the Rover V8, although for structural reasons the unit was only ever fitted into the stiffer GT bodyshell.

It was a long wait for fans of the Rover V8 engine before it finally appeared in the MGB, but this was because the car was traditionally not considered strong enough to cope with the torque.

No soft-top V8 was ever offered, although several tuning companies, most notably the British firm Costello, offered excellent V8 conversions that were practically indiscernible from factory versions.

bumper cars, and they were only partly to do with the car's looks.

New crash safety laws had forced MG to fit ungainly impact resistant rubber to the front and back of all MGBs from 1974, taking away much of the design purity, while the ride height also needed to be increased, which did little for the car's handling. This, and the fact that US-market models were constantly starved of power by ever-more stringent emissions laws, was the reason cited by then parent company British Leyland (BL) for the sad demise of the MGB. But there were other ill-advised corporate decisions that helped to engineer its downfall. A general decrease in build quality thanks to cheaper materials, the use of hideous nylon stripy seat facings and parts-bin switchgear inside, and the appalling decision to take away the car's front anti-roll bar to reduce costs

▲ MGB 1974–81

Later MGBs had thick black rubber impact-resistant bumpers to meet stringent American safety laws, and these are the ones that tend to be deliberately overlooked by collectors, making them inexpensive and fun cars to own.

▼ MGC

On the road, the MGC had little to recommend it other than extra power. It was a quick car, but the heavy engine in its nose did little for its handling abilities, while it also made the steering uncomfortably heavy.

Specifications		
Engine type: V8		Length: 4.08m (157.8in)
Displacement: 3946cc (241ci)		Width: 1.69m (66.7in)
Maximum power: 142kW (190bhp) at 4750rpm		Height: 1.32m (51.9in)
Top speed: 219kW (136mph)		Wheelbase: 2.33m (91.7in)
0–96km/h (0–60mph): 7.0sec		Weight: 1100kg (2425lbs)

◀ ▲ **MG RV8 1992**

Despite its relatively modern appearance, the MG RV8 used many of the body panels from the original MGB.

meant that the MGB wasn't half the car it used to be, and by 1981 sales had slowed to such a level that BL took the decision to close its Abingdon MG factory, despite the fact it was the only one of the company's plants that had never gone on strike! The last rubber-bumper cars were known as LE models, and featured distinctive side graphics.

MG RV8

In 1990, Rover pulled off a masterstroke when it decided to reintroduce the Mini Cooper – a car that had been absent for 20 years and was steeped in history. It was an instant hit among fans of retro motoring. To cash in on this fad, Rover looked towards its old tooling, and decided to reintroduce the MGB, albeit with a few modern tweaks, including a fuel-injected 3.9-litre (238ci) Rover V8 engine.

Eventually, 11 years after the MGB was last built, the RV8 made its debut. The car's body was essentially that of the old MGB Roadster, supplied to Rover by Heritage Ltd, which manufactured classic MGB bodyshells for restoration companies, but with added flared wheelarches to fit the new 41cm (16in) alloy wheels and fat rubber. Inside, there was hand-stitched leather and a walnut dashboard. Despite modern creature comforts, the oddball RV8 was an old-fashioned beast

Model	0–96km/h (0–60mph)	Top Speed km/h (mph)
MGA	13.7sec	163 (101)
MGB 62–74	12.2sec	167 (103)
MGC	10.0sec	194 (120)
MGB V88.	6sec	201 (124)
MGB 74–81	12.2sec	167 (103)
MG RV8	6.9sec	220 (136)
MGF/TF	8.7sec	199 (123)

underneath, with exactly the same suspension set-up as traditional MGBs and resultant ride and handling issues, largely thanks to the 187bhp (139kW) power output. Most of the 2000 RV8s sold went to Japan, although many British enthusiasts have since repatriated them.

MGF

If the RV8 reincarnated the body of the MGB, then it was the MGF that brought life back to its soul. Introduced in 1995, the mid-engined, gas-suspended roadster bore little in common with the MGB in terms of its mechanical layout, and the rounded styling bore only a passing resemblance to MGs of yore. But it was the MGF's place as an affordable, sporting ragtop from Britain's best-known domestic manufacturer that made it recall the spirit of its forebear. Priced at less than a compact family hatchback, yet with great performance and impressive handling, the F was a feisty little package, even if it did suffer from premature head gasket failure and some rattling trim issues. Replaced by the similar-looking but

Model	Years Built	Number Built
MGA	1955–62	101,470
MGB 1962–74	1962–74	356,545
MGC	1967–69	8999
MGB V8	1973–76	2591
MGB 1974–81	1974–81	155,698
MG RV8	1992–95	2000
MGF/TF	1995–	N/A

far less complex MG TF in 2002, the MG brand once again disappeared with the demise of its parent company, MG Rover, in 2005. A resurgent MG now exists in China, and builds its own cars from salvaged MG Rover tooling, while TFs are also constructed by the new owners the Nanjing Automobile Corporation, building taking place on the old Longbridge Site.

Specifications

Engine type: Inline four-cylinder twin-cam

Displacement: 1796cc (110ci)

Maximum power: 107kW (143bhp) at 7000rpm

Top speed: 211km/h (131mph)

0–96km/h (0–60mph): 7.8sec

Length: 3.91m (154in)

Width: 1.78m (70in)

Height: 1.27m (50in)

Wheelbase: 2.37m (93.5in)

Weight: 1121kg (2471lbs)

▶ ▼ **MGF VVC 1996**

MG made a remarkable return to the sports car market in 1995 with the two-seater MGF. It was a true MG sports car, despite its mid-engined, front-drive layout.

Mini
1959–2001

Dubbed 'Wizardry on Wheels' when it debuted in 1959, the Mini reinvented the way that car designers and manufacturers thought.

Mk 1

Quite possibly the most important car of the twentieth century, the original Mini redefined car design completely. Built upon a simple monocoque, Alec Issigonis's most famous design used a transverse engine, with the gearbox mounted in the sump to save space, while front-wheel drive meant that there was no need for a propshaft to run underneath the car.

The car was originally sold as either the Austin Seven Mini or Morris Mini Minor. The engine and gearbox were mounted on a subframe that bolted straight onto the car's body; at the rear there was

Specifications

Engine type: Inline four-cylinder	Length: 3.06m (120.3in)
Displacement: 848cc (51.75ci)	Width: 1.40m (55.0in)
Maximum power: 27.6kW (7bhp) at 5500rpm	Height: 1.35m (53.0in)
Top speed: 121km/h (75mph)	Wheelbase: 2.04m (80.2in)
0–96km/h (0–60mph): 26.5sec	Weight: 608kg (1340lbs)

The Mini's interior was basic, but brilliantly laid out. The steering wheel was deliberately tilted away from the cabin to create extra space, while the front parcel shelf and rear door bins were designed to add extra storage. The driving position was not exactly comfortable, but the Mini's designer Alec Issigonis said that this was deliberate because he didn't believe that people who were comfortable while driving could be concentrating properly.

◄ ▲ **Austin Mini Mk 1 1959**
Early Minis had sliding windows and hinged rather than push-button door handles. This example is an upmarket variant, with chrome wheel embellishers and front nudge bars.

◀ ▲ **Mini Cooper S 1964**

Standard Minis and Coopers were difficult to tell apart with an untrained eye.
The bonnet (hood) badge was often the only clue…

Specifications

Engine type: Inline four-cylinder	Length: 3.05m (120in)
Displacement: 970cc (59ci)	Width: 1.41m (55.5in)
Maximum power: 48.5kW (65bhp) at 6500rpm	Height: 1.35m (53in)
Top speed: 156km/h (97mph)	Wheelbase: 2.03m (80.1in)
0–96km/h (0–60mph): 10.9sec	Weight: 578kg (1275lbs)

a similar arrangement, with a single subframe holding the back wheel in place. From 1964, the dry cone suspension was replaced by a fluid-filled Hydrolastic system to improve the car's ride.

But it wasn't just the car's mechanical layout that raised a few eyebrows, as other aspects of the design were equally noteworthy, and not an inch of space was wasted. The luggage area and fuel tank, for example, sat right against the back seat, while huge door bins in the rear were designed to carry large bags or suitcases (or in the case of most Mini owners' experiences, large oil drums, as the car had a reputation for excessive oil consumption) without affecting the car's available interior space. Despite being only four metres (less than 10ft) long, the Mini had plenty of room inside for four adults. Not only that, but despite its modest engine size it was also immense fun to drive. Spot a Mk 1 by its pull-string door handles, floor-mounted starter switch and spindly magic wand-shaped gear lever.

Countryman/Traveller

Despite the Mini's ability to carry four passengers and still have plenty of usable luggage space, there were some people who needed more load space. For them, the estate (station wagon) versions of the Mini – called Traveller if you bought a Morris, or Countryman if you opted for an Austin – were perfect for the job. Based on the extended wheelbase of the Mini van and introduced in 1960, the estate models had twin rear doors, and stiffened rear suspension to cope with loads. Unlike the Morris Minor Traveller, which was similar in concept, the Mini's wooden panels on the flanks were purely decorative and not load-bearing. Both Austin and Morris variants were replaced by a Clubman estate in 1969.

Cooper

Although Alec Issigonis himself was dead against the notion of anyone travelling quickly or even necessarily enjoying the art of driving

▲ Mini Cooper S

The Mini Cooper S enjoyed remarkable motorsport success. LBL 6D is the very car in which Rauno Aaltonen and Henry Liddon drove to victory in the Monte Carlo Rally of 1967.

(which he regarded as a serious endeavour), both of which were personal bugbears of his, it wasn't long before enthusiasts cottoned on to the fact that the Mini offered brilliant handling from its unusual chassis layout.

One of the first to take advantage of this was racing car designer John Cooper, who developed a long-stroke, narrow-bore twin-carb version of the Mini's A-Series engine, producing a modest-sounding but eminently useful 55bhp (41kW). Thanks to the car's diminutive dimensions, light weight and ability to go round corners without slowing down significantly, the Cooper was enormous fun to drive, and started to find its feet in competition both on the circuits and rally stages of the world, although it would be 1964 and the dawn of the Cooper S before it achieved any major motorsport success.

Even so, earlier Coopers are very collectable, and they are prized for their luxury trim and reassuring disc brakes.

Cooper S

Probably the most famous Mini of the lot, the Cooper S proved that the Mini was a winning package by taking the winner's medal on the 1964, 1965 and 1967 Monte Carlo rallies, and would have done so in 1966 as well were it not for a technicality introduced by the rally's (French) officials, which decreed the Mini's headlamps were illegal so a Citroën could win.

While the works rally cars were doing the business in competition, Cooper S cars, or 'Cooperesses' as they became known, were proving equally successful in showrooms. By far the most common and also most rewarding variant is the 1275 S, from 1964 to 1971. Over 40,000 were built, with 76bhp (57Kw) and the ability to cruise at almost 161km/h (100mph). Other engine sizes were 970cc (59ci) and 1071cc (65ci), yet despite their comparative rarity (only 4031 1071s and 963 970s were built), they aren't worth significantly more as they existed purely for homologation, and the 1275 models are more fun to drive, yet with just the same pedigree. Cooper production ceased in 1971, as British Leyland wrongly believed that its Mini 1275GT was a worthy replacement.

▲ Mini Mk 2

The biggest difference between the Mini Mk 1 and the Mk 2 seen here was the shape of the radiator grille – it was made wider for the later cars, to improve airflow to the Mini's side-mounted radiator.

Mk 2

Visual changes between the Mini Mk 1 and Mini Mk 2 were limited to a slightly larger rear screen and a more square-shaped grille, but under the skin the differences were much more significant. Top-of-the-range SDL models now came with a 998cc (61ci) engine as standard, while all models had improved brakes and an all-syncromesh gearbox, which used the far more pleasant remote change mechanism from the Cooper in place of the original spindly lever.

Specifications

Engine type: Inline four-cylinder	Length: 3.05m (120in)
Displacement: 848cc (51.7ci)	Width: 1.41m (55.5in)
Maximum power: 25kW (34bhp) at 5500rpm	Height: 1.42m (56in)
Top speed: 105km/h (65mph)	Wheelbase: 2.03m (80.0in)
0–96 km/h (0–60mph): 21.8sec	Weight: 533kg (1176lbs)

▶ Mini Moke 1965

Originally built for military purposes, but discounted on grounds of its limited ground clearance, the Mini Moke evolved into more of a leisure vehicle, especially popular in holiday resorts.

Mini Moke

Not so much a car as a motorized buckboard, the Mini Moke was originally conceived as a military vehicle, designed to offer mobility to troops in a compact and lightweight package that could be easily freighted or air-dropped into strategically important areas. Its lack of ground clearance, low power output and inherent BMC (British Motor Corporation) reliability issues, such as a reluctance to start in wet weather, meant the forces weren't interested, so instead a civilian version was used. It had standard Mini running gear, a fold-flat windscreen and a rudimentary canvas roof; even things such as passenger seats were optional. Needless to say, the Moke didn't sell well in Britain, where it failed miserably to match the climate – but it was a huge success in Portugal, where it was built until 1994 and was a popular hire car for Western European holidaymakers.

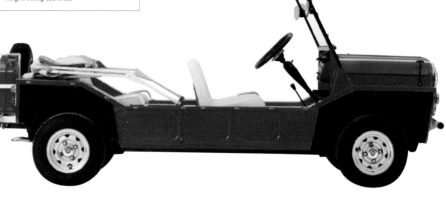

▲ Mini Mk 3

The Mk 3 was the mainstay of the Mini line-up in the 1970s, and retained 25.4cm (10in) wheels and drum brakes. This example sports Minilite alloy wheels and a Mk 1-style radiator grille.

Mk 3

Only two years after Mini Mk 2, the Mk 3 came along with some more distinctive detail changes. The most obvious was the removal of the car's external door hinges, replaced by internal ones concealed within the car's A-pillars and removing one of the earlier Mini's most common rot spots.

The doors were also made slightly larger, and were fitted with winding windows for the first time. Mk 3 models also had dry cone suspension again, in place of the Hydrolastic. This did away with some of the ride comfort of Mk 2 cars, but was much cheaper and far less troublesome, which proved popular with the Mini's target buyers.

Clubman

Intended to replace the Mini outright within two years of its launch, the Clubman was an attempt at moving the car upmarket, and giving it a modern new look. The nose, with its flat radiator grille, square wings (fenders) and central shield was a scaled-down replica of that on the new Austin Maxi hatchback, and was intended to show the broadness of the appeal in British Leyland's range.

Other changes to the Clubman included an all-new dashboard, which moved the dials away from the centre of the dashboard and into a pod ahead of the driver, plus softer vinyl seats and extra trim. On the outside, the new nose was complemented by special Clubman wheeltrims and proudly displayed British Leyland badges on the front wings.

It was clear after two years that the original Mini was still the best seller of the two, and was not going to be easy to replace. Instead, British Leyland (BL) kept the two cars on sale side-by-side for 11 years, until the original won out and the Clubman was put to pasture.

1275GT

Aside from the ungainliness of the Clubman bodyshell, there were other reasons why BL's hastily conceived 1275GT was in now way a proper replacement for the much-loved Mini Cooper.

For a start, it had only a single carburettor compared to the Cooperess's twin-carb set-up, while the low gearing that was designed

◀ Mini Clubman

The wider, flat-nosed front end of the Clubman was designed for ease of maintenance and was supposed to be a replacement for the traditional round-nose Mini, but in the end the original design outlasted it.

to compensate on the acceleration front did little more than bestow the car with dreadful fuel economy for one so small.

It was not the most auspicious start in life, but in its defence the 1275GT evolved into the pick of the Mini range during the mid- to late 1970s, as long as you were happy to live with the flat-nosed body. From 1974, all 1275GTs got 30.5cm (12in) wheels with distinctive covers, and larger disc brakes were fitted as standard. Later cars also came with Dunlop Denovo run-flat tyres – an innovation that was a practical disaster at first, but has since become commonplace on a whole host of performance cars.

1100 Special

Introduced in 1979, the only Mini to ever get the 1098cc (67ci) engine commonly found in the Morris Minor (and the unloved Austin Allegro) was the 1100 Special – a limited edition introduced to mark the Mini's twentieth anniversary.

▲ **Mini 1275GT**

Intended as a replacement for the Cooper, but lacking its performance edge and motorsport pedigree, the 1275GT was nevertheless still one of the most entertaining cars of the 1970s to drive.

Finished in an unusual metallic taupe or silver colour scheme, the Special had a fold-back canvas roof and plush interior trim, along with sill-to-sill carpeting and a revised two-dial dashboard.

It also received special gold 10-spoke alloys, which appeared briefly on the 1983 Mini Sprite Limited Edition, but were never used on any other Mini. The 1100 Special was a significant car not only for its engine, but also because it was the first anniversary Mini. It was followed by the Mini 25, Mini 30, Mini 35 and Mini 40 for each significant milestone thereafter.

Mk 4

A few tweaks were made to the Mini throughout the 1970s and 1980s, not least the welcome addition of extra soundproofing and abolition of the base model Mini 850 in 1979. But it was 1984 before BL decided to reinvest in its long-serving baby, with a raft of changes to bring it up to date.

◀ **Mini Mk 4**

For 1984, Mini got a few comfort improvements to the interior, along with the welcome addition of front disc brakes from the Austin Metro, plus larger, 30.5cm (12in) wheels to accommodate the new set-up.

▲ Mini Cooper Mk 5 Sports Pack

The ultimate Mk 5 Minis were those fitted with Rover's 'Sports Pack', offered on Cooper models. This 1999 example also has leather interior and a full-length electric roof –in such trim, it was far from cheap.

The most noticeable of these changes were the introduction of 30.5cm (12in) wheels and slightly flared plastic wheelarch extensions to accommodate the bigger rubber, while under the skin the car now got 21.6cm (8.5in) disc brakes, as fitted to the Metro, as standard equipment. Two versions were offered: the basic City and the more luxurious Mayfair, the latter of which acknowledged Mini's position as a fashion accessory rather than a means of basic transport.

Model	Years	Number Built
Mk1	1959–67	946,150
Countryman/Traveller	1960–69	206,405
Cooper	1961–69	80,495
Cooper S	1963–71	25,625
Mk 2	1967–69	359,925
Mk 3	1969–84	2,048,515
Moke	1964–94	51,000
Clubman	1969–80	473,180
1275GT	1969–80	110,670
1100 Special	1979–80	78,850
Mk 4	1984–98	Included in Mk 3
Rover Cooper	1990–2001	64,430
Mk 5	1998–2001	Included in Mk 3
Cooper Sport 500	2001	500

It was around this time that Mini special editions started to make regular appearances, too, with the Park Lane, Designer, Advantage, CheckMate and Flame all becoming the definition of what made a 'Lifestyle' Mini.

Rover Cooper
A piece of true marketing genius from Rover, the decision to approach John Cooper Garages with the idea of reviving a legendary name was inspired.

With Mini's appeal having firmly shifted away from budget motoring and more towards a role as a city accessory, Rover approached the man who had made the Mini such a success in the 1960s to once again reinvigorate its appeal.

Debuting in 1990, the 1275cc (78ci) Cooper featured classic colour schemes, including Monte Carlo Red and British Racing Green, with white roofs, 30.5cm (12in) versions of the classic Minilite alloy wheel, bonnet (hood) stripes and, on the very first cars, a decal bearing John Cooper's signature on the bonnet. The cars were initially fed through Cooper-tuned carburettors, but later Rover Coopers were fuel-injected – and all enjoyed lively performance, reminiscent of the Mini's glory days.

Rover even took the car on the Monte Carlo Rally in 1994, wearing the registration number L33 EJB. The first Monte Carlo winner, 30 years previously, was 33 EJB. This time round, though, and, unsurprisingly, it didn't win …

Mk 5
The Mini's final incarnation, the Mk 5, appeared in 1998 and just about brought the car in line with the latest legislation. Airbags were fitted for front passengers, although in such an archaic structure their worth was questionable, while Rover's new MEMS electronic engine management was introduced to keep emissions down. The Mini also got a massive hike in standard equipment, with almost all models now sold being Coopers, complete with leather interior trim, walnut dashboards, thick-pile carpets and ivory dials inside. Outside, an optional Sports Pack was introduced, with 33cm (13in) wheels and huge wheelarches, along with a centre-exit exhaust and front spoiler. Like all Minis, the Mk 5s had only four-speed gearboxes

and were as rot-prone as ever, although many were sold directly into the collector market. The Mini's role as an affordable small car was over – a new Mk 5 Cooper Sports Pack would cost you roughly the same as a VW Golf 1.6 in 1998.

Cooper Sport 500

All good things come to an end, and in October 2000 the hammer finally came down on the Mini. Its impressive 41-year sales career was stamped out by ever-tougher safety and emissions legislation, which such an old design could never have even hoped to have met. This was doubly sad, as the car's new-found appeal as a fashion accessory meant that its sales were stronger than ever – a trend that followed through to the all-new BMW-designed Mini, introduced the following year.

The last 'real' Mini, though, was the Cooper Sport 500, finished in patriotic red, white or blue, equipped with every conceivable accessory and sold out within minutes of going on sale. Although production officially ceased in 2000, many of the 500s were finished by hand in the early part of 2001, and were therefore not officially registered for a year.

Special Editions

A myriad of special-edition Minis were to appear throughout the car's 41-year life, and it would take an entire book devoted to the subject to list every one of them in turn. Special mention, however, should go to the attractive Mini Chelsea, which had leather trim and was the most luxurious pre-Rover era model; there was also the red, white and blue trio of Italian Job models introduced in 1993 to

Model	0–96km/h (0–60mph)	Top Speed km/h (mph)
Mk1	27.1sec	117 (72)
Countryman/Traveller	29.2sec	113 (70)
Cooper	14.8sec	146 (90)
Cooper S	10.9sec	157 (97)
Mk 2	26.2sec	121 (75)
Mk 3	26.2sec	121 (75)
Moke	29.0sec	113 (70)
Clubman	17.9sec	133 (82)
1275GT	13.3sec	146 (90)
1100 Special	14.5sec	142 (88)
Mk 4	19.7sec	136 (84)
Rover Cooper	11.5sec	149 (92)
Mk 5	13.1sec	149 (92)
Cooper Sport 500	11.0sec	157 (97)

commemorate the twenty-fifth anniversary of the eponymous film.

Other specials of the Rover era included the metallic purple Equinox, with a pleasing nocturnal theme to its upholstery, the basic but pretty Neon and the British Open Classic, which was finished in a classic British Racing Green colour scheme and featured tan leather trim, a wooden dashboard and a full-length retractable electric sunroof.

▶ **Mini 1100 Special**

The first of many special-edition Minis, the 1100 special was also the only Mini to officially receive the 1098cc (67ci) engine more commonly found in the Morris Minor and Austin Allegro models.

Morris Minor
1948–73

The first car created by Alec Issigonis showed the genius that lay beneath his introvert exterior. Simple yet hugely effective, the Morris Minor mobilized Britain for more than two decades.

Minor MM

With Britain rising from the ashes of World War II, and austerity widespread, the Morris Minor was designed with a very specific brief in mind – to get the nation moving again.

Styled by Alec Issigonis (of Mini fame) to offer the most practical space and simplicity, while reliant on proven powertrains, the Morris Minor was a budget-conscious car that was designed to be as well made and as easy to drive as it was good value.

Although somewhat spartan inside, the Minor was a great package. Comfortable, spacious and lively to drive, with superb roadholding for its size, it was cheap to build thanks to unitary construction and a straightforward mechanical layout – the worst point being a pre-war side-valve engine, which was lifted straight from the Morris 8. Otherwise, the car was light, and its independent front suspension made the steering feel very positive.

But the Minor had more than driver appeal. It was also cheap and easy to maintain, which was just what Britain needed. Unusual features on the MM included low-set headlights, which

Specifications		
Engine type: Inline four-cylinder		Length: 3.76m (148.0in)
Displacement: 918cc (56ci)		Width: 1.55m (61.0in)
Maximum power: 21kW (28bhp) at 4400rpm		Height: 1.45m (57.0in)
Top speed: 100km/h (62mph)		Wheelbase: 2.18m (86.0in)
0–96 km/h (0–60mph): 52.0sec		Weight: 791kg (1745lbs)

◀ ▲ **Morris Minor MM 1949**
Codenamed 'Mosquito' during its development, the original 'Lowlight' Morris Minor was Britain's most important design of the early post-war years.

were to disappear after two years, and a removable rear seat to create extra luggage space if you wanted to use it for commercial purposes.

Incidentally, the MM and all subsequent Minors were fitted with a two-piece front bumper, with a metal bridging panel in the middle. This feature existed because the management at Morris insisted that the original Issigonis-styled 'Mosquito' prototype be made wider, but this was after the moulds for the bumper had been cast …

▲ **Morris Minor Series II 'Split-Screen'**
In Minor terms the Series II 'Split-Screen' had a relatively short lifecycle. It came with a more modern-looking front end and a new A-Series engine.

Minor Series II

Better known among Minor enthusiasts as the 'Split-Screen', the Series II replaced the MM in 1952 and had raised front lamps, giving it the distinctive face that's known and loved all over the world today.

The Split-Screen saw two major advancements for the Minor, the first being a four-door bodyshell in addition to the more common two-door, and the second being the welcome introduction of a new engine. Ironically, it was Morris's merger with arch rival Austin that helped the Minor to develop into the car it always should have been, thanks to the overhead-valve 803cc (49ci) A-Series engine it shared with the Austin A30.

Series IIs also got a revised cabin, with a central speedometer, along with improved seats.

Minor 1000

The definitive version of the Morris Minor arrived in 1956, and it remained in prduction for 15 years, albeit with a few changes. The Minor 1000 got the 948cc (58ci) engine from the Austin A35, along with a close-ratio gearbox with a higher final drive, making it both more lively round town and more refined while at a

◄ **Morris Minor 1000**
The Morris Minor as most people know it – the Morris 1000 saloon (sedan) enjoyed a remarkable production run of 15 years, with only a few tweaks in between.

accordingly, as Morris didn't want the old-fashioned Minor to steal sales from its more avant-garde family model.

Not surprisingly, the Minor became a national institution in Britain, even if overseas sales were fairly slow. The car was exported in kit form, though, and was especially popular in countries where it was locally constructed, such as Australia, New Zealand, Malta, India and Ceylon (latterly Sri Lanka).

cruise. The split windscreen was replaced by a single-piece item, while flashing indicators replaced the original semaphore signals in 1961. The 948cc (58ci) engine was replaced in 1962 by a 1098cc (69ci) version of the A-Series, common to the Morris 1100. But the name wasn't changed

Minor Tourer

Almost from the start of Minor production, Morris offered a ragtop version of its popular model. This was partly in answer to customer demand, but was made much easier by the fact

Specifications

Engine type: V8	Length: 3.78m (149.0in)
Displacement: 3950cc (241ci)	Width: 1.55m (61.0in)
Maximum power: 224kW (300bhp) at 5750rpm	Height: 1.49m (58.5in)
Top speed: 201km/h (125mph)	Wheelbase: 2.18m (86.0in)
0–96 km/h (0–60mph): 5.1sec	Weight: 791kg (2400lbs)

▼ ▶ **Morris Traveller 1953 (Customized)**

Introduced in 1953, the ultra-practical Traveller came with a wood-framed rear end. The wood was actually part of the car's structure, and dry rot could (and did) spell the end of the road for many an example.

The Morris Minor Commercial was a hugely popular variant, and was also sometimes badged as an Austin to suit the requirements of both brands.

that the Minor's original unitary body was so strong that whipping the roof off was incredibly easy. Prior to 1951, the roof and sides were canvas above and beyond the doors, but from 1951 a glass side window with a metal frame was introduced, making the roof a far snugger fit and insulating the cabin from too much wind intrusion. Early Minor convertibles are nowhere near as pleasant as later cars, but their rarity makes them especially collectable.

Minor Traveller

Almost as famous as the car on which it was based, the Morris Traveller (to most people, the 'Minor' part of its name is superfluous) appeared five years after the original Minor made its debut. As far as the doors, the body was identical to that of a four-door Minor saloon (sedan), but from the rear onwards the car had aluminium panels, supported by an ash framework that was outside, rather than within, the panels. The wood was structural, so needed to be varnished and treated on a regular basis to prevent it from rotting, although the van-type rear doors did at least make it a very practical car. Britain's answer to the US 'Woodie Wagons' …

Minor Commercial

Car-derived commercials are commonplace, but mention must go to the Morris Minor van and pick-up, which are widely credited with inventing the breed. Like the Traveller, they used the front end of a four-door saloon that was literally chopped off halfway down, with a new rear added. Those used by the British postal service came with rubber wings (fenders), as its drivers were renowned for their carefree approach to driving in traffic.

Model	Years Built	Number Built
Minor MM	1948–53	176,002
Minor Series 2	1952–56	269,838
Minor 1000	1956–71	847,491
Minor Tourer	1948–69	74,960
Minor Traveller	1953–71	215,328
Minor Commercial	1954–73	300,003

Pontiac GTO
1964–

Launched in 1964 and born again 40 years later, the GTO was an exercise in rebellion that gave rise to a new breed of American classic.

1964 GTO

Widely recognized as the very first muscle car, the Pontiac GTO was the brainchild of Pontiac engineers Russell Gee and John Z. De Lorean (who later went to found the ill-fated De Lorean sports car company).

It was launched as knee-jerk reaction to parent company General Motors (GM) and its stipulation that, for political reasons, no GM division was to compete in motorsport nor use performance in any kind of marketing activity.

As a result, the GTO was originally launched as an unofficial options package on the two-door

Pontiac Le Mans. Costing $296, it comprised of an uprated 6.4-litre (389ci) V8 engine with 325bhp (242kW), with a four-barrel carburettor, twin exhausts, a three-speed floor shift Hurst gearbox, stiffer springs, wider wheels and redline tyres, while the array of options offered included a 'Tri-Power' engine upgrade to 348bhp (260kW). In this state of tune, the GTO could accelerate from 0–60mph (0–96km/h) in only 6.6 seconds – as fast as many a modern performance car.

Even faster was the Bobcat version, which was so named by dealers taking the badges from Pontiac Bonneville and Catalina models and swapping the letters around. The same sprint

Specifications

Engine type: V8	Length: 5.16m (203.0in)
Displacement: 6375cc (389 ci)	Width: 1.86m (73.3in)
Maximum power: 260kW (348bhp) at 4900rpm	Height: 1.38m (54.0in)
Top speed: 193km/h (120mph)	Wheelbase: 1.37m (115.0in)
0–96km/h (0–60mph): 6.6sec	Weight: 1418kg (3126lbs)

◀ ▼ **Pontiac GTO 1964**

There were two classic body shapes for the GTO. The quad headlamp 64, below and left, and the stacked light 66, seen right. Both were barely distinguishable from the Tempest Le Mans on which they were based.

time with the Bobcat performance upgrades was just 4.6 seconds – eye-wateringly quick even by today's standards. Weak brakes and slow-to-react steering meant that the performance was only useful on long straight stretches of road …

1966 GTO

For 1966, the GTO was given a significant restyle, with the now common 'Coke bottle' styling familiar to other American car makers, a kicked-up rear end and larger dimensions all round. Arguably not as pretty as the 1964 models, the newcomer did at least retain the stacked headlamp front end that had made the first-generation GTO so readily identifiable. By this stage, too, the muscle car concept had taken off across the United States, and GM had reluctantly been forced to back down from its anti-performance stance (a side effect, most probably, of the safety scare surrounding the Chevrolet Corvair) and allowed the GTO to become a standalone Pontiac model in its own right. Sedan, coupe and convertible models were offered, and all came with a revised interior, with black vinyl surfaces, bucket seats and walnut veneer trim.

1968 GTO

More physical changes came in 1968, with a new, curvaceous fastback body style and even longer and wider bodywork. Pontiac also took the controversial decision to delete the GTO's trademark stacked headlamps and replace them with covered twin circular lamps in the fashion of the Mercury Cougar.

Another unique feature was the addition of a new 'Endura' front bumper/nosecone, which was made out of deformable polyurethane to absorb low-speed impact. The 68 GTO was also the first car to conceal its windscreen wipers in the parked position behind the trailing edge of its bonnet (hood) – a design feature that is now commonplace on almost every car on the market. An innovator it may have been, and it was also frighteningly fast, but the GTO was starting to lose some of the purity that made the original incarnation such a desirable car.

1970 GTO

Launched in 1969, the 1970 GTO was the most powerful of the lot, with as much as 400bhp (299kW) from its Ram Air engines, which had

▶ ▼ Pontiac GTO 1966

GTOs were available in both coupe and convertible body styles. While it's the convertible models such as this that are the most collectable, it's the two-door hardtop model that is the best in terms of performance and handling.

Specifications

Engine type: V8	Length: 5.05m (199.0in)
Displacement: 6375cc (389ci)	Width: 2.03m (79.8in)
Maximum power: 418kW (360bhp) at 5200rpm	Height: 54.8in
Top speed: 201km/h (125mph)	Wheelbase: 1.39m (116.0in)
0–96 km/h (0–60mph): 6.2sec	Weight: 1612kg (3555lbs)

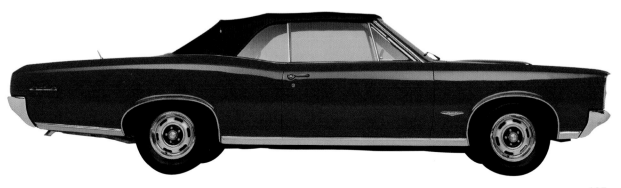

◀ ▲ Pontiac GTO 1968

The GTO received a new, more mainstream look for 1968, with more rounded coupe bodywork and a deformable 'Endura' front end that could withstand impacts of up to 8km/h (5mph).

Specifications		
Engine type: V8		Length: 4.97m (196.0in)
Displacement: 6554cc (400ci)		Width: 1.88m (74.2in)
Maximum power: 418kW (360bhp) at 5200rpm		Height: 1.24m (48.7in)
Top speed: 193km/h (120mph)		Wheelbase: 2.84m (112.0in)
0–96 km/h (0–60mph): 6.4sec		Weight: 1590kg (3506lbs)

Pontiac was just one of a series of American manufacturers to introduce hidden headlamps in its cars, on the 1968 GTO. The novel design feature debuted on the Mercury Cougar and was one of the most popular features of the muscle car scene in the late 1960s. These were times when cars were replaced on an almost annual basis, and by the time the 1970 GTO debuted these lamps had already gone by the wayside.

forced induction through bonnet-mounted air scoops, hence the name.

The most significant of these was the GTO Judge, which was named after a comedy routine on *Rowan & Martin's Laugh-In TV Show* called 'Here Comes the Judge'. The Judge was conceived as a stripped-out bargain version of the standard GTO, built to do battle with the budget-priced Plymouth Road Runner. By the time it had received styling tweaks, trim upgrades and unique wheels, however, it ended up being more expensive than the standard car.

Sadly for Pontiac, the muscle car era was starting to draw to an end – changing safety legislation,

◀ Pontiac GTO 1970

For 1970, the GTO received yet another new look. The main part of the car's body was similar, but wider than the 1968 model, while there was a new four-headlamp Endura front end.

environmental concerns and the imminent fuel crises made sales of this type of car slow down year on year. A GTO stayed in the Pontiac line-up until 1974, but by this time the car had become an emaciated, overstyled and underpowered shadow of its former self.

2004 GTO

In 2004 the GTO name rose from the ashes to appear on a new two-door coupe, using the LS2 Corvette V8 engine on a long-wheelbase four-seater platform. The car was based on the Australian-built Holden Monaro and was brought to the United States by GM's product guru Bob Lutz, who had driven one on a business trip Down Under. The GTO was never

Model	Years Built	Number Built
64 GTO	1964	32,45066
GTO	1965–66	177,29868
GTO	1967–68	169,40670
GTO	1969–74	112,4362004
GTO	2004–06	N/A

a huge success in the United States, though, because many of the brand's faithful were upset that the car wasn't built on home ground.

The 2004 GTO was also sold in the United Kingdom as the Vauxhall Monaro, and in the Middle East as the Chevrolet Lumina SS.

▼ **Pontiac GTO Judge 1969**

The GTO Judge was originally planned as a low-budget special edition, but it eventually became a GTO icon in its own right. All Judges were orange and came with magnesium alloy wheels.

One of the GTO Judge's more unusual features was its rev counter, which rather than being fitted to the dashboard was mounted on the car's bonnet (hood), directly in line of the driver's sight. As well as being a neat marketing gimmick, the cunningly hidden dial meant that there was no need to cut an additional hole in the dashboard to allow for room for the rev counter.

Specifications

Engine type: V8	Length: 4.95m (195.0in)
Displacement: 6555cc (400 ci (R/A III))	Width: 1.90m (75.0in)
Maximum power: 273kW (366bhp) at 5400rpm	Height: 1.32m (52.0in)
Top speed: 198km/h (123mph)	Wheelbase: 2.84m (112.0in)
0–96km/h (0–60mph): 6.2sec	Weight: 1589kg (3503lbs)

Pontiac Firebird
1967-2002

The GTO was the first muscle car, and with the Firebird, Pontiac tried to take on the booming 'Pony Car' market as well.

First Generation (1967–69)

Pontiac's first Firebird was the result of a clever piece of design by parent company General Motors. Sharing most of its body panels and mechanical components with the Chevrolet Camaro to keep costs to a minimum, the Firebird managed to retain an identity of its own, thanks largely to the use of a scaled-down GTO-style nose and slimmer tail lamps.

Like its arch rival the Ford Mustang, the Firebird range kicked off with a pair of six-cylinder engines of 3.8 litres (230ci) in capacity, in two states of tune. The standard car developed 165bhp (123Kw), while the sportier Sprint came with a four-barrel carburettor and developed 215bhp (160Kw). Hardtop and convertible models were offered. But it was the V8s that were the mainstay of the range in an era when fuel

▼ Pontiac Firebird 1968

Both hard and soft-top versions of the first generation Firebird were on offer, although the drop top would disappear for its replacement and not return until the fourth generation car.

Specifications	
Engine type: V8	Length: 4.81m (189.2in)
Displacement: 5735cc (350ci)	Width: 1.85m (72.8in)
Maximum power: 239kW (320bhp) at 5000rpm	Height: 1.25m (49.3in)
Top speed: 183km/h (114mph)	Wheelbase: 2.77m (109.0in)
0–96km/h (0–60mph): 6.9sec	Weight: 1696kg (3740lbs)

The key to the Firebird's appeal was similar to that of its key rival, the Ford Mustang. It was a car that you could personalize to your own tastes, and the choice of options was seemingly endless. One of the more common choices was the addition of a Hurst 'stick-shift' four-speed manual transmission, which gave a more agile feel than the more common three-speed auto.

▲ Pontiac Firebird 1973

Full-length soft-tops had disappeared from the second generation Firebird, although buyers could still enjoy wind-in-the-hair motoring to a degree, thanks to pop-out 'T-Top' panels. Full coupes such as this example were rarer.

was cheap and the environmental impact of large engines was less of a concern than it is today. The V8 was offered in a choice of 5.3-litre (326ci) or 6.6-litre (400ci) capacities, the later of which was the same 325bhp (242Kw) unit found in the GTO. A Ram Air option was also available, with hood scoops, higher flow heads, stronger valve springs and a performance camshaft.

The most famous Firebird option, though, was the 'Trans-America Performance and Appearance Package', named after the race series of the same name. The 'Trans-Am' nameplate became synonymous with the Firebird for the rest of its life, but not without causing a problem for GM, which had failed to secure rights to use the name from the stock car racing governing body, SCCA. As a result, following lengthy legal negotiations, GM had to pay royalties of $5 per car to the SCCA for every Trans-Am it sold.

Second Generation (1970–81)

GM brought the Firebird's styling closer in line with that of the Camaro for 1970, with the introduction of the Second Generation series.

The elegant, curvy shape of the original was replaced by a more angular look, complete with a distinctive polyurethane nose and steeply raked rear lamp units, both of which would stay with the car throughout is long production life. A huge variety of engines was used, initially all

Specifications	
Engine type: V8	Length: 4.86m (191.5in)
Displacement: 6555cc (400ci)	Width: 1.86m (73.4in)
Maximum power: 171kW (230bhp) at 4400rpm	Height: 1.28m (50.4in)
Top speed: 190km/h (118mph)	Wheelbase: 2.75m (108.1in)
0–96km/h (0–60mph): 9.4sec	Weight: 1708kg (3766lbs)

V8s ranging from 5.0-litres (305ci) to 6.6-litres (400ci).

A special edition 7.3-litre (455ci) model appeared in 1971 and was the last Firebird to be fitted with a true thoroughbred muscle car engine, using parts that were developed for Pontiac's NASCAR racing models. Built until 1976, the 455s are known to collectors as the 'Big Cube Birds'.

In 1974, in reaction to the fuel crisis, an inline six engine made an appearance again, this time an Oldsmobile-sourced 2.9-litre (230ci) unit, but the heart of the Firebird range still lay with the V8 models, of which there were several.

Notable versions included the Firebird Formula, which used the 6.6-litre (400ci) powerplant, and the 1976 Trans Am Anniversary,

▲ **Pontiac Firebird 1979**
Introduced in 1976 and immortalized in film, the black and gold Trans Am
Anniversary became a standalone model in its own right and remained in the
range long after the company's Golden Jubilee.

which marked Pontiac's Golden Jubilee with a
special black and gold colour scheme (either
black with gold details, or vice versa), which
found fame as Burt Reynolds' car in the Smokey
and the Bandit series of movies.

When production ceased in 1981, over a
million Second Generation Firebirds had found
homes.

▼ **Pontiac Firebird GTA 1991**
The third generation Firebird was a big seller, and enjoyed clean-cut, modern
lines. This 1991 GTA version featured revised styling and turbo power.

Third Generation (1982–1992)

Like its predecessor, the third-generation
Firebird enjoyed a longer than average
production run – although it still looked
relatively fresh and modern at the end of its life,
such was the shapliness of its original design.

Clean and modern, yet with traditional
Firebird styling cues, the car continued to be a
worthy flagship for the Pontiac range, even if the
entry-level 3.1-litre (231ci) V6 engines and later
2.5-litre (151ci) straight fours didn't live up to
the performance the sleek two-door body
suggested. The latter, in fact, could only muster
90bhp – less than most European hatchbacks of
the era.

The V8s were mighty as ever, though, but used
a Chevrolet-developed variant of GM's
legendary small block powerplant rather than
the previous Pontiac-
only unit.

The new model was
also much better in
terms of its handling
and aerodynamics. It
was the first Firebird to
be developed using a
wind tunnel, while the
car was 240kg (500lb)
lighter, which made it
much easier to drive
quickly.

Three trim levels were
offered – the entry level

Firebird, mid-range S/E and range-topping V8-only Trans Am, the latter of which found fame on the silver screen as the robotized KITT car in *Knight Rider.*

Over ten years, there were literally hundreds of Firebird special editions, engine variants and minor changes, the most significant of which came in 1989 with the Indianapolis Indy 500 Pace Car Replica, in 1991with a restyled front nose and a driver's airbag as standard, and in 1992 with the run-out 'Firehawk' edition, which came with Ferrari F40 brakes, a high-output V8 and a six-speed ZF manual gearbox.

Fourth Generation 1992–2002

With the introduction of the fourth and final generation of Firebird, Pontiac rationalized the model range quite significantly, as well as bringing it once again much closer to the Chevrolet Camaro.

The car's looks had been previewed with the 'Banshee' concept car, shown at the 2001 Detroit Auto Show, and the production model was well received in styling terms. One decision that wasn't so popular, though, was to transfer production away from the USA and to the city of Saint-Therese in Quebec, Canada; the concern of Firebird fans being that this traditional all-American Pony Car was no longer a true American product. Two engines were offered

Model	Years built	0–96km/h (60mph)	Top speed km/h/mph
First Generation	1967–69	6.0secs	189/118
Second Generation	1970–81	5.6secs	201/125
Third Generation	1982–92	4.4secs	222/138
Fourth Generation	1992–2002	5.0secs	239/149
*figures quoted are for top Trans Am model			

throughout the car's life – a 3.4-litre (250ci) V6 and a 5.7-litre (380ci) V8.

Again, myriad special edition models and tweaks came and went, the 25th Anniversary model of 1994 being the most significant with its unique white and blue colour scheme. A facelift came along in 1998, with a new four-light front end and a much revised and significantly improved interior, plus new colours including a distinctive bright purple, which was so popular it graced one in ten cars to leave the factory.

By 2002, the Firebird's hold on the American public had come to an end. Sales had slowed and GM was focusing on Corvette as its performance brand – although the Firebird's legend lives on. In 2007, three special Firebird 'Burt Reynolds Editions' were created to mark the 30th anniversary of the Smokey and the Bandit films through which the car had found global recognition.

▼ **Pontiac Firebird Fourth Generation**
Although not as sharply-styled as previous models, the fourth generation Firebird was still a smart looker, its front end distinctly different from the mechanically similar Camaro.

Porsche 911
1963–

An all-time classic, the 911 firmly established Porsche as one of the world's greatest sports car makers.

It's not just coincidence that the Porsche 911 looks like a shrunken VW Beetle, for that's in effect what it is. Designed by Ferry Porsche, who was involved with the Beetle in its early days, the 911 has an identical powertrain layout as the Beetle, with a horizontally opposed air-cooled engine adrift of the rear axle and the spare wheel mounted at the front of the car to help balance the weight.

▲ **Porsche 911 1963**

Despite dating back to 1963, the 911's lines are as pure to look at today as they were at the model's launch. It truly is a timeless shape.

Specifications

Engine type: Flat-six	Length: 4.17m (164.5in)
Displacement: 1991cc (121ci)	Width: 1.61m (63.6in)
Maximum power: 108kW (145bhp) at 6100rpm	Height: 1.32m (52.0in)
Top speed: 212km/h (132mph)	Wheelbase: 2.20m (87.0in)
0–96km/h (0–60mph): 9.0sec	Weight: 1070kg (2360lbs)

911

Designed by Ferry Porsche's eldest son, Butzi, and launched at the 1963 Frankfurt Motor Show, the Porsche 911 was a fabulous triumph of styling and engineering.

Maintaining the rear-engined rear-drive layout pioneered on the VW Beetle and used to great success on the Porsche 356, the 911 received a new 2.0-litre (121ci) six-cylinder air-cooled engine with two triple-choked carburettors. The engine sounded fabulous and offered surprisingly agile performance for its dimensions, with a five-speed gearbox as standard and all-round disc brakes further aiding its driver appeal.

Trim levels were many and various – the 911N (for Normale) was a stripped-out base model with a tempting entry price, while the 911L (for Luxus) was better equipped, with high-backed sports seats and a four-dial dash. There was also an automatic version called the Sportomatic, although this is a rather rare variant today.

The true performance potential of the 911 wasn't realized until 1966, though, and the debut of the 911S, which came with five-spoke Fuchs alloy wheels and twin exhaust pipes to differentiate it from lesser models. A higher compression ratio meant 160bhp (120kW) initially, while this went up by a further 10bhp (7kW) when the engine size was increased to 2.2 litres (134ci) in 1968. From 1971, the engine size increased again, this time to 2.4 litres (147ci), and other new features included a chin spoiler and optional rear aerofoil.

All 911S models have independent front suspension and ventilated disc brakes, while from 1968 all received flared wheelarches and a 6.4cm (2.5in) increase in the wheelbase.

A year after the first 911S appeared, a new entry-level 911 was added in the form of the 911T (which stood for Touring). Detuned to be less powerful than the standard cars, the most basic T could muster only 110bhp (82kW) and had a four-speed gearbox as standard. It was an affordable way of owning a 911, which was fast earning itself a reputation as something hugely desirable. The performance edge, however, really wasn't there ...

It returned in 1968 in the 911E (for *Einspritz* – the German word for 'injection'), a version which replaced the upmarket 911L. It had a much more healthy 140bhp (104kW) to offer from its fuel-injected 2.0-litre (121ci) engine. As with the S,

▲ **Porsche 912**

Known to many as the 'Poor Man's Porsche', the four-cylinder 912 is often overlooked, despite sharing the 911's impressive dynamic properties.

the engine size increased in 1969 and again in 1971, while alloy wheels, a comfortable cabin and self-levelling front suspension were all de rigeur for the luxury flagship of the 911 range, although even with two power increases it was never as fast as the S model.

The most desirable of the first-generation 911s, though, was the Carrera RS. Built as a homologation special for Group 4 endurance car racing, the RS eventually sold more than three times the 500 road cars required as a minimum. Available in fully stripped Sport or more upmarket (and much more popular) Touring trim, the car had a 210bhp (157kW) 2.7-litre (165ci) engine, stiffer suspension, flared rear wheelarches and optional 'Carrera RS' side graphics. Porsche used a lower-grade, lighter steel than normal to build the RS, meaning that these cars were generally even more susceptible to corrosion than normal models.

912

The 911 was a hugely popular model for Porsche, but it failed to satisfy some of the marque's aficionados, who had cherished its four-cylinder predecessor, the 356. As such, Porsche decided to offer a pared-down, four-cylinder version of the 911 using the mechanical components of the 356, but installed in the new shell. Called 912, the newcomer was virtually indistinguishable from the six-cylinder cars from

▲ Porsche 911 Targa

The 911 Targa arrived in 1967 and took its name from the Targa Florio race in Sardinia, in which Porsche had enjoyed a great deal of success over the years.

rollover hoop into which a detachable roof panel could be slotted, while a removable plastic rear screen kept any draughts at bay from the rear. A fixed-glass rear screen was optional from 1968, and this was made compulsory in 1971.

Unusually, despite costing more when new, Targa versions of 911s have always been worth significantly less than coupe models as either secondhand or classic cars, the perception being that the Targas lack the torsional stiffness and indeed the sporting image of the hardtop models. In reality, there's little to choose between the driving experience of the two.

the outside, although it remained largely the old car underneath.

Only 90bhp (67kW) was available from the 1582cc (96ci) 356 engine, which gave average acceleration at best. A four-speed gearbox was also standard fit, although a five-speed transmission was on offer as an optional extra. Dual circuit brakes were added in 1967, along with an extended wheelbase and flared wheelarches, in line with all 911 models, in 1968. After three years, sales of the 912 practically dried up, with most buyers opting for the six-cylinder 911T instead, so Porsche cancelled the model in 1969.

The 912 was briefly revived, however, in 1975 as an answer to ailing sports car sales in the United States, triggered by the fuel crises of 1973 and 1974. The 912E, as it was known, used a VW-developed fuel injection system from the 914 and was much more economical than a 911, but was also miserably slow by comparison.

Targa

Again in answer to criticisms from 356 buyers, Porsche decided to offer a fresh air variant of the 911 from 1966, although unlike its predecessor, the 911 Targa never went fully topless. To maintain structural integrity, the car had a steel

911 1973

It was all change for the 911 in 1973, with the 2.7-litre (165ci) engine that debuted in the Carrera RS being made standard across all models in the range, although there were still various different trim levels and power outputs.

At the bottom of the tree was the basic 911, with a 150bhp (112kW) version of the engine and little in the way of creature comforts. Above that was the 911S, with 175bhp (130kW) and more equipment in the cabin, and the range-topping Carrera, which used the same 210bhp (157kW) engine as the outgoing RS, but with none of the weight-saving details.

Although basically the same bodyshell as the original 911, the post-1973 cars looked quite different, thanks to the use of thick, impact-absorbent bumpers dictated as mandatory by the American market, plus deep chin spoilers on all models, which attempted to redress the styling imbalance of the new bumpers.

Two rear spoilers were offered as options on the post-1973 cars: either a modest 'ducktail' wing or the classically extravagant 'whaletail' aerofoil that was later common on the powerful Turbo models.

The engine size of Carrera models was increased in 1975 to 3.0 litres (183ci), although

Often you will hear 911s referred to as 'whaletail' versions. This is in reference to the car's optional but rather protuberant rear wing, which looked like a whale's tail. It was of great help in keeping more powerful 911 variants stuck to the road, and had a genuine purpose rather than just being a tacky styling add-on.

Specifications

Engine type: Flat-six	Length: 4.15m (163.3in)
Displacement: 2687cc (164ci)	Width: 1.61m (63.4in)
Maximum power: 157kW (210bhp) at 6300rpm	Height: 1.32m (52.0in)
Top speed: 238km/h (148mph)	Wheelbase: 2.27m (89.4in)
0–96km/h (0–60mph): 5.9sec	Weight: 980kg (2160lbs)

▲ **Porsche 911 RS 2.7 Carrera 1973**
Orange paint and black plastic trim place this 911 Carrera firmly in the 1970s. By this stage, the car had become widely regarded as one of the best sports cars in the world.

this was as a result of US emissions legislation strangling power outputs of smaller units. Although the engine was bigger, 3.0 models actually had 10bhp (7kW) less power.

911 Turbo

Although Porsche had been using turbo technology for some time in its race cars, it wasn't until 1975 that it felt brave enough to offer the technology on a road car. First presented at the 1974 Paris Motor Show and put into production the following year, the 3.0-litre (183ci) Turbo was the fastest Porsche model yet, with 260bhp (194kW) on tap courtesy of the KKK compressor, and the ability to reach at least 250km/h (155mph) with the pedal to the floor. Unusually, the first Turbos came only with a four-speed gearbox, as Porsche's five-speeder version wasn't considered strong enough to cope with the power. Other changes to compensate for the Turbo's grunt included bigger brakes, a stiffened floorpan and a standard whaletail spoiler, while inside the car air conditioning and leather trim were standard.

Altogether a fabulous, iconic car ... but the Turbo had two major faults. The first was its unpredictable on-the-limit handling, which meant that it was lethal in the wrong hands, and the second was the price, which was more than double that of the standard 911 2.7. It is, however, much admired as a classic, and worth significantly more than post-1977 turbos with larger engines.

911 1977

Several changes came in 1977, with the deletion of the 2.7-litre (165ci) engine and a 3.0-litre (183ci) unit with Bosch fuel injection made standard on all models. Power of the entry-level car was upped from 150bhp (112kW) to 180bhp (134kW), then again to 204bhp (152Kw) in 1981, meaning that even the most basic 911 was an incredibly fast machine by this stage, with the ability to top 140mph (227km/h). Prices rose in accordance with horsepower, though, making ownership less and less attainable.

Changes to the Turbo model were even greater, with the introduction of a new 3.3-litre (201ci) engine developing a colossal 300bhp (224kW). This engine would be used for the next 16 years. As with the original Turbo, a five-speed gearbox wasn't offered until 1989, when Porsche finally relented and fitted a revised version of that used in the 959 supercar. As with the earlier Turbo, the 3.3 was a real handful on the limit, while its dated cabin also counted against it – yet this made little difference to its enduring appeal. Open-top models were offered from 1987, for the first time with the turbo engine.

Convertible

For almost 20 years, Porsche hadn't been able to offer a fully open version of the 911, but those seeking complete wind-in-the-hair thrills finally got the car they'd all been waiting for in 1982. Sold alongside the Targa, rather than as its

▼ **Porsche 911 1976**

By the time Turbo models arrived, the 911's styling had evolved still further. Energy absorbent bumpers were fitted as a US market requirement, but were incorporated well into the 911's classic good looks.

The rear spoiler looked even more like a whale's tail on the original 911 Turbo, but this was because it had a purpose above that of feeding extra downforce to the car's rear end. In addition, the spoiler increased room in the engine bay to fit the intercooler, while the spoiler had integral air scoops to supply cool air directly to the turbo.

Specifications

Engine type: Flat-six	Length: 4.27m (168.3in)
Displacement: 3299cc (201ci)	Width: 1.77m (69.9in)
Maximum power: 235kW (315bhp) at 5750rpm	Height: 1.31m (51.6in)
Top speed: 270km/h (168mph)	Wheelbase: 2.27m (89.4in)
0–96km/h (0–60mph): 4.9sec	Weight: 1485kg (3274lbs)

▶ ▲ **Porsche 911 Turbo 1991**

The last-of-the-line air-cooled 911s were almost identical to the original in profile, although by this stage practically none of the components was interchangeable. One thing had remained constant through, however, and that was the 911's superb handling ability.

▼ **Porsche 911**

To take the 911 into the 1990s, the front and rear bumpers were amended, and incorporated turn signals and fog lamps at the front.

▲ Porsche 993

Launched in 1993, the 993 had a much softer look than previous incarnations of the 911 – the front end in particular looked like the legendary 959.

replacement, the Convertible featured a stiffened windscreen surround that acted as a rollover hoop, while to ensure the car maintained most of its lateral strength extra bracing was incorporated in its floor structure. With all this extra weight, the Convertible was definitely a Porsche sold for its style rather than its substance, and it attracted a completely different class of clientele to the brand. It was not so much of an enthusiasts' car, but a definite commercial opportunity that Porsche couldn't afford to miss at the time.

911 Carrera 1983

The Carrera RS started out as something special, but morphed into a standard model in the 911 range in the mid-1970s. By 1983, it had become a standalone model in its own right, and 911 buyers who didn't want a Turbo got a Carrera instead, thus weakening what had traditionally been Porsche's traditional flagship name.

Regardless, the Carrera was still a mightily impressive motor car, with a new 3.2-litre (195ci) engine that used electronic engine management and had a higher compression ratio, both of

which helped to push the power output to 231bhp (172kW).

With this much power, the normally aspirated Carrera was able to accelerate from 0–60mph (0–96km/h) in a Turbo-baiting 6.5 seconds, and on to a top speed of 228km/h (141mph).

From 1985, as the 911 became as much an icon of the 1980s as the Filofax and red trouser braces, a mild facelift occurred, adding body coloured panels to the front and rear bumpers, and including the huge whaletail rear aerofoil as standard on all models.

Carrera 2/4

Almost 26 years after the 911 first appeared, it received its first proper reskin in 1989, although the car's lines were totally unmistakable right from the outset.

Although in terms of dimensions it was almost identical to the original car, the Carrera 2

▶ Porsche Carrera 4

For the ultimate in performance and grip, the Carrera 4 offered permanent four-wheel drive. It was devilishly quick, but hardcore enthusiasts said they missed the tail-happiness of the rear-drive models.

body was actually an entirely new design, with in actuality only some of the glass being identical to that of the original 911. The Carrera 2's nose was rounder, with full-size body-coloured bumpers and painted sills and mirrors, along with larger alloy wheels and a significantly updated and more spacious cabin, providing much greater levels of comfort.

Also new was a semi-automatic Tiptronic transmission offered as an option, while those who were frightened off by the 911's legendary twitchy-tailed handling could opt for the Carrera 4, which used an all-wheel drive system based on that of the 959 supercar.

For the lily-livered, that was probably a good idea, as with the Carrera 2 Porsche had stuck resolutely to its traditional layout, with an air-cooled flat-six swinging freely behind the rear axle, and the car's increased power from its new 3.6-litre (220ci) unit was always keen to force the message home to drivers that a 911 should be treated with respect.

▼ Porsche Carrera 2

With the Carrera 2 and 4, Porsche reskinned the 911 – although it was hard to tell. The Carrera 2 seen here shared no panels at all with its predecessor.

Model	0–96km/h (0–60mph)	Top Speed km/h (mph)
911 (1963)	9.1sec	201 (124)
912	11.9sec	181 (112)
911 Targa	8.3sec	210 (130)
911 (1973)	7.6sec	206 (127)
911 Turbo	5.3sec	259 (160)
911 (1977)	6.1sec	248 (153)
911 Convertible	6.6sec	235 (145)
911 Carrera (1983)	6.5sec	228 (141)
911 Carrera 2/4	5.1sec	256 (158)
911 (993)	3.7sec	291 (180)
911 (997)	3.8sec	294 (182)

The new body and cabin were also used on the Turbo, although it retained pretty much all of its mechanical components and was still a fearsome supercar.

993

After years of sticking with the same formula, it took Porsche only four years before creating a new bodyshell for the 911 yet again, the newcomer known internally as the 993.

It had a more significant new look than the previous car, with laid-back ellipsoid headlamps replacing the 911's trademark upright items, along with front and rear bumpers that were integrated into the car's styling and were more aerodynamic as a result.

▼ **Porsche 993**

It may have looked softer and rounder, but the 993 stuck to the tried-and-tested formula of an air-cooled rear-mounted engine.

Specifications

Engine type: Flat-six	Length: 4.26m (167.7in)
Displacement: 3600cc (220ci)	Width: 1.80m (70.7in)
Maximum power: 298kW (400bhp) at 5750rpm	Height: 1.31m (51.8in)
Top speed: 290km/h (180mph)	Wheelbase: 2.27m (89.4in)
0–96km/h (0–60mph): 3.8sec	Weight: 1500kg (3307lbs)

Porsche took the opportunity presented by the 993's restyle to finally tidy up the car's rear spoiler. The original and interim

designs had always looked a little unfinished, as they weren't present in Ferry Porsche's original design, but by making the engine bay a little larger and wider Porsche could incorporate a much less flashy aerofoil on the rear of the new car.

The engine was based on the 3.6-litre (220ci) version of the Carrera 2, but now with 270bhp (201kW) of power output even in its most basic form; the chassis was thoroughly revised, with the engine remaining behind the rear axle in traditional 911 fashion. For hard-to-impress driving enthusiasts, the 993 models were the best of all of the air-cooled 911s, although critics mourned the passing of the car's original striking lines.

997

An extremely brave move by Porsche, and one that was considered a travesty by many of the marque's more traditional fans, the 1997-generation 911 (dubbed 997) came with a water-cooled engine for the first time ever. Its phenomenal driving performance and rear-mounted positioning showed Porsche hadn't forgotten its roots, but despite the car's many dynamic talents, and its sympathetically traditional styling, the loss of the trademark air-cooled burble was a crying shame.

It didn't affect sales, though, with water-cooled 911s quickly enjoying faster sales than air-cooled

▲ **Porsche 997**

With the 997, Porsche has an entirely new car on its hands. It still held on to the DNA of the original 911, but unlike all previous generations it had no panels or mechanical components in common with its forebears.

models ever had before, proving that the motor industry had moved on apace during the 911's impressive production history.

Model	Years Built	Number Built
911 (1963)	1963–69	22,333
912	1965–76	32,399
911 Targa	1967–79	38,333
911 (1973)	1973–77	37,737
911 Turbo	1975–77	2873
911 (1977)	1977–89	36,876
911 Convertible	1982–88	21,043
911 Carrera (1983)	1983–89	21,740
911 Carrera 2/4	1989–93	23,295
911 (993)	1993–97	41,008
911 (997)	1997–	N/A

Renault 5
1972–97

Renault's first take on the supermini quickly established itself as one of the major players in a rapidly growing market. Its chic style was timeless.

Mk 1

Although it looked much more modern, the first Renault 5 actually appeared in 1972, the first of a breed that would sell more than five million in a 25-year sales career.

Its most distinctive, and indeed most timeless, feature was its styling, which was mainly the work of Renault's chief designer Michael Boué, who sadly died shortly before the car was released.

Boué's intention had been to incorporate the tail lamp clusters into the car's rear pillars so that they went up the entire height of the car's rear, but this styling feature was removed at the eleventh hour – otherwise, the car went on sale exactly as Boué had first intended.

Available as a three-door only initially, the 5 had a longitudinally mounted engine that drove the front wheels – an odd arrangement that actually resulted in the car having a longer wheelbase on one side than the other, thanks to the position of the driveshafts.

Several engines were available. Three sub 1.0-litre (60ci) four-cylinder units, a 1.1-litre (77ci) and 1.3-litre (78ci) and, later, a 1.4-litre

▼ **Renault 5 Mk 2**

This battered British-registered Mk 2 is typical of the Renault 5s still doing service around the globe – more than five million were made in total.

(85ci) were all offered, while under the skin the 5 had all-independent suspension, which meant that the car possessed excellent ride and handling characteristics. Classless and stylish, the 5 became as much a symbol of France as the legendary Citroën Deux Chevaux.

Gordini

Known as the 'Alpine' in its home market, but as the Gordini everywhere else (as Chrysler owned the trademark to the Alpine name), Renault's first performance variant of the 5 had a 93bhp (69kW) version of the 1.4-litre (85ci) engine found in the standard hatchback. Available in black, blue or silver, it had distinctive quadrofoil alloy wheels, fog lamps and unique pinstripes.

It was not especially quick, but despite this the Gordini was still a great drive, thanks to superb handling, revised steering and the welcome addition of a five-speed gearbox. The set-up was good enough, thanks to a handicap system, to allow the 5 to secure first and second place in Monte Carlo Rally of 1977.

▲ **Renault 5 Gordini**

The original Gordini was one of the first-ever hot hatches. Among the Gordini's more unusual features were its high-backed 'A-Frame' sports seats and three-spoke alloy wheels.

Renault 7

Built and sold only in Spain, the Renault 7 was a four-door version of the 5, built under licence by the government-funded Spanish outlet of the French company, called FASA-Renault.

Introduced in 1974 and sold until 1986, the 7 was one of Spain's most popular cars, significantly outselling the hatchback in a market where four-door cars were very much favoured. Yet despite the car's success in Spain, and in some low-volume African markets, Renault never looked to export it anywhere else, and it remains one of the 1970s' most curious offerings.

Le Car

The appeal of the Renault 5 was global, so it came as no surprise at all that it became part of the French firm's assault on the United States when it forged an alliance with the struggling

▲ **Renault 5 Turbo**
The first-generation Turbo was a Renault 5, but really only in terms of its appearance. In reality it was a bespoke mid-engined race machine, and only the bonnet (hood), tailgate, doors and glass were the same as ordinary road cars.

Specifications

Engine type: Inline four-cylinder	Length: 3.66m (144.3in)
Displacement: 1397cc (85.25ci)	Width: 1.77m (69.9in)
Maximum power: 119kW (160bhp) at 6000rpm	Height: 1.32m (52.1in)
Top speed: 200km/h (124mph)	Wheelbase: 2.43m (95.7in)
0–96km/h (0–60mph): 7.7sec	Weight: 970kg (2138lbs)

with unique 'Le Car' side graphics. The name found amusement with French natives, where the word 'Car' actually means 'Coach' …

Turbo

Hot on the heels of its 1977 Monte Carlo Rally success, Renault decided to prepare a car for Group B rallying, and this arrived in the form of the 5 Turbo.

Instantly identifiable as a member of the 5 family, the Turbo was actually barely related to the popular supermini. It used the same doors, glass, dashboard moulding and lamp units; however, it had a turbocharged version of the 1.4-litre (85ci) engine mounted right in the middle of the car and driving the rear wheels. The unit produced a healthy 160bhp (119kW), and its low gearing gave it the ability to accelerate from 0–100km/h (0-62mph) in less than seven seconds.

More important than that, though, was the car's mid-engined layout and its effect on the Turbo's weight distribution, which was a perfect 50:50 split between front and rear. That gave it impeccable handling, and made it wonderfully easy to drive quickly, culminating in an outright victory on its first-ever world rally outing, with Frenchman Jean Ragnotti taking a popular victory in the 1978 Monte Carlo.

American Motors Corporation (AMC) in 1976. Designed exclusively for the American market and built by AMC under licence, the Renault 'Le Car' was aimed squarely at rivals such as the Honda Civic and newly introduced VW Rabbit, or Golf.

It came with a detuned 55bhp (41kW) version of the European 5's 1.4-litre (85ci) engine, coupled to a four-speed manual gearbox, and the car was essentially far better equipped than European-specification 5s; it also came complete

Supercinque

Bowing to market pressures, Renault finally answered the demands of its customers and introduced a five-door version of the 5 in 1981. Advertised as 'Supercinque; la voiture avec cinque portes et cinque vitesses' (Super Five – the car with five doors and five gears), the new model also saw the introduction of an all-new five-speed manual transmission, which was fitted to all five-door versions until the range was rationalized in 1983.

Other changes included a new design of steel road wheel, a slightly modified hatchback and a more upmarket interior, all of which were transferred into the three-door as well for the final four years of Mk 1 production.

Gordini Turbo

In the early 1980s, Renault was in the middle of a motorsport golden era. The Renault 5 had proven itself in rallies the world over, while the French manufacturer had also taken the Formula One World Constructors' Championship trophy in 1981, largely as a side effect of its expertise in turbocharging.

This was celebrated with a new road car, to replace the original Gordini. Called the Gordini Turbo, the car looked little different to its predecessor, the only telltale signs that this was anything special being restyled and wider alloy wheels, plus a wider choice of exterior colours and discreet turbo badges on the front and rear. Inside, the car also got an extra boost gauge and revised seats, with extra side supports.

With 110bhp (82kW) on tap, the vehicle wasn't exactly a rocket ship, but the Gordini Turbo was nonetheless fun, its power delivery being somewhat unpredictable, yet also entertaining, thanks to masses of turbo lag. The Gordini Turbo was also sold in the United States, unlike the original Gordini, where it was called the Le Car 2 Turbo.

Turbo 2

Two years after the original 5 Turbo disappeared, Renault revived the concept for a new homologation special, again aimed at Group B rallying. This time, though, the engine was smaller by 100cc (6ci), giving the 5 a distinct advantage because it could compete with handicap rules on its side, despite having exactly the same power output as its predecessor.It also received extra cooling, thanks to bigger air ducts behind the front doors, along with fatter tyres.

This time, the weight bias was more towards the rear, so that drivers could exploit the tail-happy characteristics on gravel or shale rally surfaces, while the ride was a lot firmer than the original Turbo. Road-going models were more

▼ **Renault 5 Gordini Turbo**
Renault replaced the original Gordini with a Turbo version to mark its successes in Formula One racing. The car suffered from torque steer, but was fun to drive.

▲ Renault 5 GT Turbo

Faster, cheaper and more fun than a Peugeot 205 GTi, the Renault 5 GT Turbo was the hot hatch to have in Europe in the late 1980s – until spiralling insurance premiums made it inaccessible to many.

civilized than before, though, with much more in the way of creature comforts, including such delights as electric windows. A number of Turbo 2s were also built with all-alloy bodywork, aimed specifically at competition customers, and with the lighter body the power could also be upped to 240bhp (179kW).

5 Mk 2

In late 1984, Renault unveiled an all-new 5 – although it was difficult to tell the difference between the two unless you got close up, such was the perfection of the original design. Michael Boué would have been very proud, though, as this time the rear lamps were faired into the bodywork and rose alongside the car's tailgate, as per his original proposal.

There were much bigger changes under the skin. Gone was the unusual longitudinal engine layout, to be replaced by a more usual transverse layout, while the car was shorter and wider overall than its predecessor, making it more entertaining to drive and giving it better grip. A diesel version was added in 1986, while a luxury leather trimmed 'Monaco' model debuted the year afterwards, and had a 1.7-litre (104ci) engine and automatic transmission. But one of the more unusual variants was the Convertible, which was sold in very small numbers between

1985 and 1989, and was built by Belgian coachbuilders EBS on Renault's behalf.

5 GT Turbo

Not to be confused with the mid-engined Turbo models, the GT Turbo appeared in 1986 and was the flagship of the second-generation 5 range. It developed 115bhp (86kW), rising to 120bhp (89kW) in 1987, and was incredibly quick, although the car did suffer from turbo lag and was prone to hot starting problems and fuel evaporation.

Despite this, it was one of the finest hot hatches of the 1980s, helped by its phenomenal grip, superb steering and excellent gearbox. The biggest criticism was that it was difficult to keep the power in check at lower speeds, and wheel spin was always prevalent.

5 Campus

Although the Clio appeared in 1990 to supposedly replace the 5, demand for a cheaper, no-frills small car from Renault meant that the 5 would enjoy a further six years in production as the 5 Campus, although there was only one rather basic trim level and a choice of two engines – a 1.1-litre (67ci) petrol or a 1.6-litre (98ci) diesel. Despite this, it remained a good seller right up until its death in 1997.

Model	Years Built	0–96km/h (0–60mph)	Top Speed km/h (mph)
5 Mk 1	1972–85	20.6sec	139 (86)
Gordini	1975–81	12.2sec	155 (96)
7	1974–86	15.7sec	133 (82)
Le Car	1976–84	13.4sec	152 (94)
Turbo	1978–79	7.8sec	201 (124)
Supercinque	1981–85	7.6sec	134 (83)
Gordini Turbo	1980–81	9.8sec	183 (113)
Turbo 2	1980–84	7.7sec	194 (120)
5 Mk 2	1985–93	14.8sec	157 (97)
GT Turbo	1986–91	7.1sec	202 (125)
Campus	1993–97	16.3sec	146 (90)

Rolls-Royce Silver Shadow
1965–92

When Rolls-Royce introduced new build methods, the best car in the world quickly became even better.

◀ **Rolls-Royce**
Silver Shadow Mk 1
Mk 1 versions of the Silver Shadow have the purest styling, with slim front bumpers and less fussy wheeltrims. This is a long-wheelbase model, which is known as the Silver Wraith for second-generation cars.

Silver Shadow I

Although it wasn't a company known for innovation, at least not since its early days, Rolls-Royce was still renowned for the exceptional quality of its engineering. The Silver Shadow was a complete break from the norm, as it was by far the most innovative Rolls in more than 50 years.

For a start, it was the British firm's first-ever unitary construction model, its monocoque crafted from thick-gauge steel to give almost the same tensile strength as the firm's more traditional separate chassis.

As well as the new build method, which unfortunately managed to harbour as many rust traps as most similar 1960s monocoques and meant that Rolls-Royce's quality reputation suffered a little, the Shadow introduced other novelties for the marque, including all-round disc brakes, split-level air conditioning and self-levelling suspension, which was developed for

Rolls-Royce by French maker Citroën.

The Silver Shadow had two choices of wheelbase available, and the European-spec Shadows differed from American models by virtue of having slimmer chrome bumpers; these were far prettier than the impact-absorbent plastic-capped ones that featured on the US cars.

Initially powered by the 6.2-litre (378ci) V8 engine that had been carried over from the preceding Silver Cloud, all Shadows from 1970 onwards received a 6.75-litre (412ci) powerplant, coupled to a GM-sourced automatic gearbox, first with four speeds, but later with a simpler and smoother three-speed set-up. The power output of the engine has always remained one of the motor industry's greatest secrets, described in the sales literature as either 'sufficient' or 'adequate'. There were certainly few complaints from buyers, although the Shadow's rather indiscreet fuel consumption did mean that it was a tremendously expensive car to run.

The rarest variant was a two-door James Young–styled two-door saloon (sedan), built from 1966 until 1969. A coachbuilt two-door

▲ **Spirit of Ecstasy**
Rolls-Royce's traditional mascot is often referred to as the Silver Lady, although its official name is actually the Spirit of Ecstasy.

body was also offered by Mulliner Park Ward, and later became a standard model in the Silver Shadow range.

Bentley T1

Despite assurances from Rolls-Royce and Bentley that the two brands were very different, and had different types of buyer, the T-Series was, in effect, little more than a badge-engineered Silver Shadow with a few detail tweaks. Initially available only in long-wheelbase form, although it was offered in both long and short versions very quickly, the T1 had a revised, more rounded radiator grille and discreet Bentley badges. Inside, the car had a more sporting feel, with less wood, firmer seats and more of a focus on the driver, rather than the passengers. Mechanically, the T1 was identical to the Silver Shadow, but

had firmer suspension settings. A super-rare two-door version, bodied by Pininfarina, is the most collectable of the lot.

Rolls-Royce Corniche

So popular were the Mulliner Park Ward two-door conversions that they became standard Rolls-Royce models in 1971. The transition was helped somewhat by the fact that Rolls-Royce had bought out the coachbuilder from Willesden, London, and was therefore able to dedicate its workforce exclusively to the task of building bespoke bodies for the Silver Shadow floorpan.

Visually, you could tell post-1971 cars apart from the earlier, tailor-made cars by their deeper radiator grilles and revised fascia, while they were also far less individual in terms of their specification. You could, of course, still choose the specification of your Rolls to a very personal level, but certain details, and in particular paint colours, were fixed by the factory.

Beautifully finished and far less rust-prone than standard Silver Shadows, most probably due to the nature in which the panels were all hand-finished, the Corniche was available as both a coupe and a convertible, of which it was the latter that was by far the most popular, outselling the hardtop by a ratio of two-to-one. Sales continued well into the 1990s (the last one was built in either 1994 or 1995, depending on who you ask), long after production of the Silver Shadow had ceased.

Bentley Corniche

If Rolls-Royce wanted to create more of a distinction between its two brands, then the introduction of the Bentley Corniche wasn't the most obvious way to go about it. It wasn't just the fact that the two-door Bentley models were dimensionally and mechanically identical to the Rolls-Royce Corniche, but also the fact that both

▶ ▲ **Bentley Corniche 1973**
'Corniche' was one of the few names to grace both a Rolls-Royce and a Bentley.
The latter, seen here, was by far the rarer of the two, as only 149 examples of the
Bentley Corniche were built in total.

cars received exactly the same model name – a
bizarre, and to this day inexplicable, move.

Irrespective of this, the Corniche possessed
the same differences from the Rolls-Royce as did
the T-Series, notably a different grille, more dials
on the dashboard and a firmer ride. It was built
in tiny numbers compared to the Rolls-Royce,
though, and was renamed the Continental, in
convertible form only, in 1984. It remained on
sale until the early 1990s.

Camargue

In a bid to move away somewhat from its rather
old-fashioned reputation, Rolls-Royce collaborated
with Italian styling house
Pininfarina to produce an all-new
model designed to supplement
the traditionally styled Corniche.
The car in question was the
Camargue, built on the Silver
Shadow platform and assembled
by Mulliner Park Ward at its
London premises.

As well detailed and luxurious
as any Rolls-Royce, the Camargue

Specifications		
Engine type: V8		Length: 517m (203.5in)
Displacement: 6750cc (412ci)		Width: 1.80m (71.0in)
Maximum power: Not quoted		Height: 1.52m (59.75in)
Top speed: 196km/h (122mph)		Wheelbase: 3.04m (119.5in)
0–96km/h (0–60mph): 9.6sec		Weight: 2184kg (4815lbs)

▶ **Bentley Corniche**
When the Corniche has its roof up, it is clear to see that
a lot of thought went into making the car as elegant as
possible, whatever the prevailing weather conditions.

▲ **Rolls-Royce Camargue 1980**
From the front, the Camargue looks distinctive, with a wider than normal grille and unique quad headlamps.

A Rolls-Royce for a brave new era? That was certainly the thinking with the Camargue, which was launched after criticism of the Silver Shadow's rather old-fashioned looks by some of the company's key customers. Styled by Pininfarina, the Camargue had a list of unique features, including faired-in indicator lenses and incongruous headlamp wipers, although the distinctive Silver Lady that graced the bonnet (hood) remained both unchanged and unmistakable. For a while, the controversial Camargue was the most expensive car on sale in Europe, which if nothing else at least ensured the vehicle's exclusivity.

was intended to be the flagship of the marque's range. Despite this, the car failed to stir the soul of many a Rolls-Royce enthusiast, thanks to its obscure, slab-sided styling.

As well as its increased price over standard Silver Shadows, the Camargue had a raised power output, which was assisted by four Solex carburettors. This made the vehicle feel notably quicker than lesser models, although as was usual for the Rolls-Royce marque the Carmague's

power outputs and performance figures were never published ...

Silver Shadow II

New for 1977, and more than just a simple facelift, the Silver Shadow II looked outwardly similar to the Series I. New impact-absorbent bumpers across the range brought US- and European-specification cars in line with each other once again. Other changes included a front air dam, new door handles and less ornate wheeltrims, but visually you'd be hard-pushed to tell a Shadow I from a Shadow II.

Drive one, though, and the changes are much more easily identified. The recirculating ball steering was replaced by a much more sure-footed and responsive rack-and-pinion set-up, while revised suspension further aided the car's handling and made it far more user-friendly.

Although it was sold for only a little over three years, the Silver Shadow II sold in such numbers that it matched over half of Series I production in such a short time – a reflection of society's growing desire for luxury items.

Silver Wraith

Although the Silver Shadow was sold in two wheelbases in its first gestation, the two models were separated for the second generation, perhaps in recognition of the fact that those buying the larger car wanted further distinction from those 'only' able to afford the shorter wheelbase.

The Silver Wraith was 10cm (4in) longer than the Shadow and came with an optional limousine dividing panel with soundproof glass. Unless the cars are seen together, it is difficult to tell a Silver Wraith apart from a Shadow II. The main telltales are a standard 'Everflex' vinyl roof and linked 'RR' monograms on the rear quarter panels.

Silver Spirit

With a thoroughly modern new look, a look that would last until 1998 without any kind of significant change, the Silver Spirit was focused on the future in its style, yet beneath the taut new skin it was little different from the Silver Shadow that preceded it. Power came from the same 6.75-litre (412ci) engine (with an undisclosed power output, in typical Rolls-Royce style), although those built from 1986 onwards had fuel injection; later Mk 2s had catalytic converters and electronic engine management to bring them bang up to date. Long-wheelbase versions were called Silver Spur and, as before, were 10cm (4in) longer than the standard saloons.

Bentley Mulsanne

More different from the Silver Spirit than the T-Series Bentleys were from Silver Shadows, the Mulsanne was nonetheless little more than a rebadged version of the Rolls-Royce car.

This time, though, the Bentley had a much more sporting image, with a completely different cabin, body-coloured exterior trim and alloy wheels. Apparently, the Bentley versions were also more powerful than the Rolls-Royces – although the power output was never disclosed, the speedometer in Bentleys read up to 270km/h (170mph), compared to 240km/h (150mph) in Silver Spirits. The Mulsanne also gave rise to a budget version, called the Bentley Eight, and a turbocharged flagship, the Turbo R, which went much further towards reclaiming Bentley's traditional sporting reputation.

Model	Years Built	Numbers Built
Silver Shadow I	1965–77	19,493
Bentley T1	1965–77	1712
Rolls-Royce Corniche	1971–94	6313
Bentley Corniche	1971–84	149
Silver Shadow II	1977–81	10,566
Bentley T2	1977–80	568
Camargue	1975–85	531
Silver Wraith	1977–80	2144
Silver Spirit	1981–98	14,366
Bentley Mulsanne	1981–92	2039

Although the Silver Spirit featured a sharp new suit, mechanically it remained the same as the Silver Shadow and variants that came before it. That meant it came with a 6750cc (412ci) V8 engine, coupled to a General Motors-sourced four-speed automatic gearbox, complete with unobtrusive column-mounted gearchange and a discreet change indicator mounted on top of the steering column.

Specifications

Engine type: V8	Length: 5.27m (207.5in)
Displacement: 6750cc (412ci)	Width: 1.88m (74in)
Maximum power: 168kW (226bhp) at 4300rpm	Height: 1.49m (58.5in)
Top speed: 203km/h (126mph)	Wheelbase: 3.06m (120.5in)
0–96km/h (0–60mph): 10.4sec	Weight: 2290kg (5049lbs)

▲ ▼ **Rolls-Royce Silver Spirit 1996**

Rolls-Royce did a good job of disguising the Silver Spirit's archaic roots when the model was introduced in 1981, with sharp, straight-edged design.

Rover P-Series models
1945–75

It may be a name that has since disappeared, but Rover was once one of the car industry's proudest and most forward-thinking marques.

10/12 and 14/16

Retrospectively known as the P1 and P2, although never officially recognized as such, the 10/12 and 14/16 Rovers were the first of the British firm's post-war offerings. The P in the name stood for 'post-war', which is why these seemingly retrograde models are worthy of mention among some of the most innovative cars of the 1950s and 1960s, for this is where the brand's sales renaissance affirmed itself.

There was nothing especially remarkable about these models, though. Elegant and well made as they were, the short-wheelbase 10 and 12 and longer, sleeker 14 and 16 were conventional in the extreme. The optional Sports Saloon body on the 14/16 models, however, was very pretty.

▼ **Rover P4**

This early P4 features a number of desirable period extras, including a roll-down radiator muff to stop the cooling system from icing up in cold weather.

P3

Visually almost indistinct from the 14 and 16, the Rover P3 (officially known as the 60 or 75, depending on horsepower) was as different beneath the skin as it was in keeping with the family line externally.

For its era, it was packed with new features that moved Rover ahead significantly. Independent front suspension with coil springs and wishbones was a feature unheard of on any rivals, and gave the car great handling, while it also benefited from hydromechanical brakes and new four- or six-cylinder engines with side exhaust valves, which were exceptionally refined. Here was a quality car, and one that kicked off Rover's thrusting new image.

P4 'Cyclops'

Introduced in 1949 as the fourth all-new Rover to appear in three years, the P4 was another revolution. Still rather upright and featuring rear 'suicide' doors, it was built on a strong separate chassis and used the six-cylinder engine from the P3 75.

The original P4's most unusual feature was its so-called 'Cyclops' headlamp, which was a third lamp mounted above the radiator grille. Although it might seem rather odd to look at, the 'Cyclops' lamp moved with the P4's steering to give a broader sweep of light when the car was cornering, an idea which preceded the swivelling head-lamps seen on the Citroën DS by six years.

P4 6-cyl

For 1954, Rover gave the P4 a facelift, losing the Cyclops headlamp and introducing a new three-piece wraparound rear window and a more chrome on the front end. At the rear, the boot (trunk) lid height was raised to create more space, and the rear lamp lenses were replaced by larger, vertical items.

Intially available as the 75, with a 2.2-litre (134ci) six-cylinder engine, the car had its engine capacity increased to 2.6 litres (159ci) in 1960. Various different power outputs were offered, with the horsepower being the same as the model number, meaning the P4 was variously known as the 90, 95, 100, 105 and 110, although the vehicles were essentially the same. Detail changes included longer front wings (fenders) from 1956, along with two options: the S specification incorporated a brake servo and overdrive, while the R specification had a two-speed automatic gearbox.

P4 4-cyl

Launched in late 1953, the lower-specification version of the P4 came with a four-cylinder engine and was markedly cheaper than the six-pot models. The 2.0-litre (121ci) engine was sourced from that used in the Land Rover and initially

◀ Rover P4 6-cyl
Six-cylinder versions of the P4 arrived in 1954 and moved the car significantly upmarket – the bigger-engined cars were much smoother and more refined.

gave 60bhp (45kW), hence the model name was Rover 60. This changed in 1959 to the 2.25-litre (139ci) petrol unit found in the Land Rover Series II, which was far better, if almost as thirsty as in its original application.

Inside, the four-cylinder models were more sparse than six-cylinder ones, with fewer instruments and a dearth of wood trim. Generally, the four-cylinder models were ignored by collectors, and most have since disappeared.

P5

As the first unitary construction Rover, the P5 was a cunning mix of the traditional and modern. Launched in 1959, at a time when there was still some resistance among more traditional buyers towards monocoque cars, the P5 successfully combined the upright Rover grille and luxurious trimmings of the company's more stately models with a hull that incorporated such modernities as torsion bar independent front suspension, servo-assisted disc brakes and power steering, the latter

▼ Rover P4
The last of the line four-cylinder P4s used the 2.25-litre (139ci) engine fitted to the Land Rover Series 2. It wasn't very refined, but was easy to maintain.

two of which were standard on all but the most basic models. Power came from a 3.0-litre (163ci) six-cylinder engine, effectively an enlarged version of that used in the P4. Aimed squarely at upmarket buyers, most P5s came with automatic transmission and leather trim, although Mk 2 models, from 1962, could be had with lowered suspension and a close-ratio manual gearbox for those who wanted a sporting Rover. Speaking of which, there were two significant developments just around the corner that would make the P5 even more of a desirable machine …

P5 Coupe

Aware that around half of P5 buyers were types who liked to be driven, and that the rest preferred to drive themselves, Rover introduced a new body style to the P5 line in 1962. Identical to the standard P5 from the floor to the base of the windscreen pillars, the P5 Coupe had a chopped and lowered roof, and lowered suspension to match. The aim was to give it a much more sporting edge than the stately saloon (sedan), which was the car of choice for chauffeur-driven owners. The Coupe had much less headroom in the rear and felt cramped, but upfront was as grand and comfortable as the saloon. The six-cylinder engine didn't offer a huge amount in terms of performance, but all that was to change.

▼ **Rover P5**
Originally known as simply the Rover Three-Litre, the P5s stately appearance hid what was actually quite an agile car underneath.

P5B

Almost by accident, Rover's head of American Operations J. Bruce McWilliams discovered, on a visit to a marine engineering company in 1961, a Buick V8 engine that General Motors had decreed past its usefulness. Admiring the compact dimensions of the all-alloy unit, he bought the plans to the unit on Rover's behalf and the engine was further developed in the United Kingdom to eradicate cooling and reliability problems that had afflicted it in its domestic market. The engine debuted in 1967 in the P5, known as the P5B (the B was for Buick) to distinguish it from six-cylinder engines. With 161bhp (120kW), the 3.5-litre (215ci) engine gave the car considerable acceleration and exceptional refinement, coupled to a three-speed automatic transmission with no manual option.

The great strength and perfect smoothness of the engine were much admired in both the saloon and coupe versions of the P5, which remained in production until 1973. They could be distinguished from non-V8 models by their Rostyle sports wheels, fog lamps, twin exhausts and rubber-faced overriders.

The P5B was the car of choice of former British Prime Minister Margaret Thatcher, who snubbed the offer of brand-new Jaguars or Rolls-Royces on official business in favour of her beloved armoured P5B.

Gas Turbine Car

Bearing in mind the company's previously staid image, Rover's experimentation with gas turbine engines in the early 1960s was a seriously forward-looking experiment. Although such vehicles were never offered as production models, at least two jet-powered prototypes were built in 1962, and these were trialled at Rover's proving ground. Rover was serious about introducing them, too. This was proven by the fact that the prototypes looked almost identical to the imminent P6 model, and that the engine bay of the P6 was designed to accommodate the unusual powertrain.

▲ ▶ Rover P5B Coupe 1971

With a lowered roof line and smaller glass area, the Rover P5B had a true coupe look. It was the first sporting P-Series Rover.

Specifications

Engine type: V8	Length: 4.74m (186.5in)
Displacement: 3528cc (215.3ci)	Width: 1.78m (70.0in)
Maximum power: 120kW (161bhp) at 5200rpm	Height: 1.45m (57.3in)
Top speed: 177km/h (110mph)	Wheelbase: 2.81m (110.5in)
0–96km/h (0–60mph): 12.4sec	Weight: 1578kg (3479lbs)

P6

This was the first ever car to win the European 'Car of the Year' award, and there was no more worthy victor than the Rover P6. Blowing any notion that Rover was a maker of old-fashioned, unadventurous models into the weeds, the newcomer proved itself an innovator in almost every respect.

The body, for example, consisted of a mixture of renewable steel and alloy panels, bolted to a skeletal base structure, while De Dion Tube back suspension and all-round disc brakes, mounted inboard on the rear axle, further added to its technical package. At the front, the suspension was even more complex, with horizontal coil springs initially designed to help incorporate the stillborn gas turbine engine.

The combination was well thought out and beautifully engineered, bestowing the P6 with roadholding and braking ability well beyond that of other cars of its era, the only downsides being a tough gearchange and fairly noisy 2.0-litre (121ci) engines.

Rover was always keen to shout about its levels of luxury, and the P5 offered plenty of comfort. Despite the car's outwardly old-fashioned looks, however, its British maker was keen not to overdo it with too much polished wood and leather. Instead, the P5's cabin was a clean and modern affair – exceptionally comfortable and well equipped, but not too showy.

Not only was the P6 a fabulous car to drive, but it was also incredibly well detailed. Inside, the cabin was simple, yet well appointed, with bucket-style front seats, standard leather and room for four adults to travel in proper comfort and style. The interior even won a safety award, thanks to its padded seatbacks and kneepads, plus a collapsible steering column.

◀ Rover P6
The P6 was a massive step forward for Rover in terms of handling, performance and ride comfort. It was certainly one of the best mainstream saloons of its era, if not the best.

In design terms, it was Rover's greatest car ever – a truly innovative saloon that was so advanced that, when production ceased 14 years later, it was still more than competitive in its class. It was, however, a victim of its own success. Survival rates are good, thanks to the interchangeable body panels, and the sheer availability of good examples means that values are lower than many less exemplary classics of the same era.

P6 Estoura
Although never an official Rover-built model, the Estoura answered the demand from some customers for a load-lugging P6 – an answer to archrival Triumph's 2000 Estate. The Estoura was converted by either HR Owen or Crayford, with panels from FLM Panelcraft. Around 160 cars in all were officially produced new, but several others were converted after the car was 12 months old, thus avoiding the extra purchase tax payable on a pricier model.

P6 V8/Rover 3500
Those who bemoaned the original P6's lack of power had their prayers answered in 1969, when Rover finally offered the ex-Buick V8 engine in the model, creating the Rover 3500 in the process. The car was vailable initially with only an automatic transmission, but the 3500S, with a

Thanks largely to an open-ended development budget in the pre-British Leyland days, Rover was allowed to create a brand-new car from the ground up, and the P6 didn't have to borrow from any other models. That meant

innovations such as a skeletal base unit and an advanced suspension system. The engine was also a new unit, but didn't quite meet expectations because it was quite noisy and not especially powerful.

Specifications

Engine type: V8	Length: 4.50m (181.0in)
Displacement: 3528cc (215.3ci)	Width: 1.68m (66.0in)
Maximum power: 137kW (184bhp) at 5200rpm	Height: 1.43m (56.3in)
Top speed: 174km/h (108mph)	Wheelbase: 2.63m (103.4in)
0–96km/h (0–60mph): 11.5sec	Weight: 1452kg (3200lbs)

▼ Rover 3500 1970
One of the most popular options on the P6 was the space-saving boot-mounted spare wheel carrier, seen here on a US-specification 3500S.

▲ Rover P6 V8

The V8 joined the P6 range in 1968 and bestowed the car with the powerplant it always deserved. Performance and refinement were second to none.

▲ Rover P6 Series 2

Series Two models saw the standard 2000 engine replaced by a 2200 unit in 1973. It had more low-down torque, although performance was little different.

manual gearbox, appeared in 1970 and turned the P6 into a genuine performance saloon.

Visually, V8 models differed from four-cylinder ones by having a much bigger air intake beneath the front bumper, while many also had the spare wheel mounted on the boot lid to create more space, as the V8 engine installation meant that the car's battery had to be moved into the boot.

Mk 2 detail changes came in 1970, with a plastic grille and simplified interior. A favourite of the British police force, the P6 V8 was fast, with accompanying impeccable handling and plenty of presence.

P6 Series 2

Although the Series 2 was billed as more advanced than the original P6, aficionados of the P6 tend to favour earlier models over the later cars. The newcomer wasn't a bad car, not least because it was still a P6 and was therefore still technically brilliant, but Rover's absorption into the British Leyland empire in 1968 meant that cost-cutting was rife and as a consequence build quality slipped.

The original leather interiors were replaced by cheap fabrics as standard, much of the chrome (including the original, rather pretty radiator grille) was replaced with plastic and the interior wood was substituted for Formica.

All four-cylinder models took a bored-out 2.2-litre (134ci) engine from 1973, with more torque to answer criticisms of the original 2.0-litre (121ci) unit.

Model	0–96km/h (0–60mph)	Top Speed km/h (mph)
10/12/14/16	N/A	108 (67) –16
P32	9.4sec	121 (75)
P4 6cyl	15.9sec (110)	162 (100) – 110
P4 4cyl	22.8sec (80)	139 (86) – 80
P5	14.5sec	163 (101)
P5B	12.4sec	175 (108)
P6 2000	14.6sec	168 (104)
P6 3500 V8	9.1sec	197 (122)
P6 2200 (Series 2)	13.4sec	163 (101)

Model	Years Built	Number Built
10	1945–46	2640
12	1945–47	4840
14	1946–48	1705
16	1946–48	4150
P3	1948–49	9111
P4 6cyl	1949–64	114,746
P4 4cyl	1953–62	15,566
P5	1959–67	48,541
P5B	1967–73	20,600
Gas Turbine Car	1962	2
P6 2000	1963–73	327,808
P6 2200	1973–77	32,270
P6 V8 (S1 and 2)	1969–77	79,057
P6 Estoura	1967–75	170

Saab 92-900
1950–93

Swedish aircraft maker Saab moved into car making in 1947, using its aircraft expertise to produce oddball cars that seemingly lasted for ever.

92/93

The first ever Saab car was conceived by Gunnar Ljungstrom and styled by Sixten Sason, both of whom were engineers for the company's aircraft division. Powered by a transverse two-stroke twin-pot engine, the 92 was mechanically simple, but incredibly lightweight and aerodynamic, which meant that it could keep pace with most traffic. Revised and made more upright for 1950 and consistently improved, the 92 became bigger and more practical each year.

In 1956, the 93 was introduced and had a new three-cylinder two-stroke engine, which when tuned and fitted with twin carburettors was

▼ **Saab 92**

Saab's motorsport career began early – this is an early two-stroke 92 model competing in the 1957 Monte Carlo Rally.

capable of producing 160km/h (100mph), while the 93's light weight made it highly popular for rallying. The cars were well made and durable, with quite a lot of curiosity value. Three-cylinder models can be spotted by virtue of their larger horseshoe-shaped grille.

95/96

Saab's move into the larger family market proved the Swedish firm's commitment to car making, and also produced its first big seller, with well over half a million 95 and 96 models produced over a 21-year lifecycle.

The 95 appeared first in 1959 and was also known as the Combi; a weirdly styled three-door estate (station wagon) car that had both aerodynamic efficiency and practicality put well ahead of any aesthetic charm. It also had a

Specifications

Engine type: Inline three-cylinder	Length: 4.04m (159.0in)
Displacement: 841cc (51ci)	Width: 1.57m (62.0in)
Maximum power: 42.5kW (57bhp) at 5000rpm	Height: 1.47m (58.0in)
Top speed: 140km/h (87mph)	Wheelbase: 2.49m (98.0in)
0–96km/h (0–90mph): 21.2sec	Weight: 844kg (1860lbs)

hidden fold-out bench seat in the rear, meaning seven people could be carried at a squeeze.

The 96 followed in 1960 and was more attractive, albeit far less practical, with its curvy saloon (sedan) bodywork. The definitive model was the GT850 (or Sport, depending on market), which further enhanced Saab's appeal among the rallying fraternity, with its lively triple-carb two-stroke engine and front disc brakes.

▲ **Saab 96 850GT 1963**
The earliest 96s built on Saab's rapidly growing reputation for oddball styling. Some critics cruelly said that the shape of the radiator grille actually resembled that of a toilet seat.

95/96 V4

Although admired by those in its home market, the two-stroke engines in Saab's most popular models were frowned upon by Western Europe and the United States. So as not to lose out in important sales markets, Saab adapted the V4 engine used in the German Ford Taunus for use in the 95

▶ **Saab 96**
Despite having a relatively low power output, the two-stroke Saab 96s were entertaining cars to drive, with surprisingly lively performance.

▲ **Saab 96 V4**

Later 96s came with V4 engines and were much quicker than early models, making them even more suited to competition use.

and 96, producing a car that was marginally more powerful and far more conventional than the two-stroke models. The V4 was rough and unrefined by comparison, but this didn't stop it selling well, with Saab's reputation for good handling and impressive crash safety preceding any negative perceptions of the raucous engine or cramped cabin.

99

In 1967 Saab introduced a much more modern and grown-up car than the 96. Again, Saab used engine technology shared with another European maker – this time Triumph and its slant-four unit, as used in the Dolomite. Although bigger inside and out, the 99 actually used much of the 96's underpinnings, with the same front double wishbone suspension and coil-sprung rigid rear axle. Initially only one body style was offered in the form of a two-door saloon; however, this was supplemented by a four-door in 1970 and a three-door hatchback Combi in 1974. The 99 set the styling precedent for Saab over the next 30 years, which helped the car to appear timeless and resulted in a long

production run; it was renamed 90 in 1984, but kept alive until 1987, 20 years after its launch. Long-lived, well engineered and impressive to drive, the 99 was a superb if oddball car.

99 Turbo

Although BMW was the first manufacturer to offer a turbocharged road car as part of its standard model range, Saab was the company that made such technology both affordable and usable without compromise on a daily basis. Using the 2-litre (121ci) slant-four engine from the standard 99, the Turbo had Bosch fuel injection and a Garrett turbo, which boosted the output from 115bhp (86kW) to 145bhp (108kW). That gave the car the ability to sprint from 0–60mph (0–96km/h) in just nine seconds, although most of the power was delivered in one ferocious burst, meaning the written performance figures didn't fully express the drama with which the 99 Turbo made its presence felt.

900

Introduced in 1978, the 900 was intended to complement, rather than replace, the 99. It used much of the smaller car's architecture to keep costs at a modest level, including its bulkhead, dashboard, windscreen, inner wings (fenders) and tailgate. Yet the 900 was longer and wider with more modern styling, although the overall look was still curiously different to anything else that was on offer.

Initially offered with a 2.0-litre (121ci) engine in different states of tune, all with a five-speed manual gearbox as standard, the 900 range was available in four different body styles, with a choice of two, three, four or five doors.

A new 16-valve engine from 1988 saw the power output increase by about 10 per cent to 133bhp (99kW), making these later cars the more eager and more fun to drive. The 900 remained in production until late 1993, by which time more than a million had been sold. Its replacement, based on the Vauxhall Cavalier platform, could never re-create its charisma.

900 Turbo

The 99 Turbo had been a big success for Saab, so it stood to reason that a 900 variant would follow, eventually outselling its predecessor by a ratio of 20 to 1. Better mannered than the 99

Turbo, without quite so much in the way of turbo lag, the 900 developed a legendary reputation of its own. This was strengthened further in 1984 when Saab upped the power output from 145 to 175bhp (108 to 130kW) by using a new twin-cam cylinder head, giving the car performance figures to rival a Porsche 911. As with all cars, the 900 Turbo was progressively updated and

Specifications

Engine type: Inline four-cylinder	Length: 4.53m (178.3in)
Displacement: 1985cc (121ci)	Width: 1.69m (66.5in)
Maximum power: 108kW (145bhp) at 5000rpm	Height: 1.44m (56.7in)
Top speed: 193km/h (120mph)	Wheelbase: 2.48m (97.5in)
0–96km/h (0–60mph): 9.1sec	Weight: 1231kg (2715lbs)

▶ ▼ **Saab 99 Turbo 1978**

The 99 Turbo was one of Saab's seminal offerings – it wasn't the first turbocharged family saloon, but it was the first to offer such technology in an affordable and sensible package.

Saab's aircraft heritage meant that aerodynamics played a big part in the company's design ethic, and it extended as far as the most minute details. These small fins, mounted on the car's rear quarter panel, actually deflected airflow away from the car and prevented it being sucked back behind, much in the same way as an aircraft's wings, and thus made the car more stable when it was driven at speed.

▲ Saab 99

In styling terms, the 99 wasn't conventionally attractive – but it did set the precedent for Saab's styling over the next two decades.

improved, and those that were sold towards the end of the 900's impressive career had fatter tyres, ventilated disc brakes and a sports interior.

900 Cabriolet

First of a breed that has since become one of the most famous soft-tops in existence, the 900 Cabriolet first appeared in 1986 (but it was 1990

Model	Years Built	0–96km/h (0–60mph)	Top Speed km/h (mph)
92/93	1950–62	N/A	100 (62)
95/96	1959–78	25.6sec	117 (72)
96 V4	1966–79	16.5sec	149 (92)
99	1967–87	12.8sec	152 (94)
99 Turbo	1977–80	8.9sec	197 (122)
900	1978–93	11.1sec	172 (106)
900 Turbo	1979–93	8.6sec	215 (133)
900 Turbo Cabrio	1986–93	8.9sec	194 (120)

before right-hand-drive production would begin). The 900's excellent build and quality interior made it a popular choice for well-heeled buyers, while removing the roof also helped the car's styling significantly. Both turbo and 16v engines were offered; almost all were sumptuously equipped.

900 1994

Under General Motors' stewardship, Saab finally put the long-serving 900 out to pasture in 1994 to introduce a new-generation car. While the newcomer's styling was unmistakably Saab, the running gear was a disappointment to fans of the marque. Gone was Saab's unusual longitudinal engine, front-wheel drive layout, to be replaced by a more conventional transverse power unit, while the chassis was derived from that of the Vauxhall Cavalier/Opel Vectra. In fairness, that meant the 900 was a decent handling car. Also, without GM's intervention, Saab may well have gone to the wall, but there's no denying that some of the brand's unique quirkiness had disappeared.

▶ Saab 900 1994

In fairness, the 900 was a decent handling car and was fairly lively to drive, while the modernized interior was well overdue.

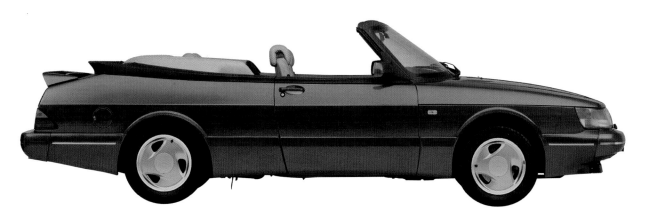

Specifications

Engine type: Inline four-cylinder	Length: 4.66m (183.5in)
Displacement: 1985cc (121ci)	Width: 1.69m (66.5in)
Maximum power: 119kW (160bhp) at 5300rpm	Height: 1.42m (56.1in)
Top speed: 211km/h (131mph)	Wheelbase: 2.52m (99.1in)
0–96km/h (0–60mph): 7.5sec	Weight: 1285kg (2833lbs)

▲ ▶ **Saab 900 Turbo Cabriolet 1993**

The original 900 was the mainstay of Saab's range for more than 20 years, but it was the convertible version, launched in 1986, that really unlocked the true potential of the car's unusual styling.

Triumph TRs
1953–81

A quintessentially British range of sports cars, the TR line ran for almost 30 years.

Roadster

Never referred to as the TR1, the Roadster was nonetheless the first Triumph sports car and where the TR line really started. Crudely constructed on a wooden frame with an unusually wide body, the Roadster used engines and running gear from the Standard Vanguard, along with the chassis from the 1800/2000 saloons (sedans) in order to keep costs to a minimum. Despite its streamlined, low-slung looks, the Roadster was not especially sporty – it was slow, heavy and cumbersome to drive.

TR2

The Roadster may not have been quick, but the TR2 more than made up for its shortcomings in this area when it replaced the larger car in 1953. Built on a separate steel chassis, the TR2 was much smaller and narrower than the earlier car,

▼ **Triumph TR2 1954**

It may have looked pretty and nimble, but the Triumph TR2 was a difficult beast to tame, with heavy steering and poor brakes.

Power for the TR2 came from the four-cylinder engine fitted to the Standard Vanguard saloon (sedan) – not a car that was renowned for its sportiness. That said, Triumph tuned the engine to deliver between 90 and 100bhp (67 and 74kW), even in its standard form. The Vanguard engine remained a stalwart of the TR line-up until the introduction of the TR5 in 1967, which used the unit from the 2.5Pi saloon.

From the TR3 onwards, TR models grew slightly more luxurious with each generation. Details such as adjustable wind deflectors, opening doors and leather seats were available in the earlier car. By the time the last-of-the-line TR7 came about, however, options went as far as automatic gearboxes and radio-cassettes – a far cry from the TR line's original hairy-chested macho image.

▲ **Triumph TR3A 1957**

You could tell a TR3A apart from a TR3 by the width of its grille. The TR3A had a wider chrome item which surrounded the indicator lamps. Earlier TR3s had a narrower one.

and, although it still used Standard Vanguard power in the form of the 1991cc (121ci) four-cylinder engine from the saloon car, the engine was tuned to deliver between 90 and 100bhp (67 and 74kW).

The handling was still a trifle adventurous, with a twitchy rear end and heavy steering, while drum brakes were prone to fade and didn't lend themselves well to sustained high-speed use.

TR3

Launched in 1955, the TR3 was effectively a TR2 with a few detail changes, notably shorter doors, a wider cabin and optional rear seats.

Other features included a more prominent radiator grille that sat flush with the front of the car, plus the option of overdrive on the top three gears to add flexibility to the car's acceleration and cruising abilities. Front disc brakes were a welcome, indeed essential, addition in 1956. Despite its modest power output and four-cylinder engine, the TR3 was a big seller in the United States, where its British ruggedness made it especially popular.

TR3A

Visually almost identical to the TR3, the TR3A was nonetheless a much improved and significantly different car to that which it succeeded. The most noticeable external differences included a wider grille, which ran the full width of the car, external door handles, sidelamps, recessed headlights and locking boot (trunk) handle. The suspension and steering were revised, and TR3As were much more responsive to drive on twisty roads as a result.

▶ **Triumph TR3**

With the roof down on a hot summer's day, the TR3 was the epitome of summer motoring. In the winter, however, life with no heater beneath a canvas roof was not all that great.

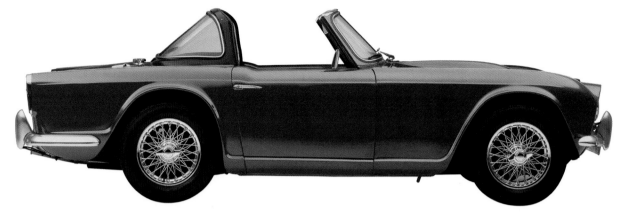

Specifications	
Engine type: Inline four-cylinder	Length: 3.93m (155.0in)
Displacement: 2138cc (130ci)	Width: 1.46m (57.5in)
Maximum power: 75kW (100bhp) at 4600rpm	Height: 1.27m (50.0in)
Top speed: 177km/h (110mph)	Wheelbase: 2.23m (88.0in)
0–96km/h (0–60mph): 10.7sec	Weight: 998kg (2200lbs)

◀ ▲ **Triumph TR4 1962**

The pin-sharp lines of the TR4 were the first example of Giovanni Michelotti's work to appear on a sporting Triumph – the start of a long and fruitful partnership.

The front-end styling of the Triumph TR4 was neatly finished, with the headlamps that were concealed beneath small humps at the edge of the bonnet (hood). The original TR4 had neatly incorporated tiny sidelamps inside the grille surround, while the TR4A and later TR5 featured a straight horizontal grille.

From 1959, the engine size was increased to 2.1 litres (128ci), with no discernible increase in power but much more torque, which made the engine far more flexible. The brakes were also improved at the same time, and it's these later cars that are the best to drive of all the early TR models.

When the TR4 appeared in 1961, Triumph kept the TR3 in production for a short while in fear that American buyers might not take to the new European-influenced styling. Known as TR3B,

these last-of-the-line cars also had an all-syncromesh gearbox.

Italia

The first Triumph penned by long-serving styling partner Giovanni Michelotti, the Italia was never an official production model. Fitted with an all-steel body built by coachbuilders Vignale and mounted on a TR3 chassis, the Italia was a beautifully pretty if little-known sports coupe. Most were sold to well-heeled Italian buyers who wanted the driver appeal of a British sports car, but with a unique Italian style.

TR4

Michelotti's first production Triumph sports car, the TR4, was styled in a manner that brought the look of the TR range right up to date, if not the technology. Sharp-suited, with angular rear fins and flat sides, plus neat hooded headlamps at the front, the TR4 was a thoroughly modern-looking car. Inside, it was neatly styled, too, with an ornate wooden dashboard and bucket seats. Yet despite the sharp looks, under the skin the

TR4 was very much a case of the same old formula. The chassis was little different to that of the TR2 or TR3, although dynamics were helped by servo-assisted disc brakes, rack and pinion steering and an all-syncromesh gearbox. Also traditional were the engines, both plucked from the Standard Vanguard. Available with the 2.1-litre (128ci) TR3A engine or the 2.0-litre (121ci) unit from the TR3, most were specified with the older, smaller powerplant, as its sub 2.0-litre (121ci) capacity made it eligible for more competitions.

TR4A

Introduced in 1964 and sold concurrently with the TR4 for slightly more than a year, the TR4A was difficult to distinguish from the standard model, despite being significantly different under the skin. Indeed, all of the external panels were identical with the exception of the front wings (fenders), which came with bigger sidelights mounted on them.

The biggest change was at the rear, which now got independent coil-sprung suspension – a simple move that did wonders for the TR4's roadholding, while a slight but noticeable power increase also made it a much more rewarding car

to drive. The only real downside is the TR4A's rarity, as production lasted for less than three years before the Standard Vanguard-sourced engines were to disappear for good.

TR5

Available for less than two years, the TR5 marks what can perhaps be regarded as the pinnacle of Triumph TR history, from a technical standpoint at least.

Based on the TR4A and identical to look at save for a power bulge in the bonnet (hood), the TR5 took bigger brakes, stiffer rear springs and quicker steering – all of which were added to cope with a significant increase in power. The reason for these modifications was the introduction of the six-cylinder 2.5-litre (152ci) engine used in the Triumph 2500 PI saloon, complete with Lucas fuel injection to help deliver 150bhp (112kW).

▼ **Triumph TR4A**

It may have looked outwardly similar in many ways, but the vast improvements in ride comfort and body control made the TR4A a much better car to drive than the standard TR4 model.

The Lucas fuelling system was troublesome, but was worth persisting with, as it improved the power output of the smooth and responsive six-pot by as much as almost 50 per cent.

TR250

Sadly for American fans of the marque, the TR5 never made its way across the Atlantic, and Triumph was instead forced to offer a US-only six-cylinder TR, which would become known as the TR250.

Forced to ditch the Lucas fuel injection system on grounds of emissions, Triumph instead gave American buyers the same 2.5-litre (152ci) engine, but fed by twin Stromberg carburettors. Ironically, a TR250 is easy to spot because of its

twin racing bonnet stripes, despite its decided lack of performance.

TR6

With no money in the bank to develop all-new models, and with the newly formed British Leyland Motor Corporation (BL) policing the Triumph purse strings, a complete ground-up replacement for the TR5 would be tricky to produce, if not impossible. Instead, Triumph went for an all-new style for the TR5's replacement.

Giovanni Michelotti was otherwise engaged, busily working on the Stag, the Dolomite and the new corporate face of the Triumph 2000, so instead of sticking with the much-admired Italian Triumph went to German style house Karmann to rework the car's looks.

The TR6, which debuted in 1969, came with new front and rear ends, with the headlamps now set out towards the edges of the wings, while the suspension was lowered to give the car a leaner stance.

The interior was revised, too, with less wood and more in the way of information, thanks to extra oil pressure and amperage dials; pressed steel sports wheels completed the visual changes. Under the skin, the TR6 received a new, thicker anti-roll bar, but apart from that it was the same

▼ **Triumph TR5 1968**

Again, you'd be hard pushed to spot the difference, but the TR5 differed from the TR4 in more than just its engine. Visual changes included a new bonnet badge and a distinct power bulge ahead of the driver.

Specifications	
Engine type: Inline six-cylinder	Length: 3.90m (153.6in)
Displacement: 2498cc (152ci)	Width: 1.47m (58.0in)
Maximum power: 112kW (150bhp) at 5500rpm	Height: 1.29m (50.9in)
Top speed: 172km/h (107mph)	Wheelbase: 2.23m (88.0in)
0–96km/h (0–60mph): 10.6sec	Weight: 1030kg (2270lbs)

Specifications

Engine type: Straight-six	Length: 4.04m (159.0in)
Displacement: 2498cc (152ci)	Width: 1.47m (58in)
Maximum power: 112kW (150bhp) at 5500rpm	Height: 1.27m (50in)
Top speed: 191km/h (119mph)	Wheelbase: 2.23m (88in)
0–96km/h (0–60mph): 8.4sec	Weight: 998kg (2473lbs)

▲ **Triumph TR6 1968**

Styling for the TR6 was the work of German coachbuilder Karmann, and was effectively a reskin of the TR4/TR5 body.

▼ **Triumph TR6**

British versions of the TR6 were more powerful than their American counterparts because they used a Lucas fuel injection system, while customers in the United States had to make do with twin Stromberg carbs.

▲ **Triumph TR7 1975**

Penned by British Leyland's star 1970s stylist, Harris Mann, the TR7 was like nothing else on the road. Its looks certainly polarized opinion.

Specifications

Engine type: Inline four cylinder	Length: 4.18m (164.5in)
Displacement: 1998cc (122ci)	Width: 1.68m (66.2in)
Maximum power: 67kW (90bhp) at 5000rpm	Height: 1.28m (49.9in)
Top speed: 177km/h (110mph)	Wheelbase: 2.16m (85.0in)
0–96km/h (0–60mph): 11.2sec	Weight: 1016kg (2240lbs)

The TR7 was the first and only British Leyland car to feature pop-up headlamps, which retracted into the bodywork in order to preserve the model's distinctive wedge-shaped profile. The only problem was that the lamps tended to get stuck in either the up or down position, and never both at the same time, meaning that many a TR7 was seen later in its life with one eye open and the other one closed.

old chassis, which could trace its roots right back to the TR2. As with the TR5 and 250, the European models had Lucas fuel injection and 150bhp (112kW), while those for the United States had to make do with twin Strombergs and 104bhp (77kW).

TR7

The mistake British Leyland made with the TR7 was not one of launching an especially bad car, but more in pretending it was a worthy successor to the brawny, macho sports cars that had worn the Triumph badge in the past. However, the TR7 wasn't actually as bad as it reputation would suggest. True, the Harris Mann–styled lines had a love-it-or-loathe-it quality and the build quality was typical of BL in the 1970s, but in terms of its handling and performance the 7 was up there with most of its rivals. The lack of a convertible at launch did it no favours with TR fans (a ragtop finally arrived in 1981), nor did the elevated ride height, a side effect of new American collision legislation. Some even went as far as to criticize the TR7 for having a four-cylinder engine derived from that of a humdrum Triumph saloon, conveniently forgetting the TR line's genesis.

TR7 Lynx

The Lynx was the TR7 that never was. It first appeared on the drawing board in 1972, three years before the TR7 coupe would go into production, and was effectively a V8-engined TR7 with a unique hatchback-cum-estate (station wagon) rear end. That may sound a little odd, but at the time of its development there were three similar models on the market – the Volvo 1800ES, Jensen GT and ubiquitous Reliant Scimitar, so Triumph's desire to enter such a market wasn't as strange as it seemed.

The Lynx emerged from the styling studio as a wholly predictable extension of the TR7 platform, relying on its front end almost unmodified, but from the scuttle line back the car was almost entirely new. The TR7 platform had its wheelbase extended by a full 30.5cm (12in), and longer passenger doors were incorporated in order to balance the side view of the car and improve access to the rear seats, as well as to make the rear deck look less estate-like and more like a coupe.

The project was signed off to the extent that production was due to start in the spring of 1978, but by this stage BL had swung from one crisis to the next and was about to indulge in yet another bout of 'plant disinvestment'. This meant closure for the Triumph plant at Speke, Merseyside, where the TR7 was built, and the transfer of production to the Rover line in Solihull. There was no room at Solihull to build more than one

body variant, so the Lynx project was canned just months before its intended production debut; a handful of completed pre-production cars are known to exist in enthusiasts' circles.

TR7 V8
Built expressly for homologation purposes, the TR7 V8 was Leyland's basis for a world rally car contender. It used the 3.5-litre (215ci) all-alloy unit from the Rover SD1 hatchback, most of which were tuned to around 300bhp (225kW), while the V8 had wider wheelarches, heavily revised rear suspension, five-speed manual transmissions and four-wheel disc brakes.

TR8
Built for only the final two years of production and aimed at the US market in particular, the TR8 was effectively what the TR7 should have been at launch. In other words, it was a complete sports car, with a choice of hard or soft tops and a genuinely lively V8 engine, sourced from Rover. If it had been around when the TR7

▼ **Triumph TR7 V8**
Although a V8 version of the TR7 wasn't officially offered until the TR8 debuted near the end of the model's production life, British Leyland had a team of V8-engined works rally cars.

Model	0–96km/h (0–60mph)	Top Speed km/h (mph)
Roadster	24.8sec	125 (77)
TR2	12.5sec	165 (102)
TR3	11.9sec	167 (103)
TR3A	10.5sec	170 (105)
TR4	10.9sec	176 (109)
TR4A	11.4sec	176 (109)
TR5	8.8sec	194 (120)
TR250	10.9sec	170 (105)
TR6	8.2sec	193 (119)
TR7	9.1sec	176 (109)
TR7 V8	6.5sec	178 (110)
TR8	7.8sec	218 (135)

Model	Years Built	Number Built
Roadster	1946–49	4501
TR2	1953–55	8628
TR3	1955–57	13,377
TR3A	1957–62	58,236
Italia	1959–63	329
TR4	1961–65	40,253
TR4A	1964–67	28,465
TR5	1967–68	2947
TR250	1967–68	8484
TR6	1969–76	94,619
TR7	1975–81	112,368
TR7 V8	1978–80	400
TR8	1979–81	2497

debuted, the car's status in the TR line-up could have been so different. As it was, the TR8 was merely an interesting footnote in the soon-to-end Triumph story, and a tragic reflection of how poor management and dreadful labour relations had thrown the British motor industry off track.

◀ ▼ Triumph TR8 1980

The TR8 was a case of too little, too late for the ailing TR line. The beefy powerplant turned the TR7 into a proper sports car, but the damage to its reputation had already been done.

Specifications

Engine type: V8	Length: 4.18m (164.5in)
Displacement: 3528cc (215ci)	Width: 1.68m (66.2in)
Maximum power: 110kW (148bhp) at 5100rpm	Height: 1.27m (49.9in)
Top speed: 193km/h (120mph)	Wheelbase: 2.16m (85.0in)
0–96km/h (0–60mph): 8.4sec	Weight: 1188kg (2620lbs)

Volkswagen Beetle
1945–2006

VW's bug-shaped compact model is the best-selling car of all-time, with more than 21 million built in a 70-year life.

Split Window

The very first VW Beetle was built in 1934, the design of Ferry Porsche and the brainchild of none other than Adolf Hitler. These early prototypes were introduced primarily as military vehicles, the idea being that their simplicity and ease of maintenance would make them ideal for mobilizing troops. The decision to use a horizontally opposed air-cooled engine added further to the appeal, with fewer moving parts to wear out or go wrong.

Never actually called the Beetle (it would be 1967 before VW adopted the car's nickname as its official moniker), the 'Type 1' almost never made it past 1945. The factory in Wolfsburg, North Germany, was destroyed during an Allied bombing campaign, and most of the production

Specifications

Engine type: Air-cooled horizontally opposed flat-four	0–96km/h (0–60mph): 16.1sec
Displacement: 1192cc (72.7ci)	Length: 4.19m (165in)
Maximum power: 22kW (30bhp)	Width: 1.55m (61in)
at 3400rpm	Height: 1.55m (61in)
Top speed: 126km/h (78mph)	Wheelbase: 2.40m (94.5in)
	Weight: 739kg (1629lbs)

▶ **VW Beetle Deluxe Sedan 1957**
The world's favourite car came in many guises – this is an early oval window variant with semaphore-style turn indicators.

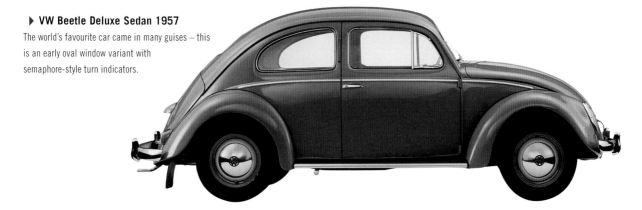

line was lost. But immediately after the war, British Army officer Major Ivan Hurst coordinated a project in the area to regenerate employment, including overseeing the reconstruction of the Volkswagen factory. The first post-war Beetles appeared later that year and were designed as cheap, accessible transport to get Germany back on its wheels. Domestic models were extremely austere, with no chrome or luxury trim, but export models were a little more luxurious, with hydraulic brakes, chrome bumpers and an optional roll-back sunroof.

Early models are easy to identify, as the rear window is split into two semi-circular pieces, with a central divider, hence the 'Split Window' name among enthusiasts. These are by far the most collectable of all Beetles, although they aren't especially pleasant to drive.

Karmann Convertible

Right from the early days, convertible Beetles were offered – and those sold officially through Volkswagen were converted by Karmann from 1949 onwards. The body was prone to flexing with the roof removed, so Karmann added extra cross members beneath the sills and around the doors, which went a long way towards addressing

the flexibility problem but added around 40kg (90lb) in weight. This wasn't so much a problem with the later powertrains (Karmann convertibles remained on sale through all generations of beetle up to 1980), but on the earlier cars with just 25bhp (19kW) it made them extremely slow and unpleasant to drive. Still, the convertible model's primary aim was to look strikingly good – something it achieved successfully, without removing any of the inherent character of the Beetle saloon (sedan).

Hebmüller

Although Karmann had been granted the contract to build the official open-top Beetle, another converter – Wuppertal-based Hebmüller – did a more distinctive two-plus-two model, with a longer rear deck and lower roof with the top up.

Also making its debut in 1949, as with the Karmann, extra strengthening was added to the sills and bulkhead, although the Hebmüller also got a stiffer rear deck panel and bespoke side windows to incorporate the new soft-top.

The hand-built nature of Hebmüller models made them significantly more expensive than the Karmann Beetles, although they were still reasonably popular with those who wanted the exclusivity of something a little different.

Sadly, a fire wiped out the Hebmüller factory within a year of production starting, and, while the Cabriolet continued after this, production never really recovered and only a handful were finished.

Oval Window

For 1954, VW introduced a few changes to the Beetle to make it more suitable for export markets – a move that would see the car become an immense success over the next decade and beyond. The cabin was better equipped and made more spacious at the rear, with a one-piece oval rear screen replacing the original split window to improve rearward visibility.

▼ **VW Beetle Hebmuller Cabriolet**
One of the rarest and prettiest Beetle variants is this, the Hebmüller Cabriolet, which was built for less than a year.

Specifications

Engine type: flat-four	Length: 4.14m (163.0in)
Displacement: 1192cc (72.7ci)	Width: 1.63m (64.2in)
Maximum power: 29.8kW (40bhp) at 3900rpm	Height: 1.50m (59.2in)
Top speed: 126km/h (78mph)	Wheelbase: 2.40m (94.5in)
0–96km/h (0–60mph): 24.6sec	Weight: 795kg (1753lbs)

▶ ▲ **VW Karmann Ghia 1961**

A Beetle beneath the skin, but definitely not in presence, the Karmann Ghia didn't
go as well as it looked – but then it did look pretty special.

New trim levels were introduced, including a De
Luxe, which received whitewall tyres and
carpets, plus an optional radio set and rubber
running boards.

Power was increased to 30bhp (22kkW),
which gave the Beetle better cruising ability and
acceleration that, while not rapid, was at least
quick enough to not embarrass itself in the cut
and thrust of city traffic.

Coupled to VW's hard-earned reputation for
quality engineering and clockwork reliability,
which made the Beetle an especially attractive
package to buyers on a budget, it is little wonder
that Beetle exports would increase year-on-year
to the extent that it became the best-selling
imported model in the United States, the United
Kingdom and Australia.

The car's simplicity and the fact that it had no
welded components, with everything bolted in
place, meant that it was also popular in
developing markets – VW set up factories in
Brazil, Mexico, Nigeria and South Africa, where
Beetle kits were assembled and sold locally.

Karmann Ghia

Karmann had already got the contract to build
official convertible versions of the Beetle, so it
was the German coachbuilders to whom Italian
styling house Ghia turned with its Virgil Exner-
designed 2+2 coupe.

Karmann put the proposal to VW, and with
the parent company's blessing the Karmann
Ghia, which had been developed in secret,
became a standalone Beetle-based model.

Using a Beetle floorpan that had been
widened by 7.5cm (3in), the car had only other
change to its mechanical layout – a front anti-
roll bar to cope with the extra weight of the shell.
Initially handbuilt, but soon far too popular for
that, the later Karmann Ghias were built on a
special line in Karmann's factory. A convertible
model arrived in 1957, while engine and
mechanical changes were in line with those of
the Beetle, meaning bigger engines in 1965 and
66, plus an automatic option in 1967. A big

change came in 1970, with thicker bumpers and a 1600cc (98ci) engine, as well as a more modern and heavily revised cabin. More than 400,000 were built in a 19-year career.

Flat Window

The Beetle's evolution continued with more styling changes in 1957, the oval rear window now replaced with a larger flat rear screen that delivered much better reversing visibility, yet somehow removed some of the car's curvaceous character. Regardless, these were the best of the

▲ Volkswagen Karmann Ghia Coupe
Early Karmann Ghias are the purest in terms of styling, and, while the convertible is the most collectable, most fans agree the coupe is the best looker.

classic Beetles to drive, with bigger brakes making a huge difference as far as driver confidence was concerned, along with a more powerful 34bhp (25kW) engine from 1960, which coincided with the introduction of syncromesh on all gears and front and rear anti-roll-bars.

Other visual changes included a deeper windscreen and a new, wider engine cover to improve access to the car's air-cooled powerplant.

The changes accelerated sales still further; by 1965 total Beetle production had exceeded eight million – not bad for a company that, 20 years previously was picking over the ashes of a burned-down factory, and

◀ VW Beetle interior
Inside a 1970s Beetle, and you can see already how there are some concessions to comfort sneaking in, such as a fuel gauge, a glove box and wiring for a radio.

was banking on building its success on a single model that was now more than 30 years old …

1200/1300

You'd be hard pushed to notice, but the 1965 Beetle was by far the most significant rework of the Beetle concept yet, with not one panel the same as the earlier car, and only the windscreen and engines interchangeable between the two.

The head and tail lamps were adjusted to make them more upright in line with the demands of US lighting regulations, the wheels were made smaller and fitted with radial tyres as standard, opening front quarterlights were introduced and the fuel filler was moved from the luggage compartment to the car's exterior. Thicker bumpers were added and the interior was also reworked, with new vinyl seat trim and wipe-clean rubber mats appearing on the basic 1200 version.

The 34bhp (25kW) engine continued unabashed on the entry-level cars, along with drum brakes, although the more powerful 1300, introduced in 1965, had more power, with 40bhp (29kW) on tap, giving it the ability to cruise at speeds of more than 110km/h (70mph) – a nod to the dawn of the motorway era.

1500

For those wanting a Beetle that had enough power to really hold its own on the open road, VW launched the largest-engined Beetle variant of the lot in 1966.

While essentially the same air-cooled flat-four engine that had powered generations of Beetles before it, the 1500's engine was bored out to 1493cc (91ci), giving it a power output of 50bhp (36kW). This may not sound like a huge

amount, but the Beetle's light weight meant that it was enough to give 129km/h-plus (80mph-plus) cruising ability, while retaining the Beetle's legendary fuel economy. The 1500 did have some reliability issues, though, most notably with the wear to the oil seals at the top of the bores, which would cause them to run even more noisily than usual and with excessive smoke.

The 1500 models had a wider track than smaller-engined cars and came with a 12-volt electric circuit, while there was also the option

▼ **VW Beetle Engine**

Beetles are tuned like all other cars – here the standard 1200cc (73ci) unit has a fast road cam and a revised ignition system.

▶ **VW Beetle 1302**

This is a later Beetle 1302, identifiable by its more rounded windscreen and wider front luggage compartment cover.

▶ **VW Beetle 1500**
A relatively rare Beetle 1500 – this one has the post-1969 body with upright front lamps, a configuration that lasted for only a year.

of an automatic gearbox for the first time.

Type 181

A rather obscure vehicle, the Type 181 was initially built for the German military as the equivalent to the Jeep of the United States or the Land Rover of the United Kingdom. It wasn't a four-wheel drive vehicle, however, and under the utilitarian four-door body was a simple Beetle chassis, which was coupled to the Beetle 1500 engine.

In 1969, VW decided to sell the Type 181 to civilians as a leisure vehicle, following the success of the British Mini Moke, which was similar in concept.

Left-hand drive only and with a simple canvas tilt in place of a proper roof, the Type 181 was officially called 'The Thing' in the United States, although this was probably much easier for foreigners to say than its official title, which was Mehrzweck-Fahrzeug Kurierwagen, meaning 'multi-purpose delivery vehicle'. Basic in layout and cheerful to drive, the 181 was built in places as far afield as Mexico and Indonesia, as well as in VW's traditional German plant located at Wolfsburg.

1302/1303

The Beetle now became even more modern. The 1302 was launched in 1970, not as a replacement to the existing models, but in addition to them. The 1302 had a 2.5cm (1in) longer wheelbase and all-new MacPherson strut front suspension with front disc

◀ **VW Beetle Karmann Cabriolet**
Karmann's interpretation of the Beetle convertible is by far the most common of the breed. It remained in production long after saloon models were stopped in Europe.

A confusing number of engines were on offer in the Beetle throughout its life, and it's not unusual to find the 'wrong' powerplant in any car. This is because changing the Beetle's engine is a straightforward job, easier, in fact, than changing a spark plug. The rear panel can be unfastened, followed by the four bolts that hold the engine in. The powerplant can then be drawn out with a trolley jack and a new one fitted in minutes.

▶ ▲ **VW Super Beetle Cabriolet 1971**
Beetle customizing takes on many forms, from the simple additional detailing seen on this relatively unmolested Karmann convertible, through to chopped and heavily modified examples.

brakes. As well as improved stopping power and handling, the 1302 had a more usable luggage compartment, as the front suspension took up far less space. It was identifiable by its extended, rounder luggage compartment lid. The 1302 disappeared after two years, to be replaced by the 1303. Changes included a bulbous wraparound windscreen, safety padded dashboard and larger rear lamp clusters. Two versions were offered – the basic 1303, which came with the Beetle 1300 engine, and the 1303S, which got a new 1584cc (97ci) unit developing 50bhp (36kW).

Mexico Beetle
Officially, VW Beetle production in Europe ceased in 1978 with a limited edition of silver

Specifications

Engine type: Flat-four	Length: 4.12m (161.8in)
Displacement: 1585cc (96.7ci)	Width: 1.58m (62.4in)
Maximum power: 45kW (60bhp) at 4400rpm	Height: (1.58m (62.4in)
Top speed: 129km/h (80mph)	Wheelbase: 2.42m (95.3in)
0–96km/h (0–60mph): 17.8sec	Weight: 860kg (1896lbs)

Model	Years Built	Number Built
Split Window	1945–53	528,793
Karmann Cabrio	1949–80	331,847
Hebmuller	1949–53	696
Oval Window	1954–65	7,267,899
Karmann Ghia	1955–74	445,300
1200/1300	1965–78	3,311,971
1500	1966–70	1,888,282
Type 181	1969–79	90,883
1302/1303	1970–75	916,713
Mexico Beetle	1978–2006	6,000,000+

'Jubilee' models to mark the car's passing. The end of German production meant that no more exports to other European Countries, the United Kingdom or the United States. But Beetle production would continue in Mexico, where the car remained the country's best-seller for another 20-plus years.

Due to the vast number of private imports, it's not unusual to find Mexican Beetles in any of the model's former export markets, where dedicated fans of the marque insisted on sourcing a replacement when their Beetles reached the end of their natural lives.

Mechanically little different from the 1967-generation beetle, the Mexican cars did come with several revisions, including the padded dashboard from the 1303 models and seats from the VW Polo for added comfort and safety. One of the most popular models was the Beetle Taxi, which had the passenger seat removed to aid entry and egress for those people wanting to travel in the rear.

Production of the Beetle finally ceased in 2005, when the car was deemed no longer environmentally friendly or safe enough to remain in production, bringing one of motoring history's most remarkable stories to a close after more than 70 years and 21 million sales.

Model	0–96km/h (0–60mph)	Top Speed km/h (mph)
Split Window	N/A	102 (63)
Karmann Cabrio	32.1sec	117 (72)
Hebmuller	N/A	99 (61)
Oval Window	23.0sec	121 (75)
Karmann Ghia	21.7sec	146 (90)
1200/1300	21.9sec	131 (81)
1500	19.1sec	138 (85)
Type181	30.1sec	110 (68)
1302/1303	18.3sec	129 (80)
Mexico Beetle	16.1sec	141 (87)

Although the very last Beetles looked almost identical to the first, there was only one component that was interchangeable between first and last, it being a metal strip used to hold the bonnet (hood) seal in place …

▼ **VW Beetle 1303S**

As close as you could get to a 'performance' Beetle, the 1303S had enough power to perform convincingly in modern traffic conditions, as well as uprated brakes and suspension.

Volkswagen Golf GTi
1976–

Initially developed in secret by a team of dedicated engineers, Volkswagen's first GTi became an icon almost overnight.

Specifications

Engine type: Inline four-cylinder	Length: 3.72m (146.5in)
Displacement: 1781cc (109ci)	Width: 1.62m (63.5in)
Maximum power: 84kW (112bhp) at 5800rpm	Height: 1.38m (54.5in)
Top speed: 172km/h (107mph)	Wheelbase: 2.40m (94.5in)
0–96km/h (0–60mph): 9.8sec	Weight: 860kg (1920lbs)

▶ ▲ **VW Golf GTi Mk I 1982**

The original and best? The Golf wasn't the first hatchback developed for a performance market, but its combination of power and handling made it the first real 'hot hatch'.

It certainly took VW's bosses by surprise. They initially (and reluctantly) agreed to build a limited run of 5000 cars at the end of 1975, in left-hand drive form only; the GTi was to be a low-volume one-off. With 110bhp (82kW) from its Bosch fuel-injected 1.6-litre (98ci) engine, the car had terrific performance and superb handling. Following its impressive introduction, in 1976 the GTi became a standard model, but it was 1979 before VW built the car for right-hand drive markets. It also received a minor facelift, with BBS alloy wheels and a five-speed gearbox as standard.

Mk 1 1.8/Campaign

Launched in 1982, the 1.8 model had only 2bhp (1.5kW) more power, but the engine had a wider spread of torque and was far more responsive. The handling was also slightly different because of stiffer springs and fatter tyres. There was also a special run-out model called Campaign, offered in a unique colour scheme and with disc wheels.

181

Mk 1 Cabriolet

Launched in 1979 as the Golf GLi, the Cabriolet picked up the GTi name in 1981 and continued until 1994 without change, despite being outdated and having a crude folding hood mechanism.

Mk 2

With the debut of an all-new Golf in 1984, VW didn't make the same mistake it did with the first generation – a GTi was in the line-up from the start. Initially available with the same engine as the GTi Mk 1 1.8, the Mk 2 wasn't the fastest hot hatchback, but had wonderful handling. A five-door car joined the line-up in 1985.

Mk 2 16v

While other manufacturers were making their cars faster by bolting on turbos, Volkswagen took a more engineering-led approach with the Golf GTi. Launched in 1986 and sold alongside the regular eight-valve model, the 16v used the standard 1.8 block, but with a new twin-cam cylinder head with four valves per cylinder and a sophisticated engine management system. This meant a power output of 139bhp (104kW) and a 0–60mph (0–96km/h) time of just eight seconds.

G60 Rallye

Not strictly a GTi, the G60 Rallye is hard to ignore. In its day it was the Golf's ultimate performance incarnation. Using a three-door GTi shell with flared arches, it had a four-wheel drive chassis developed for the more moderate Golf Syncro. Power came from the twin-cam GTi 16-valve engine, coupled to a G-Lader supercharger, giving a power output of 160bhp (119kW). As a result, the Rallye had breathtaking performance and almost glue-like grip.

Mk 3

The Golf GTi Mk 3 came with a 2.0-litre (121ci) 115bhp (86kW) powerplant, delivering reasonable but not exhilarating performance. For the first time, the GTi ceased to be something special.

Mk 4

Perhaps the Golf GTi's darkest hour in terms of driver appeal, the Mk 4 was still the best-selling GTi ever. The 1.8- and 2.0-litre (110 and 121ci) versions offered mediocre performance and little handling prowess. Turbocharged 1.8-litre (110ci) versions were moderately more interesting.

Mk 5

First shown in concept form at the 2004 Paris Motor Show, the all-new VW Golf GTi had 200bhp (150kW) on tap. With neat styling cues that hinted at the original GTi, including a red-rimmed radiator grille and red-detailed alloy wheels, the newcomer was made firmly in the mould of the original GTi. Performance was excellent, handling was impressive and for once the asking price wasn't prohibitively expensive.

Model	Years Built	0–96km/h (0–60mph)	Top Speed km/h/mph
Mk 1 1.6	1976–81	9.0sec	180/111
Mk 1 1.8	1981–84	8.3sec	183/113
Mk 1 Cabriolet	1981–94	9.1sec	178/110
Mk 2	1984–91	8.6sec	199/123
Mk 2 16v	1988–91	8.0sec	217/134
Golf Rallye G60	1989–92	7.8sec	210/130
Mk 3	1992–98	8.1sec	217/134
Mk 3 VR6	1993–98	7.1sec	223/138
Mk 4	1998–2004	8.2sec	217/134
R32	2002–04	6.4sec	248/153
Mk 5	2005–	7.2sec	236/146

Volvo 100/200 Series
1966–93

Box-like and designed very much for comfort rather than speed, Volvo's long-lived range of saloons (sedans) and estates (station wagons) put the Swedish maker firmly on the map.

144

Replacing the successful Amazon was never going to be easy, and some would argue that with the 1966 144, Volvo was trying to play it safe. To a degree, that was true – the design brief for the Swedish firm's newcomer was focused very much more on longevity and safety than it was on driving excitement or style.

Despite this, the 144 had much to recommend it. For safety's sake, the car had disc brakes all round and seatbelts as standard, while the squared-off bodywork incorporated individual crumple zones to absorb load paths in the event of an accident.

Initially, power came from the 1.8-litre (110ci) engine carried over from the Amazon, but this was increased to 2.0 litres (121ci) in 1969, although regardless of which engine you chose it was never a particular lively performer – not that this made a huge difference to the majority of traditional Volvo buyers, who weren't renowned for their raciness.

If you did want a little more in the way of performance, the 144S came with twin carburettors and 100bhp (75kW), while the 1971 144GL had Bosch fuel injection with standard overdrive, meaning 120bhp (8KkW) and much-improved cruising abilities.

Not a car renowned for its dynamism, the 144 was nevertheless incredibly well constructed, and this meant that, with careful maintenance, a 144 could last for ever …

142

On sale a year after the 144, the 142 was a two-door version of the 144 and was arguably better looking, with its long doors and four-window cabin having a much lower and leaner look than the four-door variant.

The 142 was a big seller in its native Sweden, where vehicle tax laws favoured cars with fewer doors, while in Germany the two-door also proved popular with executive buyers

◀ **Volvo 144 1967**

Simple, boxy and unobtrusive, the Volvo 140 Series did a fine job of providing safe, secure motoring to the masses.

◀ **Volvo 142**

A Volvo 142 in its natural environment, crossing an icy tundra – although the car looks suspiciously clean.

who liked to drive their own car rather than be driven. But in the United States and Britain, it was a very slow seller and was withdrawn for good in 1974.

145

Antique dealers across the globe celebrated when Volvo pulled the wraps of its 145 – a five-door estate version of the 144. Longer than the saloon but sharing its wheelbase, the 145 model had that extra length behind the rear wheelarch, meaning that there was plenty of extra space in the back for luggage.

Aside from possessing a cavernous load bay, which came with a near vertical tailgate for easy loading and unloading, the 145 was no different from the 144, sharing that car's engine and trim level options. The fuel-injected post-1972 models of the 145 are far and away the best in terms of performance and all-round flexibility.

164

Billed as a rival to the Jaguar XJ6, the Volvo 164 wasn't quite all that Volvo

said it was. Admittedly, it was fairly lively, its 3-litre (183ci) straight-six engine offering 145bhp (108Kw) at first, to 175bhp (130kW) after 1971, when fuel injection became standard. But while the car was extremely swift in a straight line, the extra power showed up the weaknesses of the 164's extended 144 chassis, and the car was always much happier cruising than being hurried along a twisty road.

Nonetheless, the 164 was well appointed, with leather as standard, and optional overdrive or automatic transmission with power steering. The 164TE, introduced in 1973, even came with standard air conditioning.

Externally, the 164 was easy to distinguish from the 140 series models by virtue of its Rolls-Royce style radiator grille and longer front wings (fenders), which incorporated the headlamps, while those built from 1970 had fog lamps set into the front slam panel.

▼ **Volvo 145**

The 145 was the first incarnation of the typical Volvo estate – a car that soon earned itself a justifiable reputation as the best load-lugger on the market.

▶ **Volvo 164**
Fans of power and luxury could opt for the Volvo 164, with a Renault-derived V6 engine. It was swift, but not as reliable as four-cylinder Volvos.

244

Volvo's new model for 1974 was more than just a facelift of the 140, so although it used many of the same panels, Volvo saw fit to give the car a new name to mark it out as something completely different.

Visibly similar, with all the same panels from the windscreen backwards and only detail changes such as new door handles and lamp clusters marking it out from the 140 series, the new 244 was more significantly different at the front. The original torsion bar front suspension of the 140 series was gone, to be replaced by MacPherson struts and coil springs, which made significant improvements to the car's handling and also made the steering far lighter on those versions not fitted with power-assisted steering – a hugely welcome modification for those who had become used to the rather unwieldy characteristics of lower specification 144s. Also new were a range of overhead camshaft four-cylinder engines, in either 2.0-litre (121ci) or 2.3-litre (140ci) form, followed by a 2.1-litre (128ci) turbo.

The new engines were both faster and more efficient than the old Amazon-based units in the 140 and along with the dynamic improvements made the 244 a much better car, yet also one that continued to enjoy the earlier model's reputation for longevity.

The 244 quickly earned itself a reputation for reliability that led to a massive increase in sales, with new factories opening in Ghent, Belgium, and Halifax, Canada, to cope with increased demand. These models were more corrosion-prone, though, than the properly winterproof Swedish-built models.

242

Although the two-door version of the 140 series had been a big seller for Volvo, the same could not be said of the 242, which

◀ **Volvo 240**
Its styling was plain, but the 240 saloon soon won a strong reputation for safety and longevity. Even Volvo's colour names were sensible – the hue of this base model British 240DL is called 'Volvo Light Blue'.

was sold in only a few markets where there was a discernible tax advantage to owning one. Otherwise, it had nothing to recommend it over the four-door, while this time the two-door styling looked quite ungainly against the 240 series chunkier front end styling.

245

By far the definitive member of the 240 series range, the 245 estate developed into the lifeblood of the Volvo brand throughout the late 1970s and 1980s.

As impressively capacious as the 145 estate, but with the dynamic improvements found in the later 244 models, the 245 is regarded as something of an icon among station wagons. Diesel models were offered in left-hand drive markets with a Volkswagen-sourced engine, but right-hand drive buyers had to wait for the 700 series Volvos to appear in 1984 before they could have an economical oil-burning variant.

264/265

As with the 164, Volvo decided a six-cylinder version of the new 200 series was essential to appeal to more upmarket buyers. This time, though, the straight-six engine of the 164 was ditched in favour of a new 2.7-litre (165ci) engine called the Douvrin, which was jointly developed by Volvo, Peugeot and Renault.

Externally, differences between the 264 and 244 were minimal, with a slightly different chrome radiator being the only noticeable change. This time, Volvo also put the V6 into the estate model, creating the 265 in the process.

Smooth and powerful, the Douvrin-engined Volvos were impressive executive cars, albeit with typically ponderous handling characteristics if compared to the likes of Mercedes and BMW. Not favoured in some European countries such as the United Kingdom, where the cost of fuel made running the V6 prohibitive, the 264 and 265 enjoyed most of their sales success in the United States, where they satisfied the demand

Specifications	
Engine type: Inline four-cylinder	Length: 4.88m (192.5in)
Displacement: 2127cc (130ci)	Width: 1.71m (67.3in)
Maximum power: 95kW (127bhp) at 5400rpm	Height: 1.43m (56.3in)
Top speed: 172km/h (107mph)	Wheelbase: 2.64m (104.3in)
0–96km/h (0–60mph): 8.9sec	Weight: 1451kg (3200lbs)

◀ ▼ **Volvo 240 GLT Turbo 1983**
The flagship of the 240 range was the 240 GLT Turbo, seen here in estate form. While not especially racy, it was a fairly swift car and was well equipped, with standard leather trim, heated seats and alloy wheels.

▶ Volvo 240 GLT Turbo
Front-end styling was different on later models, with thicker bumpers and indicator lenses that wrapped round into the front wings.

for a faster, more powerful Volvo.

262C

Quite what possessed Volvo to offer the 262C is difficult to see, other than perhaps a desire to come up with something completely different. Designed by Bertone and built in its factory in Italy on Volvo's behalf, the odd-looking two-door coupe used the bottom half of the relatively slow-selling 242, but with an unusual chopped and vinyl-covered roof. Inside, the car was hand-trimmed in Italian leather, which gave it a luxurious feel, while power came from the Douvrin V6, meaning that performance was fairly decent. The 262C was, however, very difficult to admire in terms of its styling, while the Italians managed to afflict it with their unique breed of build quality, so that the 262C had the ability to rot at a thoroughly un-Volvo-like rate, while suffering from all manner of electrical maladies to boot.

240 Series 2

In 1984, Volvo introduced the 740 and 760 models, which if anything were even more slab-sided and squared-edged than the 240 series. But rather than put the long-serving 240 models out to pasture, the Swedish firm instead facelifted the car into a form that would stay in production even after the 700-type models had been replaced.

The new look saw the 240 get larger wraparound headlamps, thicker plastic bumpers and new wheeltrims, while additional black plastic trim successfully gave the car a much more modern look without the need to resort to sheet metal changes. The cabin was also revised, with a softer, more modern dashboard and plush velour seats. The 244 and 245 names were dropped, and all models were now called 240. In estate versions, which by now accounted for more than 60 per cent of sales, a new fold-up seven-seat option was offered and proved especially popular with larger families. Despite being by now thoroughly outdated, the 240 continued to sell well, with customer demand constantly forcing Volvo to put back its proposed end of production.

The last 240s finally appeared in 1993, almost 20 years after the model first came out, yet even then there was resistance from Volvo's traditional fans to let the 240 die. More than three million examples were built in total.

Model	Years Built	0–96km/h (0–60mph)	Top Speed km/h (mph)
144	1966–74	12.6sec	163 (101)
145	1967–74	12.9sec	160 (99)
142	1967–74	12.6sec	163 (101)
164	1968–75	8.8sec	183 (113)
244	1974–82	11.4sec	172 (106)
242	1974–82	11.4sec	172 (106)
245	1975–82	12.6sec	159 (98)
264	1974–85	9.7sec	180 (111)
262C	1977–81	9.6sec	186 (115)
240 Series 2	1982–93	11.2sec	170 (105)

Glossary of Terms

Acceleration Rate of change of velocity, usually expressed as a measure of time over a given distance such as a quarter of a mile, or from rest to a given speed, such as 0–60mph (96km/h)

Air-cooled engine Where ambient air is used to cool the engine, by passing directly over fins on the cylinders and cylinder head

Alternator Electrical generator using magnetism to convert mechanical energy into an electrical output (AC)

Aluminium block Engine cylinder block cast from aluminium, usually with cast iron sleeves or liners for the cylinder bores

Anti-roll bar Transverse rod between left and right suspension at front or rear to reduce body roll

Badge engineering Selling of similar models with different manufacturer's name badges

bhp Brake horse power, 1bhp = raising 550 foot-pounds per second or 745.7 watts; 1bhp = torque x rpm/5252 with torque measured in foot-pounds

Bulkhead Panel usually separating engine from cabin compartment

Bumper Rigid addition (usually) to bodywork front and rear to prevent panel

damage in the event of collision, usually chrome-coated steel or plastic

Cabriolet Open-top car with a removable or folding roof; often abbreviated to 'cabrio'

Camshaft Engine component which controls the opening and closing of valves via lobes, either directly or indirectly

Capacity The volume of a piston measured either in cubic centimetres (cc) or cubic inches (cu in)

Carburettor Device for vaporizing fuel and mixing it with air in an exact ratio ready for combustion, via the inlet manifold

cc Cubic capacity, or cubic centimetres; the total volume of the displacement of the engine's pistons in all cylinders

Coil spring Helical steel alloy rod used for vehicle suspension

De Dion Axle/suspension system named after its inventor Count Albert de Dion, designed in 1894, where the driven axle is mounted on the chassis with universal joints at each end to keep the wheels vertical to improve handling, usually in conjunction with inboard disc brakes

Double wishbone Method of suspension where each wheel is supported by an upper and lower pivoting triangular

framework, mainly used on sportscars

Drum brake Braking system whereby friction materials (shoes) are moved radially against the inside surface of a metal cylinder (drum)

Facia or fascia A car's dashboard or instrument panel

Fender Mudguard or area of wing around wheel well

Fuel injection Direct metered injection of fuel into the combustion cycle by mechanical or electro-mechanical means, first devised in 1902

Gearbox Component of the transmission system that houses a number of gears of different ratios. Gears are selected to suit a variety of road speeds throughout the engine's rev range

Gear ratio The revolutions of a driving gear required to turn the driven gear through one revolution, calculated by the number of teeth on the driven gear divided by the number of teeth on the driving gear

Grill(e) Metal or plastic protection for the radiator, often adopting a particular style or design of an individual manufacturer to make their car recognizable

Gullwing Doors that open in a vertical arc, usually hinged along the centre of the roofline

Handbrake Brake operated manually by the driver when a vehicle is static, usually operating on the rear wheels via a cable

IFS Independent Front Suspension

Independent suspension System of suspension where all wheels move up and down independently of each other, thus having no effect on the other wheels and aiding stability

Kilowatt (kW) the standard ISO measure of horsepower (1kW = 1.3596PS or 1.341bhp)

Manifold Pipe system used for gathering or dispersal of gas or liquids

Master cylinder Brake fluid reservoir and pump in a hydraulic braking system

mpg Miles per gallon, measure of a car's fuel consumption

Muscle car U.S. term to describe a high-powered car, usually over 296kW (400bhp)

Normally-aspirated Engine charged by atmospheric pressure rather than by forced induction

OHC Overhead Camshaft engine, where the camshaft is located in the cylinder head

OHV Overhead Valve engine, where the camshaft is located in the cylinder block, the valves are in the cylinder head operated by pushrods

Quarter light Small often triangular window abutting A or C pillar, usually opened by swivelling on its vertical axis

Rack and pinion System of gearing typically used in a steering box with a toothed rail driven laterally by a pinion on the end of the steering column

Rotary engine Internal combustion engine in which power is derived from a single rotor without reciprocating pistons, and very few moving parts. Pioneered by Felix Wankel in Germany, in 1956

rpm Revs per minute, measure of crankshaft rotational speed

Running gear General description of a vehicle's underbody mechanicals, including the suspension, steering, brakes and drivetrain

Semi-elliptic spring Leaf spring suspension used on the rear axle of older cars in which the spring conforms to a specific mathematical shape

Semi-independent suspension System on a front-wheel drive car where the wheels are located by trailing links and a torsioned crossmember

Spoiler Device fitted to the front of the car, low to the ground, to reduce air flow under the car and increase down-force, thus improving roadholding at higher speeds

Synchromesh Automatic synchronization using cone clutches to speed up or slow down the input shaft to smoothly engage gear, first introduced by Cadillac in 1928

Targa Removable roof panel and rigid roll bar, named after the Targa Florio race in Sicily

Torque The rotational twisting force exerted by the crankshaft, horsepower being the measure of torque over time

Transmission General term for the final drive, clutch and gearbox. U.S. term for gearbox

Turbocharger Air pump for use in forced induction engines. Similar to a supercharger but driven at very high speed by exhaust gases, rather than mechanically to increase power output

Two-stroke An engine cycle with a power impulse every other stroke. The fuel/air mixture is compressed beneath the piston before entering the combustion chamber via ports in the cylinder wall, hence no valves or timing gear

Wheelbase The measured distance between the front and rear wheel spindles

Index

Page numbers in *italics*
refer to photographs

Picture Credits

All images supplied by Art-tech/IMP, except for the following:

Richard Dredge: 12, 14, 18, 30, 32, 33, 45, 46, 50, 62, 70, 72, 84, 130, 134, 138, 165, 171, 180, 185

National Motoring Museum: 9, 174

Phil Talbot/Rex Features: 51